Advanced Front-End Development

Building Scalable and High-Performance Web Applications with React

Nitesh Upadhyaya

Apress®

Advanced Front-End Development: Building Scalable and High-Performance Web Applications with React

Nitesh Upadhyaya
Lutz, FL, USA

ISBN-13 (pbk): 979-8-8688-1317-7 ISBN-13 (electronic): 979-8-8688-1318-4
https://doi.org/10.1007/979-8-8688-1318-4

Copyright © 2025 by Nitesh Upadhyaya

This work is subject to copyright. All rights are reserved by the Publisher, whether the whole or part of the material is concerned, specifically the rights of translation, reprinting, reuse of illustrations, recitation, broadcasting, reproduction on microfilms or in any other physical way, and transmission or information storage and retrieval, electronic adaptation, computer software, or by similar or dissimilar methodology now known or hereafter developed.

Trademarked names, logos, and images may appear in this book. Rather than use a trademark symbol with every occurrence of a trademarked name, logo, or image we use the names, logos, and images only in an editorial fashion and to the benefit of the trademark owner, with no intention of infringement of the trademark.

The use in this publication of trade names, trademarks, service marks, and similar terms, even if they are not identified as such, is not to be taken as an expression of opinion as to whether or not they are subject to proprietary rights.

While the advice and information in this book are believed to be true and accurate at the date of publication, neither the authors nor the editors nor the publisher can accept any legal responsibility for any errors or omissions that may be made. The publisher makes no warranty, express or implied, with respect to the material contained herein.

Managing Director, Apress Media LLC: Welmoed Spahr
Acquisitions Editor: Anandadeep Roy
Editorial Assistant: Kripa Joseph

Cover designed by eStudioCalamar

Cover image designed by Freepik (www.freepik.com)

Distributed to the book trade worldwide by Springer Science+Business Media New York, 1 New York Plaza, Suite 4600, New York, NY 10004-1562, USA. Phone 1-800-SPRINGER, fax (201) 348-4505, e-mail orders-ny@springer-sbm.com, or visit www.springeronline.com. Apress Media, LLC is a California LLC and the sole member (owner) is Springer Science + Business Media Finance Inc (SSBM Finance Inc). SSBM Finance Inc is a **Delaware** corporation.

For information on translations, please e-mail booktranslations@springernature.com; for reprint, paperback, or audio rights, please e-mail bookpermissions@springernature.com.

Apress titles may be purchased in bulk for academic, corporate, or promotional use. eBook versions and licenses are also available for most titles. For more information, reference our Print and eBook Bulk Sales web page at http://www.apress.com/bulk-sales.

Any source code or other supplementary material referenced by the author in this book is available to readers on GitHub. For more detailed information, please visit https://www.apress.com/gp/services/source-code.

If disposing of this product, please recycle the paper

I dedicate this book to my family, whose unwavering love and support have been the cornerstone of my journey. To my spouse, who has stood by me with patience and encouragement during the countless hours spent writing and researching, and to my children, whose curiosity and boundless energy remind me every day of the importance of learning and growth—this work is a testament to the inspiration you provide. I am deeply grateful to my mentors and colleagues, who have guided me with their wisdom and shared invaluable insights, shaping my professional path. To aspiring developers and learners, this book is written with you in mind, with the hope that it serves as a resource and a source of inspiration as you explore the ever-evolving world of React and web development. I also extend my gratitude to the open source community, whose collaborative spirit and innovative contributions have enriched the industry and motivated me to give back in the form of this book. Lastly, to everyone who has shared their knowledge selflessly, both in person and online, your generosity has been instrumental in shaping this work. This book is for all of you—those who believe in the power of education, collaboration, and innovation.

Table of Contents

About the Author xix

About the Technical Reviewers xxi

Introduction xxiii

Chapter 1: Introduction to React 1
  What Is React? 1
  A Brief History of React 3
  Why Use React? 3
    Component-Based Architecture 3
    Benefits of Component-Based Architecture 6
    Complex Applications Made Simple 6
  Virtual DOM for Performance 7
    What Is the DOM? 8
    What Is Virtual DOM? 8
    Benefits of the Virtual DOM 9
    Visualizing the Process 10
  Declarative Syntax 11
    Declarative vs. Imperative 11
    Why Declarative Syntax Is Important 12
  React Hooks 13
    Why Are Hooks Important? 13
    Core Concepts of React Hooks 13
    Custom Hooks 15

TABLE OF CONTENTS

React vs. Other Frameworks 17
The Structure of a React Application 18
What You'll Learn in This Book 19
Summary 20

Chapter 2: Setting Up Your Development Environment 21

Installing Node.js and npm 22
    Download and Install Node.js 22
    Verify Installation 23
    Updating Node.js and npm 24
Creating a React App with create-react-app 25
    Create Your First React App 25
    What create-react-app Does 27
    Understanding the Project Structure 27
    Run the Development Server 28
    Stopping the Server 30
Alternative Setup with Vite 31
    Install Vite and Create a Project 31
    Run the Vite Development Server 32
    Comparison Between Vite and create-react-app 34
Essential Tools for React Development 35
    Visual Studio Code (VS Code) 35
    Recommended Extensions for React Development 36
Setting Up Git for Version Control 37
    Download and Install Git 37
    Initial Git Configuration 38
    Initialize a Git Repository 38
    Basic Git Workflow 39
Summary 41

TABLE OF CONTENTS

Chapter 3: Components, Props, and State 43
Introduction to Components 43
Types of Components in React 44
    Functional Components 44
    Class Components 46
Props: Passing Data to Components 48
State: Managing Component Data 52
    Using State in Functional Components 52
    Using State in Class Components 53
Differences Between Props and State 55
Best Practices for Using Props and State 57
Example: Building a Simple User List Application 58
Summary 63

Chapter 4: JSX and Element Rendering 67
Introduction to JSX 67
Basic Rules of JSX 68
Rendering Elements 71
    Rendering a Single Element 72
    Rendering Multiple Elements 72
    React's Efficient Rendering 73
Embedding JavaScript Expressions in JSX 74
    Embedding Variables 74
    Conditional Rendering 75
    Calling Functions 75
Using Props for Dynamic Rendering 76

TABLE OF CONTENTS

Advanced JSX Techniques 78
    React Fragments for Grouping Elements..78
    Inline Styling in JSX..79
    Applying CSS Classes in JSX..79
    Using JSX Spread Attributes..80
    Conditional Rendering with the Logical AND (&&) Operator 80
    Rendering Lists of Elements...81
Example: Building a User Dashboard Application 81
    Features..82
Summary..87

Chapter 5: Handling Events and Conditional Rendering 89

Introduction to Event Handling..90
Event Handling in Functional Components 90
Event Handling in Class Components 92
Passing Parameters to Event Handlers 93
    Why Use Arrow Functions for Passing Parameters? 94
    Passing Multiple Parameters..95
Conditional Rendering..96
    Using if Statements 96
    Using the Ternary Operator..97
    Using the Logical && Operator 98
Creating Reusable Functions for Component Behavior......................................99
Example: Building an Interactive Login Form..100
Summary..105

TABLE OF CONTENTS

Chapter 6: Lists and Keys 107
Introduction to Lists in React 107
Rendering Lists in React 108
    Rendering Objects with Lists 108
Understanding Keys in React 109
Dynamic Lists: Adding, Removing, and Updating Items 111
Nested Lists and Complex Data Structures 113
    Recursive Rendering for Deeply Nested Structures 116
    Best Practices for Managing Lists and Keys 119
Advanced Techniques: Lazy Rendering and Virtualized Lists 119
    Lazy Loading in React 120
    Virtualization of Large Lists 121
    When to Use Lazy Loading and Virtualization 122
Example: Product List with Add-to-Cart Functionality 123
Summary 126

Chapter 7: Thinking in Components 127
Understanding Components 127
Why Adopt a Component-Based Approach? 128
Steps to Think in Components 129
Types of Components 131
    Functional Components 132
    Class Components 132
Reusability and Composition 133
Best Practices for Component Design 135
Example: Designing a Shopping Cart Page 136
    Header Component 136
    Product Component 137

TABLE OF CONTENTS

ProductList Component 137
CartSummary Component 138
Composing the Page.. 138
Common Challenges When Thinking in Components....................................... 140
Summary.. 141

Chapter 8: Styling Your Application...143

Importance of Styling in React Applications 143
Adding Styles Using Traditional CSS 145
    Pros of Using Traditional CSS 146
    Cons of Using Traditional CSS... 146
Inline Styling in React 147
    Pros of Inline Styling.. 148
    Cons of Inline Styling... 149
CSS Modules... 149
    How CSS Modules Work 150
    Pros of CSS Modules 151
    Cons of CSS Modules 151
CSS-in-JS Libraries... 152
    Dynamic Styling.. 153
    Theming Support.. 154
Using Preprocessors (SCSS/SASS) 155
    Features of SCSS/SASS 156
    How to Use SCSS/SASS in React... 158
Styling with Frameworks (Bootstrap, Tailwind)... 159
Responsive Design Techniques 161
Best Practices for Styling 164
Summary.. 165

x

TABLE OF CONTENTS

Chapter 9: Lifecycle Methods and Hooks 167
   Understanding the Component Lifecycle 168
   Lifecycle Methods in Class Components... 169
      Mounting Phase.. 169
      Updating Phase 171
      Unmounting Phase 171
   Hooks for Functional Components 172
      Using useEffect for Side Effects 172
      Managing State with useState 174
   Advanced Hooks for Lifecycle Scenarios 175
   Example: A Timer Component with Cleanup 176
   Common Challenges and Solutions 179
   Best Practices for Lifecycle Management...................................... 180
   Summary... 180

Chapter 10: Managing State with Context and Redux 183
   Understanding State Management in React 183
   React Context API... 184
   Introduction to Redux Toolkit 187
      Core Features of Redux Toolkit... 187
   Connecting Redux Toolkit with React Components....................... 191
   Comparing Context API and Redux Toolkit 193
   Best Practices for State Management 193
   Example: Building a Shopping Cart with Redux Toolkit................ 194
      Step 1: Define the Cart Slice... 194
      Step 2: Configure the Store 196
      Step 3: Provide the Store to the Application 196
      Step 4: Build the Shopping Cart Component 197
   Summary... 201

TABLE OF CONTENTS

Chapter 11: Form Handling and Validation 203
Controlled vs. Uncontrolled Components 203
Controlled Components 203
Uncontrolled Components 205
Handling User Input 206
OnChange Event 207
OnSubmit Event 208
Combined Event 209
Event Object 211
Form Validation 212
Client-Side Validation 212
Real-Time Validation 214
Using Third-Party Libraries 216
Formik 216
React Hook Form 218
Example: Checkout Form 220
Summary 224

Chapter 12: Routing and Navigation 227
Understanding Routing in SPAs 228
How SPAs Handle Routing 228
Setting Up React Router 229
Core Concepts of React Router 231
Route Matching 232
Navigating Between Pages 233
Nested Routes 234
Protected Routes 236

TABLE OF CONTENTS

Lazy Loading Routes 237
Error Handling 239
Example: Simple Blog Navigation with React Router 241
    Page Implementations 243
Summary 246

Chapter 13: Optimizing Performance 247

Understanding React's Rendering Behavior 247
    Symptoms of Bottlenecks 248
    Tools for Identifying Bottlenecks 249
Preventing Unnecessary Re-renders 249
    React.memo 249
    useCallback and useMemo 250
Code Splitting and Lazy Loading 252
Optimizing State Management 254
    Avoiding Deeply Nested State 254
    Using Selectors in Redux 254
Optimizing Large Lists 255
    Virtualization 256
Optimizing Images and Media 257
    Lazy Loading Images 257
    Responsive Images 258
Network Performance 259
    Caching with React Query 259
    Prefetching Data 261
Summary 262

TABLE OF CONTENTS

Chapter 14: Testing Your Application 265
Why Testing Matters.. 265
    The Testing Pyramid 266
Setting Up a Testing Environment 267
    Configuring Jest 268
    Configuring React Testing Library 268
    Configuring Cypress 269
Unit Testing 269
Integration Testing 271
End-to-End Testing.. 272
Snapshot Testing... 274
    How Snapshot Testing Works 276
Mocking and Stubbing 276
    Mocking API Calls 277
Summary... 279

Chapter 15: Security Best Practices 281
Common Security Risks in React Applications.. 282
    Cross-Site Scripting (XSS).. 282
    Cross-Site Request Forgery (CSRF).. 282
    Sensitive Data Exposure... 283
    Insecure API Endpoints 283
Securing React Components.. 283
    Sanitizing User Inputs... 284
    Escaping Output 285
Authentication and Authorization 287
    Secure Authentication 287
    Role-Based Access Control (RBAC)... 288

TABLE OF CONTENTS

Securing API Requests 291
    Using HTTPS 291
    Securing Tokens 292
    Preventing CSRF Attacks 292
    Example: CSRF Token Implementation 293
Data Protection 293
    Encryption 293
    Masking Sensitive Information 294
Dependency Management 295
Secure Deployment 296
Security Testing 297
    Static Analysis Tools 297
    Penetration Testing 298
    Conducting Penetration Testing 299
Summary 300

Chapter 16: Accessibility and Internationalization 301

Introduction to Accessibility and Internationalization 302
Implementing Accessibility in React 303
Testing for Accessibility 307
    Writing Automated Tests for Accessibility 308
Internationalization (i18n) in React 310
    Setting Up react-i18next 311
Summary 315

Chapter 17: Deployment and Continuous Integration 317

Preparing Your React App for Deployment 318
    Optimizing for Production 319
    Setting Up Environment Variables 320
    Creating a Build 321

TABLE OF CONTENTS

Deployment Platforms 322
    Popular Deployment Platforms 323
    Deploying to Netlify 323
    Deploying to Vercel 324

Continuous Integration and Deployment (CI/CD) 326
    What Is CI/CD? 326
    Setting Up CI/CD with GitHub Actions 326
    Automating Tests and Builds 330

Monitoring and Error Tracking in Production 331
    Setting Up Sentry for Error Tracking 332

Summary 334

Chapter 18: Integrating Third-Party Services and APIs 337

Introduction to Third-Party Services 338
    Why Use Third-Party Services? 338
    Examples of Popular Services 338

Working with REST APIs 339
    Fetching Data with fetch 339
    Using Axios for Fetching Data 342
    Handling API Errors Gracefully 344

GraphQL Integration 346
    What Is GraphQL? 347

Payment Gateway Integration 351

Integrating Firebase with React 355

Summary 358

TABLE OF CONTENTS

Chapter 19: Advanced Component Patterns 361

Higher-Order Components (HOCs) 362

    Use Cases and Limitations 363

Render Props 364

    Comparing Render Props with HOCs 366

Compound Components 366

Controlled and Uncontrolled Components 369

Custom Hooks 371

Summary 374

Chapter 20: Building a Real-World Retail Store App 377

Setting Up the Project 378

    Folder Structure 379

    Why This Structure? 381

Adding Mock Data 381

    Creating the Mock Data File 381

Organizing Product Images 383

    How Mock Data Fits into the App 383

Building Core Pages and Components 384

    Product Page (Home) 384

    Product Card 385

    Product Details Page 387

State Management with Redux 389

Setting Up Redux 390

    1. Creating the Store 390

    2. Creating the Retail Slice 391

    3. Connecting Redux to the App 393

xvii

TABLE OF CONTENTS

Checkout with Stripe 394
    1. Installing Stripe Dependencies 394
    2. Cart Page 395
    3. Creating the Checkout Page 399
    4. Creating the Checkout Form 401
Routing 404
    Adding Routes 404
Deployment 406
    1. Building the App 406
    2. Deploying to Netlify 407
    3. Testing the Deployed App 408
Summary 408

Index **411**

About the Author

Nitesh Upadhyaya is a distinguished Solution Architect with over 15 years of experience in designing and delivering scalable, high-performance web applications and complex distributed architectures enhanced with AI. He holds a master's degree in Computer Science from California State University, Long Beach, where he laid the foundation for his innovative work in technology.

Currently working at GlobalLogic, a Hitachi Group company, Nitesh drives enterprise solutions across diverse industries. He is a Senior Member of IEEE, an honor that recognizes his significant contributions to engineering and technology, and a Fellow of the Soft Computing Research Society, highlighting his leadership in computational research.

Nitesh's achievements have been recognized globally, including being honored with the 40 Under Forty Award by *Achievers World Magazine* for his exceptional contributions to the tech industry. He is also a prolific writer and educator, having published influential research papers in esteemed conferences such as IEEE. Additionally, he is a technical content reviewer for leading publishers and frequently delivers guest lectures at universities and conferences, covering cutting-edge topics like artificial intelligence, machine learning, and generative AI.

ABOUT THE AUTHOR

Driven by a deep passion for empowering developers and advancing technology, Nitesh is committed to simplifying complex concepts, fostering innovation, and mentoring the next generation of engineers. Through his expertise, mentorship, and contributions to the tech community, he has established himself as a trusted leader in software architecture and AI-driven solutions.

About the Technical Reviewers

Naveen Shandilya serves as the Director of Engineering at GlobalLogic, a Hitachi Group company specializing in digital product engineering. A highly experienced IT professional, he brings extensive expertise in both technology and management. He holds a master's degree in IT and a bachelor's degree in Computer Science. As a technical reviewer, he ensures precision, clarity, and consistency in complex concepts, enabling readers to grasp the subject with ease. Driven by a passion for knowledge sharing, Naveen is committed to upholding the highest standards in technical content.

Pooja Padmani is a Senior Front-End Developer with expertise in web development, a strong background in computer science, and hands-on experience in the tech industry. With ten years of experience, she has contributed to a variety of projects across multiple domains, including healthcare, education, telecommunications, transportation, and logistics.

ABOUT THE TECHNICAL REVIEWERS

Passionate about coding, she specializes in optimizing front-end architecture, enhancing user engagement, and staying at the forefront of industry trends. She also enjoys reviewing technical literature to ensure clarity, accuracy, and practical value for fellow developers. Through thoughtful critique and feedback, she strives to support authors in delivering high-quality resources that empower the tech community.

Introduction

Welcome, and thank you for choosing this book as your guide to mastering React! Whether you are a beginner just starting your journey into front-end development or an experienced developer looking to deepen your understanding of React, this book is designed to equip you with the skills and knowledge needed to create powerful, dynamic, and scalable web applications.

React has transformed the way developers build user interfaces, offering a robust, component-based approach that simplifies development and enhances performance. As one of the most popular JavaScript libraries, it is used by companies ranging from startups to industry giants. This book aims to bridge the gap between theory and practice, taking you from the foundational concepts of React to advanced topics, with practical, real-world applications along the way.

Whom This Book Is For

This book is intended for developers at all skill levels:

- **Beginners**: You'll learn the fundamentals of React, including components, state, props, and event handling, and progressively build your confidence through hands-on examples.

- **Intermediate Developers**: You'll explore advanced topics like state management, hooks, performance optimization, and working with third-party libraries.

INTRODUCTION

- **Experienced Developers**: You'll find in-depth discussions about best practices, architecture, and modern tools in the React ecosystem to enhance your existing knowledge.

What This Book Covers

The structure of this book has been carefully planned to provide a step-by-step learning experience:

- **Chapter 1: Introduction to React** sets the stage by exploring React's history, its importance, and how it fits into the modern development ecosystem.

- **Chapter 2: Setting Up Your Development Environment** walks you through installing the necessary tools, such as Node.js, npm, and Vite, and setting up a project with best practices in mind.

- **Chapter 3: Components, Props, and State** dives into React's core concepts, helping you understand how to create reusable, dynamic components.

- **Chapter 4: JSX and Element Rendering** explains the syntax of JSX and its role in rendering user interfaces.

- **Chapter 5: Handling Events and Conditional Rendering** focuses on interactivity, teaching you how to handle user actions and conditionally display elements.

- As the book progresses, you'll delve into topics like state management with Redux, React Router for navigation, back-end integration, and deployment using platforms like Netlify or Vercel.

In the final chapters, we bring everything together by building a **real-world retail store application**, demonstrating how to use the concepts covered in the book to create a complete, functional project. This app includes features like product listings, a shopping cart, and Stripe-based payment integration.

What You'll Gain

By the end of this book, you'll have

1. A deep understanding of React's core principles and how to use them effectively
2. The ability to design, build, and deploy scalable web applications
3. Practical experience through hands-on coding exercises and a full-scale project
4. Insights into best practices, common pitfalls, and how to stay up to date in the ever-evolving React ecosystem

A Final Note

Writing this book has been a labor of love, combining years of practical experience and insights gained from working with React in real-world projects. My hope is that this book will empower you to build amazing applications, inspire you to tackle challenging problems, and instill confidence in your abilities as a developer.

Whether you are reading this book to solve a specific problem or to expand your horizons, I encourage you to experiment, ask questions, and, most importantly, have fun along the way. Let's dive into React and explore the endless possibilities it offers!

CHAPTER 1

Introduction to React

Congratulations on beginning your journey with **React**! In this book, we're going to explore everything you need to know to build modern, scalable web applications using React, one of the most popular libraries for front-end development.

In this chapter, we'll lay the foundation by exploring

- **What React is** and why it stands out
- A brief history of React and how it evolved into the powerful tool we use today
- **Why developers love React** and how it can transform your projects

By the end of this chapter, you'll understand why React has become a favorite among developers and be ready to start building your first components.

What Is React?

React is a **JavaScript library for building user interfaces**, originally developed by Facebook in 2013. It's designed to handle only the view layer, the part of your application that users see and interact with. Unlike frameworks like Angular that attempt to handle everything, React focuses solely on the UI, making it flexible and easy to integrate with other libraries or frameworks for functionality beyond the view.

CHAPTER 1   INTRODUCTION TO REACT

At its core, React provides a powerful, efficient way to build components that represent specific parts of your user interface. With React, you can create isolated, reusable components, each managing its own logic and UI, and combine them to form complex, interactive applications. Let's break it down!

1. **Library, Not a Framework**: React doesn't dictate how you build your app. Instead, it provides the building blocks (like components) that you can assemble in any way you like.

2. **Component Based**: Everything in React revolves around components. Think of components like LEGO blocks—you can use them individually or combine them to create complex interfaces.

React simplifies UI development in several ways. It allows you to write declarative code, where you define what your app should do, and React takes care of the how. Its **Virtual DOM** ensures blazing-fast updates, even for large applications, making it highly efficient. Moreover, getting started with React is simple—you only need basic knowledge of HTML, CSS, and JavaScript, making it accessible to beginners.

Note   React is a library, not a full framework. This gives you flexibility to pick and choose other libraries or tools based on your project's needs.

A Brief History of React

React's journey began at Facebook,[1] where it was created to address issues the company faced in managing complex UIs. Developers at Facebook struggled to maintain fast, efficient applications while keeping code readable and reusable. React solved these problems with its **component-based architecture** and **Virtual DOM**, which we'll dive into shortly.

Since its open source release in 2013, React has undergone significant evolution. In 2015, React 0.14 introduced stateless functional components, simplifying component creation. Then, in 2016, React 15 improved rendering performance and stability. But the most transformative update came in 2019 with the introduction of **React Hooks**—a feature that allows you to manage state and lifecycle events in functional components. Today, React is maintained by Meta (formerly Facebook) and has a massive community of contributors and a rich ecosystem of tools and libraries.

Why Use React?

So, what makes React so popular, and why should you consider it for your project? Here are some compelling reasons.

Component-Based Architecture

React's component-based architecture allows you to build your application in small, reusable chunks called components. Each component can manage its own state, handle events, and update independently, which makes it easy to build and maintain complex UIs. Think of components

---

[1] React was originally developed at Facebook by Jordan Walke in 2011 and open-sourced in 2013. It was initially used for Facebook's newsfeed feature and later adopted across the platform.

CHAPTER 1   INTRODUCTION TO REACT

like building blocks: you can use a single component for a button, a form, or even an entire page layout. This modularity encourages reusability and keeps your code organized. Let's break it down!

1. **Encapsulate UI and Logic**: Each component is responsible for its own behavior and appearance, making it easier to understand and debug.

2. **Promote Reusability**: Once a component is created, you can reuse it in multiple places without rewriting code.

3. **Support Modularity**: By breaking down your UI into smaller pieces, you create a more organized and maintainable codebase.

React offers two primary types of components: **functional components** and **class components**. Functional components are the simplest type, defined as JavaScript functions, and are the most used today. On the other hand, class components are older and include lifecycle methods and state management but are gradually being replaced by functional components with hooks due to their simplicity and efficiency.

Imagine you're designing a house: each room (e.g., bedroom, kitchen, living room) is a **component** and has its own properties, like dimensions and purpose, and is self-contained. Moreover, you can reuse similar designs (e.g., multiple bedrooms) across different houses. Similarly, in a React app, a `button` component can be reused on multiple pages, a navbar component can provide consistent navigation across the entire app, and a form component can handle user input wherever needed.

Here's a simple example of how you can create and reuse a `Button` component in React. Listing 1-1 illustrates the implementation of a reusable `Button` component, and Listing 1-2 shows how this component is used within the `App` component as the entry point of the application.

Listing 1-1. Button Component

```
// Button.js
import React from 'react';

const Button = ({ label, onClick }) => {
  return <button onClick={onClick}>{label}</button>;
}

export default Button;
```

Listing 1-2. App Component

```
// App.js
import React from 'react';
import Button from './Button';

const App = () => {
  const handleAddToCart = () => alert('Added to cart!');
  const handleCheckout = () => alert('Proceeding to checkout!');

  return (
    <div>
      <Button label="Add to Cart" onClick={handleAddToCart} />
      <Button label="Checkout" onClick={handleCheckout} />
    </div>
  );
}

export default App;
```

In this example, the Button component is a reusable UI element. Its behavior can be customized by passing props such as label for the button text and onClick for the action to be triggered when the button is clicked.

The `App` component demonstrates how this reusable `Button` component can handle multiple functionalities, such as adding an item to the cart or proceeding to checkout, using separate event handlers.

Benefits of Component-Based Architecture

The component-based architecture offers several benefits. First, it promotes *reusability*, allowing you to write components once and use them throughout your application or even in other projects. For example, a `UserProfile` component can display user information on a dashboard, settings page, or profile page. Second, it ensures a clear *separation of concerns*, where each component manages its own responsibilities, making it easier to isolate and fix bugs. For instance, if the cart button isn't working, you only need to debug the `Button` component. Third, the self-contained nature of components *simplifies testing*, as you can test them individually without worrying about the rest of the application. Finally, this approach *accelerates development* since teams can work on different components simultaneously, speeding up the overall process.

Complex Applications Made Simple

Let's extend the idea of components to a more complex application, such as a *shopping cart*. In this example, a `Header` component displays the logo and navigation links, while a `Product List` component shows a grid of products with images, names, and prices. A `Cart` component handles the items in the user's cart, and a `Checkout` component manages the final steps of the purchase process. Each of these components can be independently developed and tested before being combined to create the final application. Figure 1-1 illustrates the UI structure of an ecommerce application.

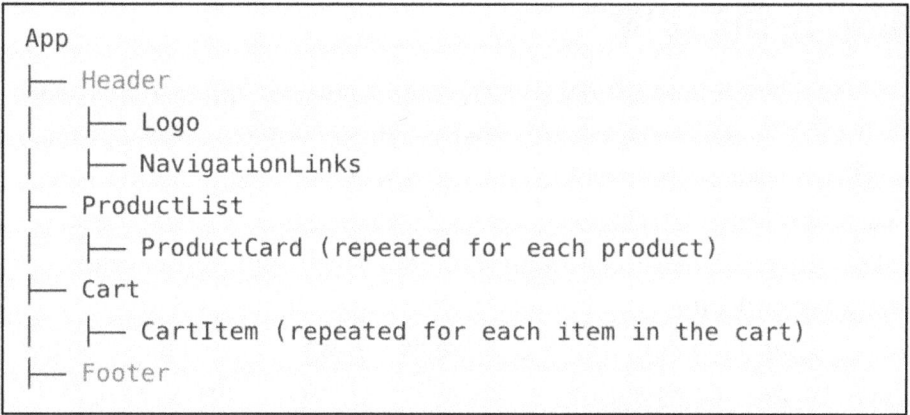

Figure 1-1. *UI structure of an ecommerce application*

React's component-based architecture is one of its greatest strengths, allowing developers to create modular, reusable, and scalable UIs. Whether you're building a single button or a multipage application, components provide the foundation for a maintainable and efficient codebase. By mastering components, you'll unlock the true potential of React and pave the way for building dynamic and interactive web applications.

Virtual DOM for Performance

One of React's core innovations is the **Virtual DOM**.[2] To understand its significance, let's first explore the challenges of working with the traditional **DOM**.

---

[2] The Virtual DOM in React enables efficient updates by comparing the virtual DOM with the actual DOM and updating only the necessary elements. More information can be found at React's Official Documentation.

CHAPTER 1   INTRODUCTION TO REACT

What Is the DOM?

The Document Object Model (DOM) represents your application's user interface (UI) as a tree structure, where each element (e.g., div, button, input) is a node in the tree. Web browsers use the DOM to render your application's content. However, directly updating the DOM can be slow and resource-intensive, especially in modern web applications with interactive and complex UIs. Each update triggers a series of processes, including recalculation of styles, where the browser recalculates CSS for affected elements; repainting, where visible elements are redrawn; and reflow, where the browser recalculates the layout for affected parts of the page. While these updates may not be noticeable in small applications, they can lead to performance bottlenecks in larger, more dynamic applications.

What Is Virtual DOM?

React introduces the Virtual DOM, a lightweight in-memory representation of the real DOM, to address performance challenges. Instead of interacting with the real DOM directly, React first updates the Virtual DOM. It then compares the updated Virtual DOM with its previous version through a process called "**diffing**." Based on this comparison, React calculates the minimal set of changes needed to update the real DOM, a process known as "reconciliation." Finally, only the affected parts of the real DOM are updated, ensuring faster and more efficient rendering.

Think of the Virtual DOM as a **"middle manager"** between your app's UI and the real DOM:

1. Instead of constantly disrupting the real DOM, React sends a clear, optimized **"to-do list"** of changes.
2. This reduces unnecessary work and ensures your app remains fast and responsive.

Imagine you're editing a large document. Without the Virtual DOM, you make changes directly on the printed document. Each edit requires reprinting the entire document, wasting time and paper. With the Virtual DOM, you make edits on a draft copy (Virtual DOM) and only reprint the sections of the document that have changed.

Benefits of the Virtual DOM

The Virtual DOM offers several key benefits. First, it significantly improves performance by optimizing updates, ensuring that the UI remains smooth even during frequent changes. This makes it particularly efficient for complex applications handling real-time data. Second, it simplifies updates with its declarative approach—you specify what you want to update, and React determines the most efficient way to achieve it. Finally, the Virtual DOM ensures cross-browser compatibility by abstracting away browser-specific quirks, providing consistent behavior across different browsers.

Let's consider an ecommerce site where the price of a product updates dynamically based on user interactions. Listing 1-3 demonstrates how React's Virtual DOM efficiently handles updates by focusing only on the elements that have changed, and Listing 1-4 shows how this component is used within the App component as the entry point of the application.

Listing 1-3. Product Component

```
// Product.js
import React from 'react';

const Product = ({ price }) => {
  return <h1>Price: ${price}</h1>;
}

export default Product;
```

Listing 1-4. App Component

```
// App.js
import React from 'react';
import Product from './Product;

const App = () => {
  const [price, setPrice] = React.useState(100);
  const increasePrice = () => setPrice(price + 10);

  return (
    <div>
      <Product price={price} />
      <button onClick={increasePrice}>Increase Price</button>
    </div>
  );
}
```

When the button is clicked, the price value updates in the Virtual DOM. React then compares the updated Virtual DOM with its previous version and identifies that only the <h1> element displaying the price has changed. As a result, React updates the real DOM exclusively for the <h1> element, leaving the rest of the page untouched.

Visualizing the Process

React's use of the Virtual DOM to optimize updates can be visualized as a step-by-step process. Initially, the Virtual DOM and the real DOM are in sync. When a change is detected, such as a state update, it triggers changes in the Virtual DOM. React then performs a process called "diffing," where it compares the new Virtual DOM with its previous version to identify differences. Based on these differences, React calculates the smallest number of changes required in a process known as "reconciliation." Finally, only the affected parts of the real DOM are updated, ensuring efficient and smooth updates.

Note The Virtual DOM is one of React's most powerful features for optimizing performance. By minimizing direct interaction with the real DOM, React reduces the time it takes to render updates, making applications feel more responsive.

Declarative Syntax

React's **declarative syntax** allows you to focus on describing **what** the UI should look like at any given state, while React takes care of the details on **how** to achieve it. This approach simplifies your code by eliminating the need for complex, step-by-step DOM manipulation.

Declarative vs. Imperative

- **Declarative Approach (React)**: You specify the desired outcome, and React determines how to update the UI.

- **Imperative Approach (Traditional JavaScript)**: You provide detailed instructions to update the DOM, such as finding an element and manually modifying it.

Think of declarative syntax as placing an order at a restaurant: You tell the server *what* you want (e.g., "a cheeseburger"). The server handles *how* it gets prepared and served. In contrast, the imperative approach would require you to specify each step (e.g., "grill the patty, add cheese, toast the bun")—time-consuming and prone to errors.

CHAPTER 1   INTRODUCTION TO REACT

Why Declarative Syntax Is Important

Declarative syntax is important for several reasons. First, it simplifies code by reducing complexity and improving readability. By allowing React to handle the "how," there's less room for errors, which leads to fewer bugs caused by manual DOM manipulation. Additionally, declarative code enhances maintainability, making it easier to understand and manage, especially in large applications. Here's a simple example of how React's declarative syntax simplifies updating the UI as illustrated in Listing 1-5.

Listing 1-5. Conditional Rendering

```
// App.js
const App = () => {
  const [submitted, setSubmitted] = React.useState(false);

  const handleSubmit = () => {
    setSubmitted(true);
  };

  return (
    <div>
      {!submitted ? (
        <button onClick={handleSubmit}>Submit</button>
      ) : (
        <p>Thank you for submitting!</p>
      )}
    </div>
  );
}
```

The explanation is straightforward: React uses declarative updates, meaning the submitted state determines whether the button or the "Thank You" message is displayed. React automatically updates the DOM based on the state, eliminating the need to manually add or remove elements.

React Hooks

Introduced in **React 16.8**, **Hooks** have revolutionized the way developers write React components. They allow you to manage **state** and handle **side effects** directly in **functional components**, eliminating the need for class components in many scenarios. Before Hooks, managing state and lifecycle methods required using class components, which often led to complex, hard-to-read code. With Hooks, functional components became just as powerful while remaining simpler and more reusable.

Why Are Hooks Important?

1. **Simplified Code**: Hooks reduce boilerplate code, making your components easier to read and maintain.

2. **Logic Reusability**: With custom hooks, you can extract and reuse logic across multiple components.

3. **Functional over Class**: By enabling state and lifecycle management in functional components, Hooks have largely replaced the need for class components.

Core Concepts of React Hooks

React provides several built-in Hooks, each designed for specific purposes. The useState Hook enables you to add and manage state in functional components, while the useEffect Hook handles side effects such as data fetching, subscriptions, or logging. The useContext Hook offers a way to share data across the component tree without the need for prop drilling. Additionally, you can create custom Hooks to encapsulate reusable logic, making your code more modular and maintainable.

CHAPTER 1   INTRODUCTION TO REACT

Imagine your React app as a house: the state represents the current conditions in the house, such as whether the lights are on or off. Side effects, on the other hand, are the actions triggered by state changes, like turning on the lights notifying the electric meter to start recording energy usage. Hooks, such as useState and useEffect, function as the switches and mechanisms that manage these interactions seamlessly.

Here's a simple example as shown in Listing 1-6 that demonstrates how Hooks make managing state and side effects easy.

Listing 1-6. Counter Example with Hooks

```
// App.js
import React, { useState, useEffect } from 'react';

const App = () => {
  const [count, setCount] = useState(0); // Initializing state

  // Logging the count whenever it changes
  useEffect(() => {
    console.log(`Count updated: ${count}`);
  }, [count]); // Dependency array ensures this runs only when
               'count' changes

  return (
    <div>
      <p>Count: {count}</p>
      <button onClick={() => setCount(count +
      1)}>Increment</button>
    </div>
  );
}

export default App;
```

CHAPTER 1 INTRODUCTION TO REACT

The example demonstrates the usage of `useState` and `useEffect`. The `useState` Hook initializes the `count` variable with a value of 0 and provides the `setCount` function to update the state. Every time `setCount` is called, react re-renders the component with the updated state. Meanwhile, the `useEffect` Hook runs after the component renders. In this example, it logs the updated `count` value to the console whenever the count changes, showcasing how side effects can be managed effectively. Table 1-1 provides a comprehensive list of all React Hooks along with their respective purposes.

Table 1-1. *Commonly Used Hooks in React*

Hook	Purpose
useState	Manages local state in a component
useEffect	Handles side effects like API calls, subscriptions, or DOM updates
useContext	Shares global state across components without passing props manually
useReducer	An alternative to useState for managing more complex state logic
useRef	Accesses DOM elements or stores mutable variables without causing re-renders
useMemo	Optimizes performance by memoizing expensive computations

Custom Hooks

One of the most powerful aspects of Hooks is the ability to create **custom Hooks**. A custom Hook is simply a JavaScript function that uses built-in Hooks to encapsulate reusable logic. For example, let's create a custom Hook to track window width as shown in Listing 1-7.

Listing 1-7. Building Simple Custom Hook

```js
// CustomHook.js
import { useState, useEffect } from 'react';
const useWindowWidth = () => {
  const [width, setWidth] = useState(window.innerWidth);

  useEffect(() => {
    const handleResize = () => setWidth(window.innerWidth);
    window.addEventListener('resize', handleResize);

    return () => window.removeEventListener('resize',
    handleResize); // Cleanup
  }, []);

  return width;
}
// Using the custom Hook in App.js component
const App = () => {
  const width = useWindowWidth();

  return <p>Current window width: {width}px</p>;
}
```

Hooks are a game changer in React development. Before their introduction, managing state and lifecycle events required more verbose and error-prone class components. Developers needed to understand and implement lifecycle methods like `componentDidMount` and `componentDidUpdate`, and reusing logic across components was challenging without patterns like higher-order components (HOCs) or render props. Hooks simplify this process by colocating state and effects within functional components, keeping related logic together. Additionally, complex patterns like HOCs are often unnecessary, as custom Hooks make logic reuse more straightforward and maintainable.

React vs. Other Frameworks

React is not the only framework in the JavaScript ecosystem. Let's take a quick look at how it compares to other popular frameworks. Table 1-2 highlights the comparison between React and other frameworks.

- **Angular**: Angular is a complete framework, providing everything from data binding to routing and services. It's powerful but often comes with a steeper learning curve and a larger bundle size due to its comprehensive features.

- **Vue.js**: Vue offers a similar component-based architecture and is also popular for its simplicity and ease of use. Vue's syntax is often seen as more approachable, but React's ecosystem and community support are generally larger.

Table 1-2. React Comparison with Other Frameworks

Features	React	Angular	Vue
Learning Curve	Moderate	Steep	Easy
Component Architecture	Yes	Yes	Yes
State Management	Redux	Built-in	Vuex
Ecosystem Support	Large	Large	Growing
Flexibility	High	Moderate	High

React's **flexibility**, **performance**, and **ecosystem** make it an ideal choice for many projects, especially those that require scalability and a modular approach.

CHAPTER 1   INTRODUCTION TO REACT

The Structure of a React Application

Now that you know what makes React unique, let's look at the basic structure of a React application:

1. **Components**: The core building blocks of a React app. Each component represents a part of the UI and can range from a single button to an entire layout.

2. **State and Props**: Components manage their own state, holding data they need to render. Props allow components to share data with each other, creating connections between components.

3. **JSX Syntax**: React uses JSX (JavaScript XML), which looks like HTML but lets you write JavaScript within your UI. JSX makes React code easy to read and visually connects JavaScript with the HTML-like elements it creates.

4. **Event Handling**: React allows you to handle user interactions like clicks and form submissions easily, making applications interactive and responsive.

Tip   If you're new to JSX, think of it as HTML with JavaScript embedded in it. JSX allows you to combine logic and UI in a way that is more readable and easier to maintain.

CHAPTER 1   INTRODUCTION TO REACT

What You'll Learn in This Book

This book is designed to take you from a complete beginner in React to building advanced, production-ready applications. It's structured to guide you step by step, gradually introducing concepts with practical examples. Here's a quick preview of what's in store:

Early Chapters

- You'll start with the **fundamentals** of React, learning how to create and render components, use JSX syntax, and manage data using state and props. These chapters will also introduce you to core concepts like event handling and conditional rendering, giving you the building blocks for interactive UIs.

Middle Chapters

- Once you're comfortable with the basics, we'll dive into **advanced concepts** like managing state effectively with React Hooks, Context API, and Redux. You'll learn how to handle forms, manage user input, and build dynamic, multipage applications using **React Router**. These chapters will include hands-on projects to solidify your understanding.

Final Chapters

- The final chapters focus on **real-world challenges**: performance optimization, security best practices, and ensuring accessibility in your applications. You'll apply everything you've learned to build a complete **retail store application**, integrating features like product listings, shopping carts, and checkout functionality. This project will give you the confidence to build your own scalable React applications.

CHAPTER 1   INTRODUCTION TO REACT

Summary

React is a powerful and flexible JavaScript library that has redefined how developers build modern user interfaces. Its component-based architecture promotes modularity and reusability, making it easier to manage even the most complex applications. By leveraging the Virtual DOM, React delivers exceptional performance, ensuring smooth and responsive user experiences.

The declarative nature of React simplifies development by focusing on what the UI should look like, leaving the how to React. This approach not only makes code more predictable but also significantly reduces bugs.

In this chapter, you've gained a foundational understanding of React's key features and its place in modern web development. As you move to the next chapter, you'll set up your development environment and start building your first React components.

Get ready to turn concepts into code—let's dive in!

CHAPTER 2

Setting Up Your Development Environment

In this chapter, we'll set up everything you need to start building applications with React. Setting up a well-configured development environment is essential to ensure a smooth workflow and optimize productivity. We'll cover the installation of **Node.js** and **npm**, creating your first React app using both **create-react-app** and **Vite**, and some essential tools that will help streamline your development process, including **VS Code**, extensions, and **Git** for version control.

By the end of this chapter, you'll have a complete React setup ready to go, so you can jump straight into building your applications.

CHAPTER 2   SETTING UP YOUR DEVELOPMENT ENVIRONMENT

Installing Node.js and npm

Node.js[1] is a JavaScript runtime that allows you to run JavaScript on your local machine, outside of a browser. **npm** (Node Package Manager) comes bundled with Node.js and is used to install libraries and packages, including React. Here's how to set it up.

Download and Install Node.js

Visit the Node.js official website and download the installer for your operating system. There are usually two versions available: **LTS (Long-Term Support)** and **Current**. For stability, it's generally recommended to download the LTS version. After downloading the installer, run it and follow the installation prompts. The installer will also set up npm for you. Figure 2-1 illustrates the Node.js website's download section, highlighting the LTS version.

Figure 2-1. *Node.js website showing the LTS version download option*

---

[1] Node.js was created by Ryan Dahl in 2009. It allows JavaScript to run outside the browser, making it possible to build server-side applications with JavaScript. For more information, visit the Node.js documentation.

CHAPTER 2　SETTING UP YOUR DEVELOPMENT ENVIRONMENT

Verify Installation

Once installed, you can verify that Node.js and npm are properly installed by opening your terminal (or Command Prompt on Windows) and running the commands. Listing 2-1 demonstrates how to check the installed versions of Node.js and npm. Figure 2-2 provides an example output for these commands.

Listing 2-1. Verify Version for Node and npm

```
node -v
npm -v
```

```
niteshupadhyaya@Niteshs-MacBook-Pro ~ % node -v
npm -v

v23.3.0
10.9.1
niteshupadhyaya@Niteshs-MacBook-Pro ~ %
```

Figure 2-2. *Output of Node.js and npm version verification in the terminal*

You should see the version numbers for both Node.js and npm. If you don't see these, it might mean there was an issue with the installation, and you may need to try reinstalling or consult the Node.js documentation for troubleshooting tips.

Tip　If you're new to the command line, start by practicing simple commands like cd to change directories or ls (or dir on Windows) to list files. Basic command-line skills will make you more efficient as a developer.

Updating Node.js and npm

If you already have Node.js installed, you may want to update to the latest version to ensure compatibility with the latest packages and features. To update npm, you can run the command shown in Listing 2-2. Figure 2-3 displays the output of updating npm using the terminal.

Listing 2-2. Updating npm

```
npm install -g npm
```

```
niteshupadhyaya@Niteshs-MacBook-Pro ~ % npm install -g npm
(node:18528) ExperimentalWarning: CommonJS module /opt/homebrew/lib/node_modules/npm/no
de_modules/debug/src/node.js is loading ES Module /opt/homebrew/lib/node_modules/npm/no
de_modules/supports-color/index.js using require().
Support for loading ES Module in require() is an experimental feature and might change
at any time
(Use `node --trace-warnings ...` to show where the warning was created)

changed 18 packages in 1s

25 packages are looking for funding
  run `npm fund` for details
niteshupadhyaya@Niteshs-MacBook-Pro ~ %
```

Figure 2-3. Terminal output for updating npm to the latest version

To update Node.js, visit the Node.js website and download the latest installer, or use a tool like **nvm (Node Version Manager)**, which allows you to switch between multiple Node.js versions.

CHAPTER 2   SETTING UP YOUR DEVELOPMENT ENVIRONMENT

Creating a React App with create-react-app

The **create-react-app**[2] tool is a popular, beginner-friendly way to set up a React project. It handles the initial configuration and setup for you, so you can focus on building features right away. Let's walk through creating a React app using create-react-app.

Create Your First React App

In your terminal, navigate to the folder where you want to create your project. For example, if you want to create it in your "Projects" folder, you can use the command shown in Listing 2-3.

Listing 2-3. Navigate to Projects Folder

```
cd ~/Projects
```

Next, run the command in Listing 2-4 to create a new React app.

Listing 2-4. Create my-first-app

```
npx create-react-app my-first-app
```

Replace `my-first-app` with your desired project name. The `npx` command is a package runner tool that comes with npm and allows you to execute packages without installing them globally. Figure 2-4 shows the terminal output of running the `npx create-react-app` command and prompting the user to proceed.

---

[2] create-react-app is maintained by the React team and provides a standardized project structure. You can explore the repository and more detailed configuration options on its GitHub page.

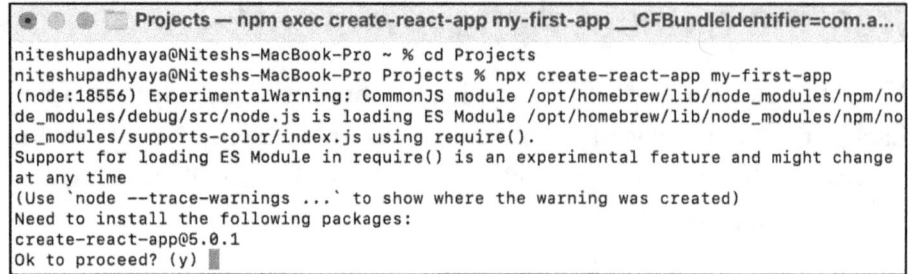

Figure 2-4. Initial terminal output when running `npx create-react-app`, *prompting for user confirmation*

Enter y to proceed. Once the execution is complete, a success message will appear, providing details about the available commands you can use. Figure 2-5 shows an example of this success message.

Figure 2-5. Success message after initializing a new React app, listing available commands

CHAPTER 2   SETTING UP YOUR DEVELOPMENT ENVIRONMENT

What create-react-app Does

This command creates a project folder (my-first-app), installs all necessary dependencies, and configures the initial file structure. Inside the project folder, you'll see folders like src (where your source code goes) and public (which contains static files like index.html). Figure 2-6 displays the structure of the project folder after running the `create-react-app` command.

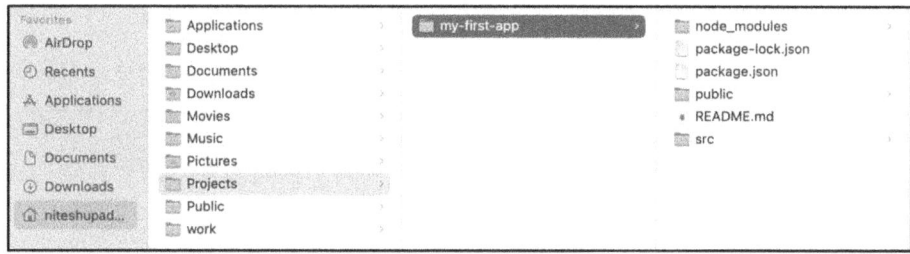

Figure 2-6. *File structure of a newly created React app project folder, including src and public directories*

Note   create-react-app is optimized for simplicity and ease of use, making it a great choice for new projects or if you're just starting out with React.

Understanding the Project Structure

After creating the app, navigate into the project folder and list the files. The project includes files like

- `src/index.js`: The entry point for your React application

- `src/App.js`: The main app component, a good place to start editing

- `public/index.html`: The HTML template for your application

27

CHAPTER 2   SETTING UP YOUR DEVELOPMENT ENVIRONMENT

These files and folders are set up for you, allowing you to focus on coding instead of configuration. Figure 2-7 highlights the contents of the src folder, while Figure 2-8 showcases the public folder structure.

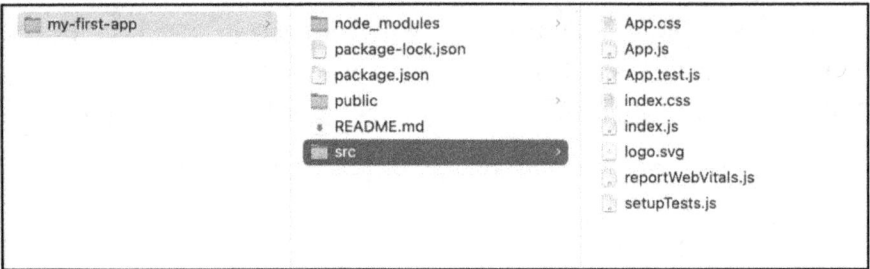

Figure 2-7. File structure of the `src` folder in a newly created React app

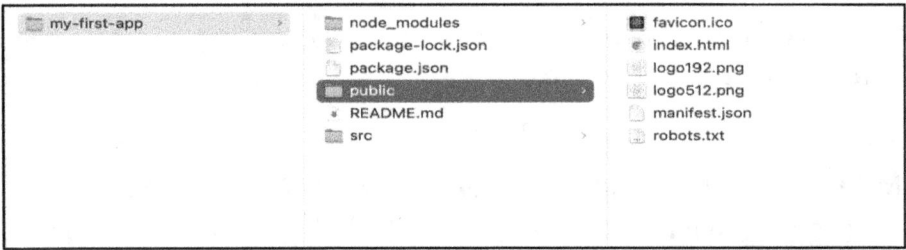

Figure 2-8. File structure of the `public` folder in a newly created React app

Run the Development Server

To start the development server, use the commands shown in Listing 2-5.

Listing 2-5. Start the Server

```
cd my-first-app
npm start
```

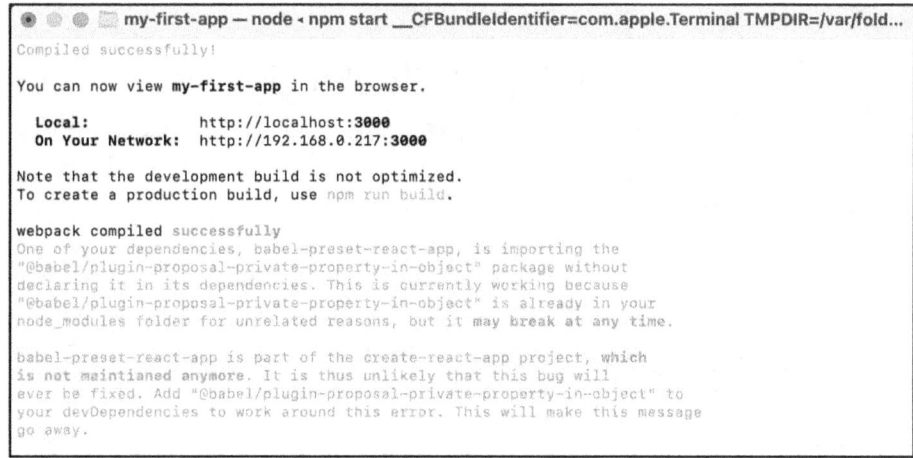

Figure 2-9. *Terminal output after starting the React development server*

This command starts a local development server and opens your app in the browser at http://localhost:3000. Any changes you make in your code will automatically reload in the browser, allowing you to see updates instantly. Figure 2-9 shows the terminal output when starting the development server, and Figure 2-10 displays the default React app in the browser.

CHAPTER 2   SETTING UP YOUR DEVELOPMENT ENVIRONMENT

Figure 2-10. *Default React app running in the browser at* `http://localhost:3000`

Stopping the Server

To stop the development server, go to the terminal where the server is running and press Ctrl+C (or Cmd+C on macOS). This will stop the server and free up the port for other uses.

Tip   The local development server with auto-reloading is a great way to see changes in real time. Remember to stop the server when you're done working for the day.

CHAPTER 2   SETTING UP YOUR DEVELOPMENT ENVIRONMENT

Alternative Setup with Vite

Vite[3] is a newer build tool that provides faster development and better optimization for modern JavaScript applications. While create-react-app is great for beginners, Vite is an alternative for developers seeking faster build times, especially for larger projects.

Install Vite and Create a Project

To create a new React project using Vite, execute the commands as shown in Listing 2-6.

Listing 2-6. Create New Project with Vite

```
npm create vite@latest my-vite-app -- --template react
cd my-vite-app
npm install
```

```
my-first-app — npm create vite@latest my-vite-app --template react __CFBundleIdentifier=com.apple....
niteshupadhyaya@Niteshs-MacBook-Pro my-first-app % npm create vite@latest my-vite-app -- --template react
cd my-vite-app
npm install

(node:19756) ExperimentalWarning: CommonJS module /opt/homebrew/lib/node_modules/npm/node_modules/debug/src
/node.js is loading ES Module /opt/homebrew/lib/node_modules/npm/node_modules/supports-color/index.js using
 require().
Support for loading ES Module in require() is an experimental feature and might change at any time
(Use `node --trace-warnings ...` to show where the warning was created)
Need to install the following packages:
create-vite@6.0.1
Ok to proceed? (y)
```

Figure 2-11. *Terminal output during the process of creating a new React project with Vite*

---

[3] Vite is a fast build tool created by Evan You, the creator of Vue.js. Vite offers faster builds and Hot Module Replacement (HMR), which improves the development experience. For more, see the Vite documentation.

31

During the process, you will be prompted to proceed by entering y. Once completed, the terminal will display a Done message along with details about available commands for your new project. Figure 2-11 shows the terminal output when running the Vite project creation command, and Figure 2-12 displays the successful completion message after installation.

Figure 2-12. *Completion message and available commands after setting up the Vite project*

Run the Vite Development Server

To start the Vite development server, use the command shown in Listing 2-7.

Listing 2-7. Run Development Server

```
npm run dev
```

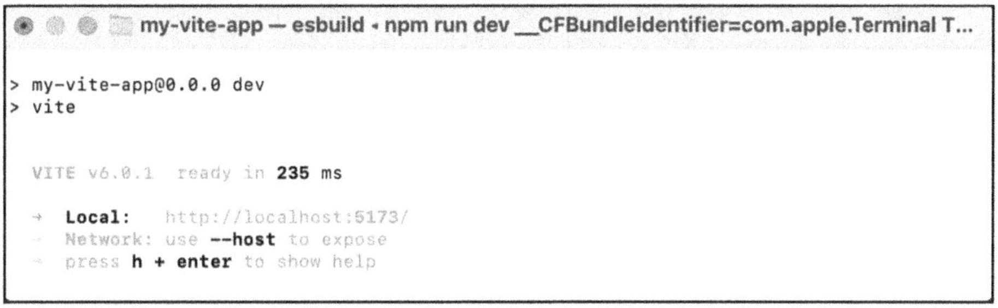

CHAPTER 2   SETTING UP YOUR DEVELOPMENT ENVIRONMENT

```
> my-vite-app@0.0.0 dev
> vite

  VITE v6.0.1  ready in 235 ms

  ➜  Local:   http://localhost:5173/
  ➜  Network: use --host to expose
  ➜  press h + enter to show help
```

Figure 2-13. *Terminal output after starting the Vite development server*

The terminal will output a local server URL, typically http://localhost:5173/, where your application can be accessed. Like create-react-app, Vite supports hot reloading, enabling you to see code changes reflected in the browser instantly. Figure 2-13 displays the terminal output after starting the development server, and Figure 2-14 shows the default Vite + React app in the browser.

CHAPTER 2 SETTING UP YOUR DEVELOPMENT ENVIRONMENT

Figure 2-14. *Vite + React app displayed in the browser at* `http://localhost:5173`

Comparison Between Vite and create-react-app

Vite offers superior performance compared to create-react-app, as it utilizes ES Modules for bundling and Hot Module Replacement (HMR), which significantly optimizes development speed. In terms of configuration, Vite is more flexible, allowing for greater customization. However, this flexibility may require additional setup for advanced use cases compared to the more straightforward configuration of create-react-app.

> **Caution** If your project requires complex configuration or third-party integrations, Vite may require additional setup compared to create-react-app. Consider your project's needs before deciding which tool to use.

Essential Tools for React Development

A well-rounded development environment includes tools that improve productivity and code quality. Let's set up some essential tools to enhance your React workflow.

Visual Studio Code (VS Code)

VS Code[4] is a lightweight and powerful code editor developed by Microsoft. It's highly customizable, with extensions available for virtually every programming language, including React.

- **Download and Install VS Code**

    Visit Visual Studio Code and download the installer for your operating system. Follow the on-screen instructions to complete the installation.

- **Basic Configuration**

    Open VS Code and adjust your settings, such as themes, font size, and default formatting options. These configurations will improve your workflow and comfort while coding.

---

[4] Extensions can greatly enhance your coding experience. The Visual Studio Code marketplace offers thousands of extensions across various programming languages and tools.

Tip VS Code's integrated terminal allows you to run terminal commands without leaving the editor, making it convenient to manage your development workflow.

Recommended Extensions for React Development

To get the most out of VS Code, here are some recommended extensions:

- **ESLint**: Helps you maintain clean and consistent code by identifying syntax errors and enforcing coding standards

- **Prettier**: Automatically formats your code, ensuring consistency and readability

- **ES7 React/Redux/GraphQL/React-Native Snippets**: Adds helpful code snippets for React, making it faster to create components and import modules

- **Bracket Pair Colorizer**: Helps you match opening and closing brackets with color coding, useful for complex nested code

- **GitLens**: Adds Git superpowers to VS Code, making it easier to manage version control within the editor

Note Extensions like ESLint and Prettier help enforce code standards, reducing bugs and ensuring a cleaner codebase.

CHAPTER 2   SETTING UP YOUR DEVELOPMENT ENVIRONMENT

Setting Up Git for Version Control

Git[5] is a version control system that lets you track changes in your code, collaborate with other developers, and revert to previous versions when necessary. If you're working on personal projects, Git is invaluable for managing your code history, and if you're collaborating, it's essential for seamless teamwork.

Download and Install Git

Visit the Git website to download and install Git for your operating system. Follow the installation instructions. Figure 2-15 displays the Git download page.

Figure 2-15.   *Git website download page for selecting the appropriate version*

---

[5] Git was developed by Linus Torvalds in 2005 and is widely used for version control in software development. A helpful beginner's guide can be found in the Git documentation.

37

Initial Git Configuration

After installing, open your terminal and configure your name and email (these will be associated with your Git commits). Listing 2-8 shows how to configure `Git` with username and email address.

Listing 2-8. Configure Git with Username and Email Address

```
git config --global user.name "Your Name"
git config --global user.email your.email@example.com
```

After completing the setup, you can run `git config --global --list` to verify whether the user credentials have been successfully configured as illustrated in Figure 2-16.

```
niteshupadhyaya@Niteshs-MacBook-Pro my-vite-app % git config --global --list
user.name=Nitesh Upadhyaya
user.email=niteshupadhyaya@gmail.com
niteshupadhyaya@Niteshs-MacBook-Pro my-vite-app %
```

Figure 2-16. *Terminal output showing username and email configuration in Git*

Initialize a Git Repository

To initialize a Git repository, navigate to your project directory and run the command as shown in Listing 2-9.

Listing 2-9. Initialize Git Repository

```
git init
```

This command initializes an empty Git repository in your project folder, setting up the necessary `.git` directory. Figure 2-17 displays the terminal output after running the `git init` command, which also provides guidance on setting the default branch name for your repository.

CHAPTER 2   SETTING UP YOUR DEVELOPMENT ENVIRONMENT

```
niteshupadhyaya@Niteshs-MacBook-Pro my-vite-app % git init
hint: Using 'master' as the name for the initial branch. This default branch name
hint: is subject to change. To configure the initial branch name to use in all
hint: of your new repositories, which will suppress this warning, call:
hint:
hint:   git config --global init.defaultBranch <name>
hint:
hint: Names commonly chosen instead of 'master' are 'main', 'trunk' and
hint: 'development'. The just-created branch can be renamed via this command:
hint:
hint:   git branch -m <name>
Initialized empty Git repository in /Users/niteshupadhyaya/Projects/my-first-app/my-vite-app/.git/
niteshupadhyaya@Niteshs-MacBook-Pro my-vite-app %
```

Figure 2-17. *Terminal output after initializing a Git repository in the project directory*

Basic Git Workflow

Stage Changes: Add your changes to the staging area as illustrated in Listing 2-10.

Listing 2-10. Stage Modified Files

```
git add .
```

Commit Changes: Commit your changes with a message describing the update as illustrated in Listing 2-11. Figure 2-18 shows the terminal output after staging and committing changes.

Listing 2-11. Commit Changes

```
git commit -m "Initial commit"
```

```
niteshupadhyaya@Niteshs-MacBook-Pro my-vite-app % git add .
niteshupadhyaya@Niteshs-MacBook-Pro my-vite-app % git commit -m "Initial commit"
[master (root-commit) 7b64c7e] Initial commit
 13 files changed, 4611 insertions(+)
 create mode 100644 .gitignore
 create mode 100644 README.md
 create mode 100644 eslint.config.js
 create mode 100644 index.html
 create mode 100644 package-lock.json
 create mode 100644 package.json
 create mode 100644 public/vite.svg
 create mode 100644 src/App.css
 create mode 100644 src/App.jsx
 create mode 100644 src/assets/react.svg
 create mode 100644 src/index.css
 create mode 100644 src/main.jsx
 create mode 100644 vite.config.js
niteshupadhyaya@Niteshs-MacBook-Pro my-vite-app %
```

Figure 2-18. *Terminal output after staging changes and committing the initial commit*

Push to Remote Repository (Optional): If you're using a platform like GitHub, create a repository there and push your code as shown in Listing 2-12.

Listing 2-12. Push to Repository

```
git remote add origin https://github.com/yourusername/my-first-app.git
git push -u origin main
```

Tip Use meaningful commit messages. A clear commit history makes it easier to track changes and understand project progress.

Summary

By now, you should have everything you need to start building with React. We've covered the essential steps to set up your development environment, beginning with the installation of Node.js and npm, the foundational tools for React development. We then explored two popular ways to initialize a new React project: **using create-react-app**, the tried-and-true method offered by Facebook's React team, and **Vite**, a modern, fast, and opinionated alternative that optimizes for a smoother development experience.

Additionally, we configured **VS Code** as your IDE, set up essential extensions to enhance productivity, and ensured Git was installed for version control, so you can track your changes and collaborate seamlessly. These tools and workflows are designed to empower you, allowing you to focus on building your application without worrying about setup hassles.

In the next chapter, we'll dive into React's core concepts: components, props, and state. These are the building blocks of any React application, enabling you to create dynamic, interactive interfaces. With your environment fully configured, you're ready to start experimenting with React code. So, let's take a deeper look into what makes React such a powerful library for front-end development!

CHAPTER 3

Components, Props, and State

In React, everything revolves around components, which form the building blocks of your application's user interface. Components are reusable pieces of UI that can manage their own data and behavior through **state** and receive external data through **props**. In this chapter, we'll dive into the core concepts of React components, explore the differences between **functional** and **class components**, and introduce props and state management.

By the end of this chapter, you'll have a solid understanding of how to create and use components, manage their state, and pass data to them in a way that builds a dynamic and interactive user interface.

Introduction to Components

A **component** in React is essentially a JavaScript function or class that returns a piece of UI. Components allow you to break down your application into smaller, self-contained units, making your code more organized and reusable. React components can be as simple as a button or as complex as an entire page layout. Figure 3-1 illustrates the folder structure for organizing React components within the src directory.

CHAPTER 3   COMPONENTS, PROPS, AND STATE

Before we dive into creating components, let's organize our project:

1. Navigate to the src folder in your React project.
2. Create a folder named components to store all your components.
3. Inside components, create two subfolders:
   - **functionalComponents**
   - **classComponents**

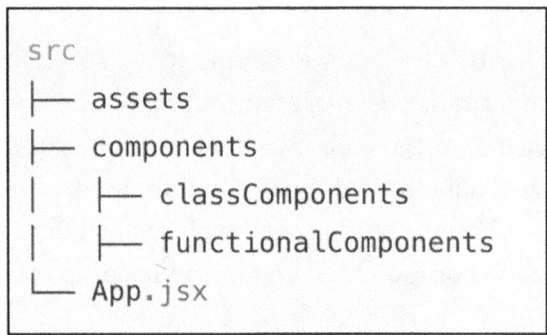

Figure 3-1. *Folder structure showing the organization of functional and class components in a React project*

Types of Components in React

React supports two main types of components: ***functional components*** and ***class components***.

Functional Components

Functional components are JavaScript functions that return a React element. They're the most common way to create components in modern React, especially since the introduction of **Hooks**. Functional components are simple and lightweight, making them ideal for components that don't require advanced features like lifecycle methods. Inside the functionalComponents folder, create a file named Greeting.jsx and add the code shown in Listing 3-1.

Listing 3-1. Greeting Functional Component

```
// Greeting.jsx
const Greeting = () => {
  return <h1>Functional Based Component!</h1>;
}
export default Greeting;
```

To render this component, open App.js in the src folder and import the Greeting component and use it as shown in Listing 3-2. Figure 3-2 shows the rendered output of the Greeting functional component.

Listing 3-2. Entry Point of Application—Functional Component

```
// App.jsx
import Greeting from './components/functionalComponents/Greeting.jsx';
import './App.css'

const App = () => {
  return (
    <div>
      <Greeting />
    </div>
  );
}
export default App;
```

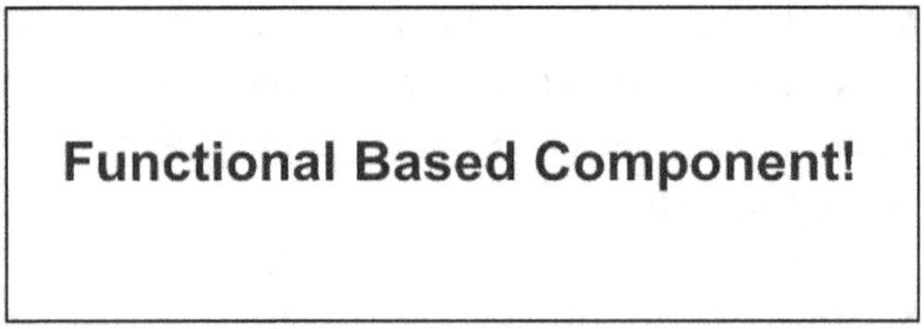

Functional Based Component!

Figure 3-2. Output of the Greeting *functional component rendered in the browser*

In this example, Greeting is a functional component that returns an h1 element with the text "Functional Based Component!". When you run the development server, this output will be displayed in the browser.

Class Components

Before the introduction of Hooks, **class components** were the standard for creating more complex components. Class components are created using ES6 classes and provide additional features like **lifecycle methods**. Although functional components with Hooks have largely replaced class components, it's still useful to understand them, as you may encounter class components in legacy codebases. Inside the classComponents folder, create a file named Greeting.jsx and add the code shown in Listing 3-3.

Listing 3-3. Greeting Class Component

```
// Greeting.jsx
import React, { Component } from 'react';
class Greeting extends Component {
  render() {
    return <h1>Class Based Component!</h1>;
  }
}
export default Greeting;
```

To render this component, open App.js in the src folder and import the Greeting component and use it as shown in Listing 3-4. Figure 3-3 shows the rendered output of the Greeting class component.

Listing 3-4. Entry Point of Application—Class Component

```jsx
// App.jsx
import Greeting from './components/class-components/Greeting.jsx';

const App = () => {
  return (
    <div>
      <Greeting />
    </div>
  );
}

export default App;
```

Class Based Component!

Figure 3-3. *Output of the Greeting class component rendered in the browser*

In this example, Greeting is a class component that extends React.Component and has a render method that returns the h1 element with the text "Class Based Component!". When you run the development server, this output will be displayed in the browser.

> **Note** While functional components are recommended for new development, understanding class components is beneficial for working with legacy React code.

Props: Passing Data to Components

Props (short for "properties") are a way of passing data from a parent component to a child component. Props are **read-only** and cannot be modified by the child component; they're meant to provide information that a component needs to render properly.

When implementing a functional component, `Props` are passed as an argument to functional components and can be used within the component. Let's update our **Greeting.jsx** file inside the functionalComponents folder to use props as shown in Listing 3-5.

Listing 3-5. Greeting Functional Component—with Name Prop

```
// Greeting.jsx
const Greeting = ({ name }) => {
  return <h1>Hello, {name}!</h1>;
}
export default Greeting;
```

To render this component, open `App.js` in the src folder and import the `Greeting` component and use it as shown in Listing 3-6. Figure 3-4 shows the rendered output.

CHAPTER 3   COMPONENTS, PROPS, AND STATE

Listing 3-6. *Entry Point of Application—Functional Component with Name Prop*

```
import Greeting from './components/functionalComponents/Greeting.jsx';
import './App.css'
const App = () => {
  return (
    <div>
      <Greeting name="John" />
    </div>
  );
}
export default App;
```

Hello, John!

Figure 3-4. *Output of the Greeting functional component that receives a name prop rendered in the browser*

In this example, name is a prop passed to the Greeting component, allowing it to display "Hello, John!" dynamically.

When implementing a class component, Props are accessed via the this.props object. Let's update our Greeting.jsx file inside the classComponents folder to use props as shown in Listing 3-7.

49

Listing 3-7. Greeting Class Component—Props Accessible via this.props

```jsx
// Greeting.jsx
import React, { Component } from 'react';
class Greeting extends Component {
  render() {
    return <h1>Hello, {this.props.name}!</h1>;
  }
}
```

To render this component, open `App.js` in the src folder and import the Greeting component and use it as shown in Listing 3-8. Figure 3-5 shows the rendered output.

Listing 3-8. Entry Point of Application—Class Component Props Accessible via this.props

```jsx
import Greeting from './components/classComponents/Greeting.jsx';
import './App.css'

const App = () => {
return (
   <div>
     <Greeting name="Jane" />
   </div>
  );
}
export default App;
```

CHAPTER 3   COMPONENTS, PROPS, AND STATE

Hello, Jane!

Figure 3-5. *Output of the* `Greeting` *class component that receives prop via* `this.props` *rendered in the browser*

In this example, name is a prop passed to the Greeting component, allowing it to display "Hello, Jane!" dynamically.

React allows you to set **default props** for components to ensure they have default values if no prop is provided. Additionally, **prop types** can be used to enforce type-checking on props, helping to prevent bugs by ensuring components receive the correct types of data as shown in Listing 3-9.

Listing 3-9. Using Default Props and Prop Types

```
import PropTypes from 'prop-types';
function Greeting({ name }) {
  return <h1>Hello, {name}!</h1>;
}

Greeting.defaultProps = {
  name: 'Guest'
};

Greeting.propTypes = {
  name: PropTypes.string
};

export default Greeting;
```

CHAPTER 3 COMPONENTS, PROPS, AND STATE

> **Tip** Using default props and prop types improves your code's reliability and makes your components easier to understand and maintain.

State: Managing Component Data

State is a way to manage data within a component that can change over time. Unlike props, which are passed from parent to child, state is **internal to a component** and can be updated by the component itself. When state changes, react automatically re-renders the component to reflect the new state.

Using State in Functional Components

Functional components use the **useState Hook** to manage state. The useState Hook returns an array with two elements: the current state and a function to update it as shown in Listing 3-10. Moreover, Figure 3-6 displays the rendered output of the Counter component, where the count starts at zero and increments each time the button is clicked.

Listing 3-10. Simple Counter Component Using useState

```
import React, { useState } from 'react';
import './Counter.css';

function Counter() {
  const [count, setCount] = useState(0);

  return (
    <div className="counter-container">
      <p className="counter-text">Count: {count}</p>
```

```
    <button className="counter-button" onClick={() =>
    setCount(count + 1)}>
      Increment
    </button>
  </div>
);
}
export default Counter;
```

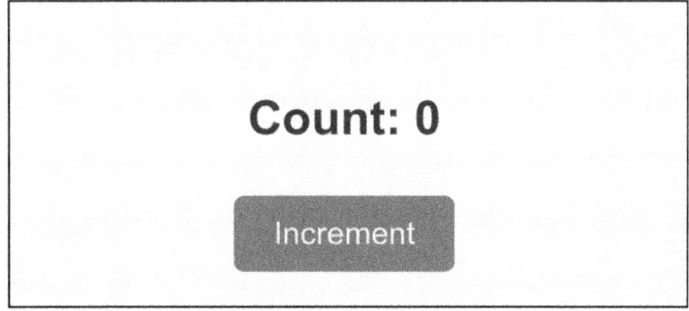

Figure 3-6. *Output of the Counter component using the useState Hook*

In this example, count is the state variable, and `setCount` is the function to update count. Each time the button is clicked, `setCount` updates the count, causing the component to re-render.

Using State in Class Components

In class components, state is managed using the `this.state` object and updated using `this.setState`. Here is an example of a simple counter component implemented as a class component in Listing 3-11.

Listing 3-11. Simple Counter Component in Class Components

```
import React, { Component } from 'react';
import './Counter.css'; // Import the CSS file

class Counter extends Component {
  constructor(props) {
    super(props);
    this.state = { count: 0 };
  }

  increment = () => {
    this.setState((prevState) => ({ count: prevState.count
    + 1 }));
  };

  render() {
    return (
      <div className="counter-container">
        <p className="counter-text">Count: {this.state.
        count}</p>
        <button className="counter-button" onClick={this.
        increment}>
          Increment
        </button>
      </div>
    );
  }
}

export default Counter;
```

CHAPTER 3 COMPONENTS, PROPS, AND STATE

In this example, this.state.count holds the current state, and this.setState updates the count, causing the component to re-render with the updated value. Each time the "Increment" button is clicked, the increment method updates the state by incrementing the count value. Figure 3-7 shows the rendered output of the Counter class component, displaying the count and the increment button.

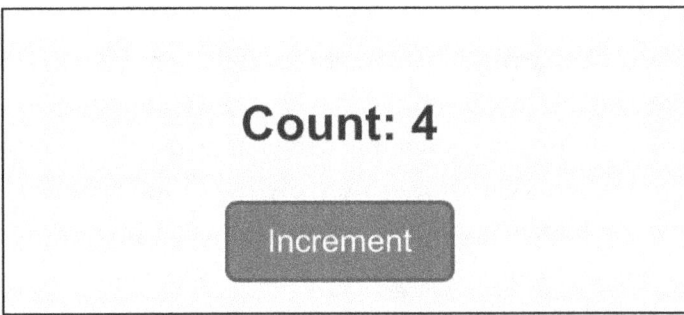

Figure 3-7. Output of the Counter class component using this.state and this.setState

---

Caution In class components, avoid directly modifying this.state; always use this.setState to update state.

Differences Between Props and State

In React, both props and state play essential roles in managing data, but they serve different purposes and are handled differently. Understanding the distinction between them is critical for building effective and maintainable components. Refer to Table 3-1 for a comparison between props and state.

CHAPTER 3   COMPONENTS, PROPS, AND STATE

1. **Props**: These are short for "properties" and are used to pass data from a parent component to a child component. Props are read-only, meaning the receiving component cannot modify them directly. Props make components more reusable and customizable since you can pass different values for each instance.

2. **State**: Unlike props, which are passed down from the parent, state is managed within the component itself. It represents data that can change over time. Components can modify their own state, and when the state updates, React re-renders the component to reflect the new data. State is typically used for data that changes dynamically, like form inputs or toggle switches.

Table 3-1. *Comparison Between Props and State*

Feature	Props	State
Definition	Data passed from parent to child	Data managed within the component
Mutability	Read-only	Can be modified
Purpose	Pass information	Store dynamic data
Access in Functional Components	Direct (as function arguments)	useState Hook
Access in Class Components	this.props	this.state

CHAPTER 3   COMPONENTS, PROPS, AND STATE

Best Practices for Using Props and State

When working with **props** and **state** in React, following best practices can help you build clean, maintainable, and efficient components. One of the key principles is to **keep state local** to the component whenever possible. State should only be used for data that changes over time and is specific to the component. For shared or static data, consider using props or context instead. Overusing state can unnecessarily complicate components and make them harder to maintain, so it's important to use props and context wherever appropriate. For example, if managing multiple pieces of related state, it's often better to group them into a single object for easier handling and fewer bugs.

When passing data through props, it's a good idea to **destructure props** directly in the component function. This simplifies your code by removing repetitive references to the `props` object, making it more readable and concise. Another essential best practice is to use `PropTypes` to validate the data type of props. This ensures that the correct type of data is passed to your components, helping you catch potential bugs early during development. Additionally, setting **default props** provides fallback values for props that aren't explicitly passed, which can prevent unexpected behaviors in your application.

To further maintain a clean codebase, avoid mutating state directly. Always use the appropriate updater functions, such as `setState` in class components or the `useState` updater in functional components, to ensure React can properly track and re-render updates. Similarly, try not to pass excessive props to child components; only pass what is necessary to keep the code simple and easier to understand. For cases where child components need to communicate back to parent components, it's a good idea to use **callback functions** passed as props. This allows child components to trigger specific actions in their parents, ensuring a clear flow of data and events.

57

By adhering to these best practices, you can make your React components more predictable, reusable, and easier to debug. Whether managing state locally, passing data through props, or leveraging validation with PropTypes, these principles will help you create scalable and robust applications.

Note Following best practices for props and state can make your code more predictable and easier to debug.

Example: Building a Simple User List Application

In this section, we'll build a **User List Application** that demonstrates everything we've discussed so far—**props**, **state**, **default props**, **destructuring**, and React best practices. This application will display a list of users with their name, email, and activity status. Users can toggle their activity status dynamically using a button. This example ties together all the concepts to create a simple yet practical React application.

We begin with the **App component**, which serves as the main entry point of the application as shown in Listing 3-12. Inside this component, we initialize the state with a list of users, each represented as an object containing `id`, `name`, `email`, and `isActive` properties. To handle changes in user activity, we define a `toggleUserActivity` function that takes a user's ID as an argument. This function maps through the user list, toggling the `isActive` property for the user with the given ID while keeping the rest of the state intact. This approach ensures the state is updated immutably, following React's best practices. The `App` component then passes the user data and the toggle function to the `UserList` component via props, enabling child components to access and interact with the data. Here's how the `App` component is implemented.

CHAPTER 3   COMPONENTS, PROPS, AND STATE

Listing 3-12. App.jsx—Entry Point of Application

```
// App.jsx
import React, { useState } from 'react';
import UserList from './components/UserList';

const App = () => {
  const [users, setUsers] = useState([
    { id: 1, name: 'John Doe', email: 'john@example.com',
    isActive: true },
    { id: 2, name: 'Jane Smith', email: 'jane@example.com',
    isActive: false },
  ]);

  const toggleUserActivity = (id) => {
    setUsers((prevUsers) =>
      prevUsers.map((user) =>
        user.id === id ? { ...user, isActive: !user.isActive
        } : user
      )
    );
  };

  return (
    <div>
      <h1>User List</h1>
      <UserList users={users} toggleActivity={toggleUser
      Activity} />
    </div>
  );
}

export default App;
```

CHAPTER 3 COMPONENTS, PROPS, AND STATE

The `UserList` component acts as a middle layer, receiving the list of users and the toggle function as props from the App component. It iterates through the user list using the map method and renders a `User` component for each user. This component demonstrates how to pass data and actions to child components via props as shown in Listing 3-13. The implementation of the `UserList` component is as follows.

Listing 3-13. User List Functional Components

```
// UserList.jsx
import React from 'react';
import User from './User';
import './UserList.css';

const UserList = ({ users, toggleActivity }) => {
  return (
    <div className="user-list-container">
      <h1 className="user-list-title">User List</h1>
      {users.map((user) => (
        <User
          key={user.id}
          id={user.id}
          name={user.name}
          email={user.email}
          isActive={user.isActive}
          toggleActivity={toggleActivity}
        />
      ))}
    </div>
  );
}

export default UserList;
```

Next, the User component displays individual user details. It uses **destructuring** to extract props like id, name, email, isActive, and toggleActivity. This component renders the user's name, email, and activity status. It also includes a button that, when clicked, calls the toggleActivity function with the user's ID as an argument, allowing the parent component to update the user's state as shown in Listing 3-14. Here's the implementation of the User component.

Listing 3-14. User Functional Components

```
// src/components/User.jsx
import React from 'react';
import PropTypes from 'prop-types';
import './UserList.css';

const User = ({ id, name, email, isActive,
toggleActivity }) => {
  return (
    <div className="user-card">
      <h2>{name}</h2>
      <p>Email: {email}</p>
      <p className="user-card-status">Status: {isActive ?
      'Active' : 'Inactive'}</p>
      <button
        className={`user-card-button ${isActive ? 'deactivate'
        : 'activate'}`}
        onClick={() => toggleActivity(id)}
      >
        {isActive ? 'Deactivate' : 'Activate'}
      </button>
    </div>
  );
}
```

CHAPTER 3   COMPONENTS, PROPS, AND STATE

```
// PropTypes and defaultProps (optional, as in your
original code)
User.propTypes = {
  id: PropTypes.number.isRequired,
  name: PropTypes.string.isRequired,
  email: PropTypes.string.isRequired,
  isActive: PropTypes.bool,
  toggleActivity: PropTypes.func.isRequired,
};

User.defaultProps = {
  isActive: false,
};

export default User;
```

The **User** component showcases several key best practices. It uses PropTypes to enforce type checking for the props it receives, ensuring that the component behaves as expected and avoids runtime errors. The component also defines a default prop for `isActive`, setting its value to `false` if it's not explicitly provided. By using destructuring, the component avoids repetitive references to `props`, keeping the code clean and readable.

When you run the application, the `App` component renders the `UserList` component, which in turn renders a `User` component for each user in the list. Each User displays the user's name, email, and activity status, with a button to toggle the activity status between "Active" and "Inactive." Clicking the button triggers the `toggleUserActivity` function in the App component, updating the state and re-rendering the UI with the updated status. Figure 3-8 shows the rendered output of the application with a list of users and their respective activity statuses.

Figure 3-8. *Rendered output of the application displaying a user list with activity toggle functionality*

This application demonstrates the practical application of React concepts like **state management**, **props**, **default props**, **destructuring**, and PropTypes. By following best practices, you can create reusable, predictable, and maintainable components that are easy to scale. With this understanding, you're now well equipped to build dynamic, interactive applications in React.

Summary

In this chapter, we explored the fundamental building blocks of React: **components**, **props**, and **state**. Components, which are the core units of a React application, allow you to divide your user interface into smaller, reusable, and self-contained pieces. We discussed two types of components—**functional components**, which are lightweight and modern, and **class components**, which are older but still relevant for legacy codebases. Both types of components serve to render dynamic UI elements, with functional components being the preferred choice for new development due to their simplicity and the introduction of Hooks.

We delved into **props**, the mechanism for passing data from parent components to child components. Props are immutable, making them ideal for customizing and reusing components while ensuring a unidirectional data flow. Using props, we demonstrated how to pass user information to child components, enabling dynamic content generation. To make our code cleaner and more readable, we also introduced the concept of **destructuring props**, a best practice that simplifies how props are accessed within a component.

The chapter also introduced **state**, a mechanism for managing component-specific data that can change over time. Unlike props, state is mutable and allows components to exhibit interactive behavior, such as toggling user activity or updating form fields. By keeping state local to the component that owns it and updating it immutably, we ensured a predictable and maintainable structure. We also explored how state and props work together to create dynamic applications by using state to manage data and props to pass it down the component tree.

To tie all these concepts together, we built a small application—a **User List Application**—that demonstrated how to use components, props, and state in harmony. This practical example showcased how to

- Pass data from parent to child components using props

- Use state to manage user activity and update the UI dynamically

- Implement best practices like destructuring props, validating data with **PropTypes**, and setting **default props** to ensure robust and error-free components

Finally, we emphasized best practices for managing state and props effectively, including keeping state local, avoiding overuse of state, and ensuring data validation. These practices not only make your React components easier to maintain but also improve performance and reliability.

With this chapter, you now have a solid understanding of how to create and manage components, work with props to pass data between them, and leverage state for dynamic interactions. These concepts form the backbone of React development, enabling you to build reusable, interactive, and scalable applications. In the next chapter, we'll delve into **JSX and element rendering**, where you'll learn how to combine JavaScript with HTML-like syntax to define the structure of your components and render them dynamically.

CHAPTER 4

JSX and Element Rendering

In React, **JSX** (JavaScript XML) is the syntax that allows us to write HTML-like code within JavaScript. JSX is an essential part of React because it makes code more readable, intuitive, and directly linked to the visual structure of your application. This chapter will cover the basics of JSX, how to render elements, how to make use of JavaScript expressions within JSX to create dynamic content, and how to use props in JSX for dynamic rendering. We'll also dive into some advanced topics, such as React Fragments, inline styling, and conditional rendering.

By the end of this chapter, you'll understand how to use JSX effectively and render elements based on dynamic data.

Introduction to JSX

JSX, short for **JavaScript XML**, is a syntax extension for JavaScript that allows developers to write code resembling HTML directly within their JavaScript files. Despite its similarity to HTML, JSX is not HTML. Instead, it's a powerful abstraction that combines the visual structure of HTML with the dynamic capabilities of JavaScript. Before JSX is rendered to the browser, tools like Babel compile it into standard JavaScript, making it understandable by the browser's JavaScript engine. This conversion

CHAPTER 4 JSX AND ELEMENT RENDERING

process bridges the gap between a declarative syntax that is easy for developers to read and JavaScript's imperative execution. For example, consider the JSX snippet in Listing 4-1.

Listing 4-1. Sample JSX Snippet

```
const element = <h1>Hello, World!</h1>;
```

Here, `<h1>Hello, World!</h1>` looks like an HTML element but is JSX. Behind the scenes, React's compiler translates this into a `React.createElement` function call, which generates an object representing a DOM node. This process ensures that JSX is not only readable but also performant and compatible with React's virtual DOM.

The primary advantage of JSX is that it enables developers to write UI code in a declarative manner, where the focus is on **what the UI should look like** rather than the procedural steps to achieve it. By allowing you to combine markup with JavaScript logic, JSX creates a seamless development experience, empowering you to build complex UIs with clarity and efficiency.

Basic Rules of JSX

JSX, while resembling HTML, follows its own set of rules and syntax conventions to ensure seamless integration with JavaScript and React's component system. Understanding these rules is essential to avoid common errors and fully leverage JSX's power in building dynamic user interfaces.

One of the foundational rules of JSX is that every JSX expression must have only **one root element**. This requirement enforces a clear hierarchy and ensures that React can correctly manage the virtual DOM. For instance, the JSX snippet in Listing 4-2 is invalid because it attempts to return two sibling root elements.

CHAPTER 4   JSX AND ELEMENT RENDERING

Listing 4-2. Invalid JSX Expression

```
// This will cause an error
const invalidElement = <h1>Hello</h1><p>World</p>;
```

To fix this issue, wrap both elements within a single parent element, such as a `<div>`. This creates a single root element, satisfying JSX's requirements as illustrated in Listing 4-3.

Listing 4-3. Valid JSX Expression

```
const validElement = (
  <div>
    <h1>Hello</h1>
    <p>World</p>
  </div>
);
```

While this example uses a `<div>` as the parent element, modern React allows the use of a shorthand syntax called **fragments** (`<>` and `</>`), which avoids adding unnecessary wrapper elements to the DOM as shown in Listing 4-4.

Listing 4-4. Valid JSX Expression with Fragments

```
const validElementWithFragment = (
<>
    <h1>Hello</h1>
    <p>World</p>
</>
);
```

Another critical rule of JSX is that **every tag must be closed**, even for self-closing elements like `<img>` or `<br>`. While HTML allows unclosed tags, JSX enforces stricter syntax to avoid ambiguities. For example, an `<img>` tag must include a forward slash (/) before the closing angle bracket, as shown in Listing 4-5.

Listing 4-5. Self-Closing JSX Expression

```
const element = <img src="logo.png" alt="Logo" />;
```

This syntax ensures that JSX is consistent and unambiguous, especially when dealing with nested components or complex UI structures.

One of JSX's most powerful features is the ability to embed **JavaScript expressions** directly within the mark up using curly braces ({}). This allows you to dynamically insert values, call functions, or evaluate expressions, enabling a high degree of flexibility in defining your UI. For instance, you can use JavaScript variables to personalize a greeting as shown in Listing 4-6.

Listing 4-6. Embedded JS into JSX Expression Using Curly Braces

```
const name = "Alice";
const element = <h1>Hello, {name}!</h1>;
// Outputs: Hello, Alice!
```

Tip JSX expressions are not strings. They are JavaScript expressions that compile into React.createElement() calls, which build the component tree for React.

These curly braces can contain any valid JavaScript expression, including function calls, conditional statements, and mathematical operations as shown in Listing 4-7 with additional examples.

Listing 4-7. JSX Expression Additional Examples

```
const currentTime = new Date().toLocaleTimeString();
const element = <p>The current time is {currentTime}.</p>;
```

This dynamic nature makes JSX far more powerful than static HTML, as it allows you to integrate logic and data directly into your markup. It's important to note that **JSX expressions are not strings**. They are JavaScript objects that are transformed into `React.createElement` function calls by React's compiler. This process constructs the component tree, allowing React to efficiently manage updates to the DOM.

By adhering to these basic rules, JSX provides a robust yet flexible syntax for building user interfaces. These rules not only ensure that your JSX code is syntactically correct but also make your components predictable and easy to debug. As we move forward, these principles will form the foundation for creating dynamic and interactive React applications.

Rendering Elements

In React, rendering elements is the process of defining what should appear on the screen. Elements are the smallest building blocks of the React user interface, comparable to DOM nodes in the traditional HTML DOM. These elements describe what you want to see on the screen at any point in time, and React ensures that the actual DOM reflects these descriptions. Rendering is at the heart of React's declarative programming paradigm, allowing you to focus on describing the UI without worrying about how to manipulate the DOM.

To render elements, React relies on the `ReactDOM.render` method. This method takes two arguments: the element to render and the DOM container where the element should be displayed. Let's explore rendering with practical examples.

CHAPTER 4   JSX AND ELEMENT RENDERING

Rendering a Single Element

Rendering a single element is straightforward. Consider the example in Listing 4-8, where we render a simple "Hello, React!" message to the screen.

Listing 4-8. Rendering One Element

```
import React from 'react';
import ReactDOM from 'react-dom';

const element = <h1>Hello, React!</h1>;

ReactDOM.render(element, document.getElementById('root'));
```

In this example, the constant element holds a JSX representation of a React element. The ReactDOM.render method inserts this element into the DOM container with the ID root. If you inspect the browser, you'll find that the rendered output appears as shown below:

```
<div id="root">
  <h1>Hello, React!</h1>
</div>
```

Here, React efficiently translates your JSX into actual DOM nodes and updates the browser display accordingly.

Rendering Multiple Elements

To render multiple elements, they must be wrapped in a single root element. This is because React enforces a single root element in JSX to maintain a clear and predictable structure. You can use a <div> as a wrapper or, for cleaner code, utilize React fragments (<> </>) to avoid adding unnecessary elements to the DOM. Here's an example that renders multiple elements in Listing 4-9.

Listing 4-9. Rendering Many Elements

```
const element = (
  <>
    <h1>Hello, React!</h1>
    <p>Welcome to learning JSX!</p>
  </>
);

ReactDOM.render(element, document.getElementById('root'));
```

In this example, the <h1> and <p> elements are wrapped inside a fragment, ensuring that they share a single root. React renders these elements into the DOM container specified. The resulting DOM structure looks like Listing 4-10.

Listing 4-10. Rendering Many Elements DOM Visualization

```
<div id="root">
  <h1>Hello, React!</h1>
  <p>Welcome to learning JSX!</p>
</div>
```

This approach helps keep your DOM clean and free from unnecessary wrappers, which is especially useful when dealing with large, nested components.

React's Efficient Rendering

One of the standout features of React is its ability to render changes efficiently. Unlike traditional DOM manipulation, where entire sections of the DOM might be replaced or re-rendered, React compares the current state of the virtual DOM to its previous state. It identifies the parts of the DOM that have changed and updates only those parts. This process, known as **reconciliation**, ensures that React applications are not only fast but also highly responsive.

For instance, if you update the content of a specific element, React will only update that particular DOM node rather than re-rendering the entire page. This selective update mechanism is a key reason why React is considered more performant than traditional DOM manipulation libraries.

> **Note** React re-renders only the parts of the DOM that have changed, making it more efficient than traditional DOM manipulation.

Embedding JavaScript Expressions in JSX

One of JSX's most powerful features is its ability to embed JavaScript expressions directly into your code using curly braces ({}). This capability allows you to seamlessly integrate dynamic values, perform calculations, or even call functions within your JSX, making it more flexible and dynamic than static HTML.

Embedding Variables

Variables in JSX can be embedded directly into the markup, enabling you to dynamically populate content. For instance, you might want to display a personalized welcome message based on a user's name. You can achieve this by embedding the variable representing the name inside curly braces as shown in Listing 4-11.

Listing 4-11. Embedding Variables

```
const name = "React Developer";
const element = <h1>Welcome, {name}!</h1>;
```

In this example, the name variable is dynamically inserted into the JSX, and React renders the greeting: Welcome, React Developer! This demonstrates how JSX allows you to bind JavaScript variables to your user interface effortlessly.

Conditional Rendering

JSX also supports conditional rendering, enabling you to display different elements or content based on a condition. The ternary operator is commonly used for this purpose, as it provides a concise way to implement conditional logic directly within JSX as illustrated in Listing 4-12.

Listing 4-12. Conditional Rendering

```
const isLoggedIn = true;
const element = <h1>{isLoggedIn ? "Welcome back!" : "Please sign in."}</h1>;
```

Here, the `isLoggedIn` variable determines whether the user is greeted with "Welcome back!" or prompted to "Please sign in." React evaluates the JavaScript expression inside the curly braces and renders the appropriate message. Conditional rendering is particularly useful in creating interactive user interfaces, such as displaying login/logout buttons or user-specific content.

Calling Functions

In addition to embedding variables, JSX allows you to call JavaScript functions to generate content dynamically. This is particularly helpful for scenarios like formatting data or combining multiple variables as shown in Listing 4-13.

Listing 4-13. JavaScript Function in JSX

```
const formatName = (user) => {
  return `${user.firstName} ${user.lastName}`;
}

const user = { firstName: "Alice", lastName: "Doe" };
const element = <h1>Hello, {formatName(user)}!</h1>;
```

In this example, the formatName function takes a user object and returns the full name. The JSX then calls this function inside curly braces, dynamically generating the greeting: Hello, Alice Doe!. By leveraging functions, you can keep your JSX clean and focus on logic within separate methods, improving code readability and maintainability.

Caution JSX expressions should remain simple. Avoid embedding complex logic directly in JSX; instead, move it to a function or method for better readability.

Using Props for Dynamic Rendering

Props play a crucial role in React by allowing parent components to pass data to child components, enabling the rendering of dynamic, personalized content. When combined with JSX, props provide a powerful mechanism for creating flexible and reusable components. For example, a parent component can pass a name prop to a child component to render personalized greetings as shown in Listing 4-14.

CHAPTER 4 JSX AND ELEMENT RENDERING

Listing 4-14. Passing Props to a Functional Component

```
const Welcome = (props) => {
  return <h1>Hello, {props.name}!</h1>;
}
const element = <Welcome name="Alice" />;
ReactDOM.render(element, document.getElementById('root'));
```

In this example, the name prop is embedded within the JSX using curly braces ({}), allowing the Welcome component to display a customized message based on the value passed. To make the code cleaner, you can destructure props directly in the function's parameter list as shown in Listing 4-15.

Listing 4-15. Destructuring Props in Functional Component

```
const Welcome = ({ name }) => {
  return <h1>Hello, {name}!</h1>;
}
```

Similarly, for class components, props are accessed via the this.props object, as shown in Listing 4-16.

Listing 4-16. Destructuring Props in Class Components

```
class Welcome extends React.Component {
  render() {
    return <h1>Hello, {this.props.name}!</h1>;
  }
}
```

By integrating props seamlessly into JSX, React enables components to render personalized and dynamic content based on the data they receive. This approach fosters reusability, as components can adapt to different contexts without modification.

> **Tip** Using props effectively allows you to create flexible and reusable components that can adapt based on the data they receive.

Advanced JSX Techniques

As you grow more comfortable with JSX, you'll encounter scenarios that require more advanced techniques to handle styling, grouping, and conditional rendering effectively. These techniques not only make your code cleaner but also enhance its readability and maintainability.

React Fragments for Grouping Elements

In JSX, you must wrap multiple sibling elements in a single parent element to satisfy its requirement for a single root. While you could use a `<div>` as a wrapper, doing so unnecessarily adds extra nodes to the DOM, which can clutter your output and affect performance. React Fragments provide a cleaner solution by allowing you to group multiple elements without adding extra nodes as shown in Listing 4-17.

Listing 4-17. Grouping Fragment Using React Fragments

```
function App() {
  return (
    <>
      <h1>Welcome to React</h1>
      <p>Enjoy learning JSX!</p>
    </>
  );
}
```

In this example, the empty angle brackets (<> </>) are shorthand for React Fragments. They group the <h1> and <p> elements without introducing an unnecessary <div> in the DOM.

Inline Styling in JSX

JSX supports inline styling, but unlike HTML, styles must be defined as JavaScript objects with camel-cased property names. This approach ensures that styles are dynamic and programmatically controllable as shown in Listing 4-18.

Listing 4-18. Inline Style JSX

```
const element = <h1 style={{ color: 'blue', fontSize: '20px' }}>Hello, React!</h1>;
```

Here, the `style` attribute accepts a JavaScript object, allowing you to define styles directly within your JSX. Inline styling is useful for dynamic styles that depend on variables or user interactions.

Applying CSS Classes in JSX

To apply CSS classes to elements, JSX uses the `className` attribute instead of `class` as illustrated in Listing 4-19. This distinction prevents conflicts with the `class` keyword in JavaScript.

Listing 4-19. JSX with CSS Classes

```
const element = <h1 className="header">Styled Header</h1>;
```

By using `className`, you can style your components with external CSS, combining the declarative power of JSX with the flexibility of traditional CSS.

CHAPTER 4   JSX AND ELEMENT RENDERING

Using JSX Spread Attributes

The spread operator (...) in JSX allows you to pass all properties of an object as props to a component, making it a convenient way to handle multiple props dynamically as illustrated in Listing 4-20.

Listing 4-20. Spread Operator with JSX

```
const user = { name: "Alice", age: 25 };
const element = <UserProfile {...user} />;
```

In this example, all properties of the user object (name and age) are passed to the UserProfile component as props. This technique is particularly useful when dealing with components that require numerous props.

Conditional Rendering with the Logical AND (&&) Operator

JSX allows you to conditionally render elements using the logical && operator. This approach renders the second expression only if the first is true, providing a concise alternative to ternary operators when there's no else case as shown in Listing 4-21.

Listing 4-21. Conditional Rendering with Logical AND (&&) Operator

```
const showMessage = true;
const element = <div>{showMessage && <p>Welcome to our site!</p>}</div>;
```

In this example, the <p> element is rendered only if showMessage is true. This technique is a common pattern for rendering optional UI elements, such as notifications or tooltips.

Rendering Lists of Elements

When rendering lists in React, you use the map method to iterate over an array and return a list of JSX elements. To optimize rendering, React requires that each list item has a unique key prop. This helps React efficiently update the DOM by tracking which items have changed, been added, or been removed as shown in Listing 4-22.

Listing 4-22. Rendering List Using Map

```
const numbers = [1, 2, 3];
const listItems = numbers.map((number) =>
<li key={number}>{number}</li>);
const element = <ul>{listItems}</ul>;
```

In this example, the array of numbers is mapped to <li> elements, each with a unique key. Without unique keys, React cannot accurately identify updates, which may lead to unexpected behavior.

Note Keys help React identify which items have changed, enhancing rendering performance.

Example: Building a User Dashboard Application

The **User Dashboard** will display a greeting, user information, and a list of tasks assigned to the user. It will also use conditional rendering to show a "No tasks available" message if the task list is empty.

CHAPTER 4   JSX AND ELEMENT RENDERING

Features

1. Display user data (name, email) using props.
2. Render a dynamic task list with conditional rendering.
3. Use React Fragments to group elements without adding unnecessary DOM nodes.
4. Style elements using both inline styles and CSS classes.
5. Use state to manage the list of tasks and allow users to add or remove tasks.

Here's how the complete application might look. Listing 4-23 illustrates the code for the entry point.

Listing 4-23. Interactive User Dashboard

```
// UserDashboard.jsx
import React, { useState } from "react";
import "./App.css"; // Import CSS for styling

function UserDashboard({ user }) {
  const [tasks, setTasks] = useState(user.tasks);

  const addTask = () => {
    const newTask = `Task ${tasks.length + 1}`;
    setTasks([...tasks, newTask]);
  };

  const removeTask = (index) => {
    const updatedTasks = tasks.filter((_, i) => i !== index);
    setTasks(updatedTasks);
  };
```

```jsx
return (
  <>
    {/* Greeting Section */}
    <header style={{ textAlign: "center", color: "blue",
    margin: "20px 0" }}>
      <h1>Welcome, {user.name}!</h1>
      <p>Your email: {user.email}</p>
    </header>

    {/* Task Section */}
    <main className="dashboard">
      <h2>Task List</h2>
      {tasks.length > 0 ? (
        <ul>
          {tasks.map((task, index) => (
            <li key={index}>
              {task}{" "}
              <button
                onClick={() => removeTask(index)}
                style={{ marginLeft: "10px" }}
              >
                Remove
              </button>
            </li>
          ))}
        </ul>
      ) : (
        <p>No tasks available. Add a task to get started!</p>
      )}
```

CHAPTER 4 JSX AND ELEMENT RENDERING

```
        <button onClick={addTask} className="add-task">
          Add Task
        </button>
      </main>
    </>
  );
}
export default function App() {
  const user = {
    name: "Alice Doe",
    email: "alice@example.com",
    tasks: ["Buy groceries", "Finish React project"],
  };

  return <UserDashboard user={user} />;
}
```

Figure 4-1 showcases the User Dashboard in action, displaying the greeting, user details, and a dynamic task list.

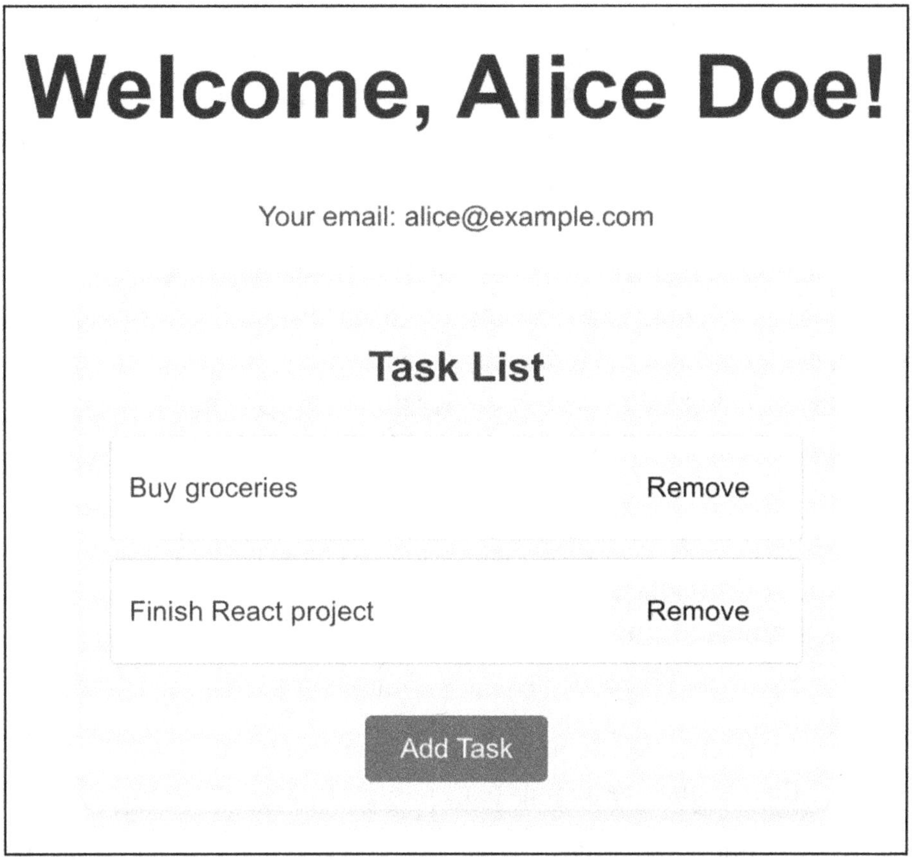

CHAPTER 4 JSX AND ELEMENT RENDERING

Welcome, Alice Doe!

Your email: alice@example.com

Task List

Buy groceries   Remove

Finish React project   Remove

Add Task

Figure 4-1. *User Dashboard showing a personalized greeting, user details, and a task list with add and remove functionality*

The UserDashboard component uses **React Fragments** (`<> </>`) to group the greeting and task sections without adding unnecessary DOM elements, ensuring a clean structure. The user object is passed as a **prop**, allowing dynamic rendering of the user's name, email, and tasks. For **state management**, the `useState` hook is employed to manage the task list, enabling users to add or remove tasks with dynamic updates to the UI. The application demonstrates **conditional rendering** by displaying a message encouraging the user to add tasks when the tasks array is empty. The task list is rendered dynamically using the **map** method, with each task assigned a unique key for efficient updates and rendering. Finally, the dashboard incorporates **styling** through a combination of inline styles (e.g., for the header) and CSS classes (e.g., for the "Add Task" button), showcasing flexibility in React styling approaches.

For simplicity and clarity, the entire **User Dashboard** application has been implemented in a single App.jsx file. However, in a real-world project, it is a best practice to break your application into smaller, reusable components. For example, you could create separate components for the header, task list, and task item, each handling its specific functionality and styling.

Here's an example of how you might structure these components:

1. UserHeader.jsx: Handles displaying the user's name and email
2. TaskList.jsx: Manages and renders the list of tasks
3. TaskItem.jsx: Represents individual tasks with their respective actions (e.g., remove task)

These components would then be imported and rendered in App.jsx to keep the code organized and maintainable. This modular approach not only improves readability but also makes testing and reusing components across different parts of your application much easier.

By presenting the entire application in a single file, we aim to focus on teaching key concepts without introducing complexity. As you advance, you'll see how separating components into individual files helps manage larger applications effectively.

Summary

In this chapter, we delved into JSX, a syntax extension for JavaScript that is integral to React development. By combining JavaScript with HTML-like syntax, JSX simplifies the process of writing and maintaining React code, making it both more readable and powerful. We started by understanding the basic rules of JSX, emphasizing that every JSX expression must have a single root element and that all tags must be properly closed. These foundational rules ensure that your React code adheres to the structural integrity required by the library.

Next, we explored how React renders elements to the DOM using the ReactDOM.render method. This process allows developers to efficiently define what appears on the screen, whether it's a single element or a group of elements wrapped in React Fragments to avoid unnecessary DOM nodes. Additionally, we discussed embedding JavaScript expressions within JSX, highlighting how variables, functions, and conditional logic can dynamically influence what is rendered, enhancing the flexibility and interactivity of your components.

The chapter also revisited props, illustrating how they enable dynamic rendering by passing data from parent components to child components. Through practical examples, we demonstrated how props can be destructured for cleaner and more concise code, and we reviewed their usage in both functional and class components. While props remain a cornerstone of React's reusability, this chapter connected them explicitly with JSX to showcase their practical implementation.

Toward the end, we introduced advanced JSX techniques that further extend its capabilities. These included React Fragments for grouping elements without extra DOM nodes, inline styling for dynamic and programmatic control over styles, and the use of the spread operator to pass multiple props at once. We also examined conditional rendering and the efficient handling of lists using unique keys, reinforcing React's declarative nature and rendering optimization.

CHAPTER 4   JSX AND ELEMENT RENDERING

By integrating these concepts into a cohesive sample application, such as the User Dashboard, you saw how to apply JSX rules, dynamic props, state, and advanced rendering techniques to build an interactive and modular user interface. The chapter not only laid a strong foundation for working with JSX but also emphasized how it serves as a bridge between JavaScript's logic and HTML's structure.

With a solid understanding of JSX and rendering elements, you are now prepared to tackle more complex topics. In the next chapter, we'll dive into handling events and conditional logic, equipping your components with the tools to respond to user interactions and adapt dynamically to changing states. As we progress, your ability to build truly interactive and responsive applications will take center stage.

CHAPTER 5

Handling Events and Conditional Rendering

Interactivity and dynamic user interfaces are central to modern web applications, and React excels in enabling both. Event handling allows you to manage user actions like clicks and form submissions, using a clean, declarative syntax tailored for React's components. Conditional rendering complements this by dynamically adjusting the UI based on the application's state or user input.

In this chapter, we'll explore event handling in functional and class components, highlighting key techniques like state management with useState and context binding. We'll also cover conditional rendering methods, including if statements, ternary operators, and logical operators, with practical examples. To tie it all together, we'll build an interactive login form that demonstrates these concepts in action.

By the end of this chapter, you'll be equipped to handle user interactions and create dynamic, responsive React applications.

CHAPTER 5   HANDLING EVENTS AND CONDITIONAL RENDERING

Introduction to Event Handling

Event handling in React is inspired by JavaScript's traditional event model but is tailored for the React environment. Events like clicks, form submissions, or keyboard presses can be handled using React's declarative approach, making your code cleaner and easier to maintain. React event handlers differ from their JavaScript counterparts in two significant ways: they use camelCase naming conventions (e.g., `onClick` instead of `onclick`), and instead of passing a string of code, you provide actual functions as handlers. These enhancements ensure better integration with React's component model and lifecycle.

Similarly, conditional rendering allows you to dynamically adjust what is displayed on the screen based on the application's state or user input. Whether you need to show a "Loading" spinner while waiting for data or display alternate content for logged-in vs. guest users, conditional rendering provides the flexibility to create personalized user experiences.

By combining event handling and conditional rendering, you can build robust and interactive web applications that respond seamlessly to user actions. This chapter will cover the core principles of handling events and explore the various ways to implement conditional rendering, ensuring you have the tools to build dynamic, user-driven interfaces.

Note   Remember to use camelCase for event handlers in React, like onClick and onChange, instead of the lowercase JavaScript conventions. This ensures that React recognizes them as valid events.

Event Handling in Functional Components

In functional components, event handling becomes simpler and more intuitive with the use of React's `useState` hook. This hook allows you to manage the component's state without the need for class syntax or explicitly binding this. Functional components are now the preferred way to handle events in modern React development because they are cleaner, more concise, and easier to maintain. Consider the example in Listing 5-1, where a basic click counter increments each time a button is clicked.

Listing 5-1. Click Counter

```
// Counter.jsx
import React, { useState } from 'react';
const ClickCounter =()=> {
  const [count, setCount] = useState(0);
  const handleClick = () => {
    setCount(count + 1);
  };
  return (
    <div>
      <p>You clicked {count} times</p>
      <button onClick={handleClick}>Click me</button>
    </div>
  );
}
export default ClickCounter;
```

In this example, the handleClick function is passed as the onClick event handler for the button. When the button is clicked, handleClick updates the count state variable using the setCount function provided by useState. React then re-renders the component, displaying the updated count.

> **Tip** For functional components, consider using arrow functions in event handlers to keep your code concise. However, avoid inline arrow functions in cases where performance is a concern, as they create new functions on every render.

Event Handling in Class Components

In class components, event handling introduces additional complexity due to the need to bind methods to the component instance. Without this explicit binding, event handlers lose their context, resulting in errors. However, with proper understanding, class components can still effectively manage events and state changes. The example in Listing 5-2 demonstrates toggling a button's state between "ON" and "OFF" using a class component.

Listing 5-2. Toggle Button

```jsx
// Toggle.jsx
import React, { Component } from 'react';
class Toggle extends Component {
  constructor(props) {
    super(props);
    this.state = { isToggled: false };
    this.handleToggle = this.handleToggle.bind(this);
  }
  handleToggle() {
    this.setState(prevState => ({ isToggled: !prevState.
    isToggled }));
  }
```

CHAPTER 5   HANDLING EVENTS AND CONDITIONAL RENDERING

```
  render() {
    return (
      <button onClick={this.handleToggle}>
        {this.state.isToggled ? 'ON' : 'OFF'}
      </button>
    );
  }
}
export default Toggle;
```

Here, the `handleToggle` method is explicitly bound to the class instance in the constructor using `this.handleToggle = this.handleToggle.bind(this)`. Each click on the button toggles the `isToggled` state between `true` and `false`, which changes the button's label from "ON" to "OFF" and vice versa.

Caution   Avoid forgetting to bind this in class component methods that handle events, such as `this.handleClick = this.handleClick.bind(this);`, in the constructor. Without this binding, your event handler won't have the correct context, causing errors.

Passing Parameters to Event Handlers

In many cases, event handlers need to perform context-specific actions based on additional data or parameters. React allows you to pass parameters to event handlers by wrapping the handler function in an arrow function. This ensures the handler receives the appropriate arguments without being immediately invoked when the component renders. Consider the example in Listing 5-3, which demonstrates how to greet a user by passing their name as a parameter.

Listing 5-3. Greeting User with a Parameter

```jsx
// GreetUser.jsx
const greetUser = (name)=> {
  alert(`Hello, ${name}`);
}

export default function App() {
  return (
    <div>
      <button onClick={(() => greetUser(("John")}>Greet</button>
    </div>
  );
}
```

In this example, the greetUser function accepts a name parameter and displays a personalized greeting in an alert dialog. The onClick event handler uses an arrow function to pass the string "John" as an argument to greetUser. This ensures that the function is called only when the button is clicked, rather than immediately during rendering.

Why Use Arrow Functions for Passing Parameters?

React's event handlers are designed to trigger functions when the corresponding user action occurs. However, directly calling a function with arguments inside the onClick attribute (e.g., onClick={greetUser("John")}) would execute the function immediately during the component's render

CHAPTER 5   HANDLING EVENTS AND CONDITIONAL RENDERING

phase. By wrapping the function in an arrow function (e.g., onClick={() => greetUser("John")}), you create a new function that is invoked only when the event is triggered. This approach is both intuitive and powerful, allowing you to add contextual data to your event handlers while maintaining React's declarative syntax.

Passing Multiple Parameters

Let's extend this concept by passing multiple parameters. Consider a scenario where you want to display a personalized message with both the user's name and their age as shown in Listing 5-4.

Listing 5-4. Greeting a User with Multiple Parameters

```
// GreetUser.jsx
const greetUser = (name, age) => {
  alert(`Hello, ${name}! You are ${age} years old.`);
}
export default function App() {
  return (
    <div>
      <button onClick={() => greetUser("Alice",
      30)}>Greet</button>
    </div>
  );
}
```

In this example, the greetUser function takes two parameters: name and age. The arrow function within the onClick event handler passes both parameters to greetUser, allowing the function to construct a detailed, dynamic message.

> **Note** When passing parameters to event handlers, wrapping them in an arrow function (e.g., `onClick={() => handleClick(param)}`) ensures they are called only when triggered, rather than immediately.

Conditional Rendering

Conditional rendering is a fundamental concept in React that enables components to dynamically adjust their output based on specific logic or conditions. By controlling what is rendered on the screen, you can provide a highly interactive and personalized user experience. React offers several approaches to implement conditional rendering, depending on the complexity of the condition and the desired readability of your code.

Using if Statements

When dealing with more complex conditions, using if statements outside of JSX provides a clear and straightforward way to control what is rendered. For instance, consider the example in Listing 5-5, where a message is displayed based on the user's login status.

Listing 5-5. Conditional Rendering Using if Statements

```
// Message.jsx
const Message = (props) => {
  const isLoggedIn = props.isLoggedIn;
  if (isLoggedIn) {
    return <h1>Welcome back!</h1>;
```

```
  } else {
    return <h1>Please sign in.</h1>;
  }
}
```

In this example, the `Message` component checks the value of `isLoggedIn`. If it is `true`, it renders a welcome message; otherwise, it prompts the user to sign in. This approach is particularly useful when the conditional logic is complex or spans multiple lines.

Using the Ternary Operator

For simpler conditions, the ternary operator provides a concise inline alternative to if statements. It allows you to directly embed the condition and its corresponding outputs within JSX. The example in Listing 5-6 illustrates this.

Listing 5-6. Conditional Rendering Using the Ternary Operator

```
// Message.jsx
const Message = (props) => {
  const isLoggedIn = props.isLoggedIn;
  return isLoggedIn ? <h1>Welcome back!</h1> : <h1>Please sign up.</h1>;
}
```

Here, the `Greeting` component returns one of two elements based on the value of `isLoggedIn`. The ternary operator is ideal for short, straightforward conditions that fit neatly on a single line, making the code both compact and readable.

Using the Logical && Operator

When you want to render content only if a condition is true, the logical && operator offers a minimalistic solution. This method is particularly useful when there is no "else" case. The example in Listing 5-7 illustrates this.

Listing 5-7. Conditional Rendering Using the Logical && Operator

```jsx
// Mailbox.jsx
const Mailbox = (props) => {
  const unreadMessages = props.unreadMessages;
  return (
    <div>
      <h1>Hello!</h1>
      {unreadMessages.length > 0 && <h2>You have
      {unreadMessages.length} unread messages.</h2>}
    </div>
  );
}
```

In this example, the <h2> element is rendered only if unreadMessages.length is greater than zero. If the array is empty, nothing is displayed. This concise syntax avoids the need for additional if statements, keeping the code clean and efficient.

Caution Be cautious when using conditional rendering with complex expressions. Overly complex conditions can make your JSX difficult to read and debug. If your conditional logic is complex, consider extracting it into a separate function.

CHAPTER 5   HANDLING EVENTS AND CONDITIONAL RENDERING

Creating Reusable Functions for Component Behavior

Encapsulating logic within reusable functions is a key practice for maintaining clean and modular React components. By isolating specific behaviors into functions, you can not only simplify your components but also enhance their reusability and testability. Functions that handle repetitive or common logic can significantly reduce code duplication and make your application easier to manage.

Consider the example in Listing 5-8, where a toggle button switches between "ON" and "OFF" states. The logic for toggling the state is encapsulated within a function, ensuring that the component remains organized and focused on its purpose.

Listing 5-8. Toggle Button with Function

```jsx
// ToggleButton.jsx
import React, { useState } from 'react';

const ToggleButton = () => {
  const [isOn, setIsOn] = useState(false);

  const toggle = () => setIsOn(!isOn);

  return <button onClick={toggle}>{isOn ? 'ON' : 'OFF'}
  </button>;
}

export default ToggleButton;
```

In this example, the `toggle` function is responsible for updating the state variable `isOn`. Each time the button is clicked, the `toggle` function toggles the state between `true` and `false`. By separating this logic from the JSX, the component remains clean and focused on rendering, while the function handles the behavior.

This approach not only improves code readability but also makes the logic reusable. For instance, the same `toggle` function could be adapted for other components that require similar functionality, such as toggling visibility, enabling/disabling features, or switching themes.

> **Tip** Use keys in lists to help React identify which items have changed, been added, or removed. This is especially important when rendering lists conditionally, as it optimizes re-rendering.

Example: Building an Interactive Login Form

To consolidate the event handling and conditional rendering concepts discussed in this chapter, let's create an interactive login form. This form will handle user input, validate login credentials, and display a personalized welcome message upon successful login. By incorporating React's state management, event handling, and conditional rendering, we can demonstrate how to build dynamic and responsive user interfaces.

The complete application is designed to provide a functional and interactive login form. Listing 5-9 illustrates the code for the `LoginForm.jsx` file, which serves as the entry point of the application.

Listing 5-9. Interactive Login Form

```jsx
// LoginForm.jsx
import React, { useState } from 'react';
import './LoginForm.css';

const LoginForm = () => {
  const [username, setUsername] = useState('');
```

CHAPTER 5   HANDLING EVENTS AND CONDITIONAL RENDERING

```
  const [password, setPassword] = useState('');
  const [isLoggedIn, setIsLoggedIn] = useState(false);
  const [errorMessage, setErrorMessage] = useState('');

  const handleSubmit = (event) => {
    event.preventDefault();
    if (username === 'user' && password === 'password') {
      setIsLoggedIn(true);
      setErrorMessage('');
    } else {
      setErrorMessage('Invalid credentials. Please try
      again.');
    }
  };

  const handleLogout = () => {
    setIsLoggedIn(false);
    setUsername('');
    setPassword('');
  };

  return (
    <div className="login-form-container">
      {isLoggedIn ? (
        <div className="welcome-message">
          <h1>Welcome, {username}!</h1>
          <button onClick={handleLogout}
          className="logout-button">
            Logout
          </button>
        </div>
      ) : (
        <form onSubmit={handleSubmit} className="login-form">
```

CHAPTER 5   HANDLING EVENTS AND CONDITIONAL RENDERING

```
        <h2>Login</h2>
        {errorMessage && <p className="error-message">
        {errorMessage}</p>}
        <label>
          Username:
          <input
            type="text"
            value={username}
            onChange={(e) => setUsername(e.target.value)}
            className="input-field"
          />
        </label>
        <label>
          Password:
          <input
            type="password"
            value={password}
            onChange={(e) => setPassword(e.target.value)}
            className="input-field"
          />
        </label>
        <button type="submit" className="login-button">
          Login
        </button>
      </form>
    )}
    </div>
  );
}

export default LoginForm;
```

CHAPTER 5 HANDLING EVENTS AND CONDITIONAL RENDERING

The login form is rendered when the user is not logged in, as shown in Figure 5-1. The login form includes input fields for the username and password, along with a "Login" button. It also provides an error message if the submitted credentials are invalid. This screen is displayed when the isLoggedIn state is false, prompting the user to enter their credentials to proceed.

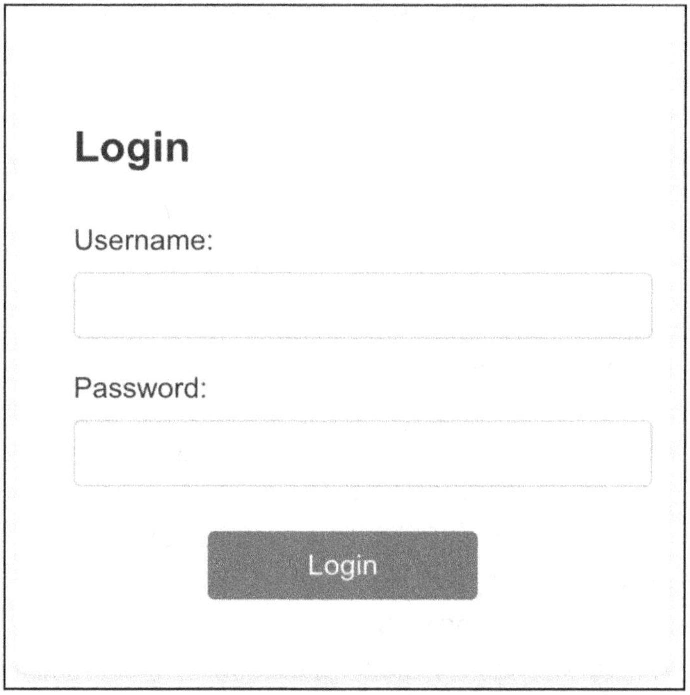

Figure 5-1. *Login form displaying input fields for username and password with a "Login" button*

The welcome screen is dynamically rendered when the user successfully logs in as shown in Figure 5-2. The welcome screen consists of a personalized greeting (Welcome, {username}!) and a "Logout" button. This screen is displayed when the isLoggedIn state is true.

103

CHAPTER 5   HANDLING EVENTS AND CONDITIONAL RENDERING

Figure 5-2. *Welcome screen displaying a personalized greeting and a "Logout" button after successful login*

The interactive login form showcases essential React concepts, providing a seamless and user-friendly experience. The application leverages **event handling** to manage key interactions, such as form submission and logout actions. The `handleSubmit` method validates user input, preventing default browser behavior and ensuring the credentials are checked. Similarly, the `handleLogout` method handles the logout process, resetting the application state to its initial values.

The form and welcome message toggle dynamically using **conditional rendering** based on the isLoggedIn state. This ensures that the user only sees the appropriate interface, enhancing usability. **State management** is implemented using the useState hook, which tracks the `username`, `password`, `isLoggedIn`, and `errorMessage` states, enabling real-time updates to the UI.

The application also incorporates **CSS styling** to create a clean and modern interface, emphasizing the importance of aesthetics in enhancing user experience. Upon entering valid credentials (username as "`user`" and password as "password"), the application updates the isLoggedIn state and displays a personalized welcome message. If the credentials are invalid, an error message appears without reloading the page. The "Logout" button resets the state, redirecting the user back to the login form.

CHAPTER 5   HANDLING EVENTS AND CONDITIONAL RENDERING

This implementation demonstrates React's powerful features, including state management, conditional rendering, and event handling, while maintaining a professional design that prioritizes user interaction and experience.

Summary

In this chapter, we delved into the critical concepts of handling user interactions and dynamically controlling the display of content in React applications. We began by exploring event handling, understanding how to manage user actions such as clicks and form submissions in both functional and class components. The chapter highlighted the differences in event handling syntax between functional components, which leverage hooks like useState, and class components, which require explicit binding of event handlers to ensure the correct context.

Next, we examined conditional rendering, an essential tool for creating responsive and interactive user interfaces. We covered various techniques, including the use of if statements for complex conditions, ternary operators for inline logic, and the logical && operator for concise conditional rendering. Each method was explained with practical examples to illustrate how to adapt the UI based on dynamic conditions effectively.

To solidify these concepts, we built a practical application: an interactive login form. This example showcased how to handle form submission events, validate user inputs, and use conditional rendering to display a personalized welcome message upon successful login. The login form also demonstrated clean UI design and state management, tying together the chapter's key themes in a cohesive, real-world scenario.

This chapter equipped you with the skills to create dynamic and user responsive React applications by combining event handling, state management, and conditional rendering. In the next chapter, we will

CHAPTER 5   HANDLING EVENTS AND CONDITIONAL RENDERING

take these skills further by focusing on rendering lists efficiently. You'll learn how to dynamically generate lists of items, the role of unique keys in tracking component updates, and strategies to manage data-driven UIs effectively. With these tools, you'll be ready to build React applications that handle collections of data seamlessly.

CHAPTER 6

Lists and Keys

Introduction to Lists in React

Lists are a foundational aspect of React applications, allowing developers to dynamically render collections of data, such as products, users, or messages. React efficiently handles lists by transforming arrays into components, enabling interactive and dynamic user interfaces. Keys, an essential feature in React, play a critical role in helping React identify changes in lists, optimize rendering, and improve overall performance.

Whether you are building an ecommerce product grid, a to-do list, or a social media feed, understanding how to render lists, manage dynamic data, and use keys correctly is critical. This chapter introduces these concepts with practical examples and explores advanced techniques like lazy rendering and virtualization for handling large datasets.

Note Lists in React are often combined with state management techniques to handle dynamic data updates, making them integral to most interactive applications.

CHAPTER 6   LISTS AND KEYS

Rendering Lists in React

In React, rendering lists is done using the `map()` function, which iterates over an array and transforms it into a set of React components. For example, a list of numbers can be easily displayed as shown in Listing 6-1.

Listing 6-1. Rendering a List of Numbers

```
const NumberList = (props) => {
  const numbers = props.numbers;
  return (
    <ul>
      {numbers.map((number) => (
        <li key={number}>{number}</li>
      ))}
    </ul>
  );
}
const numbers = [1, 2, 3, 4, 5];
ReactDOM.render(<NumberList numbers={numbers} />, document.getElementById('root'));
```

Here, the `map()` function creates a list of `<li>` elements for each number. Notice the use of the key attribute, which helps React identify and optimize updates to each list item.

Rendering Objects with Lists

Lists often consist of objects rather than primitive data types. You can use the `map()` function to render specific object properties as illustrated in Listing 6-2.

Listing 6-2. Rendering a List of Users

```
const users = [
  { id: 1, name: 'Alice' },
  { id: 2, name: 'Bob' },
  { id: 3, name: 'Charlie' },
];

const UserList = () => {
  return (
    <ul>
      {users.map((user) => (
        <li key={user.id}>{user.name}</li>
      ))}
    </ul>
  );
}
ReactDOM.render(<UserList />, document.getElementById('root'));
```

Tip Always include a key when rendering lists to ensure React can efficiently track changes to list items.

Here, each user object is rendered as a list item. The `id` property is used as a unique key for each list element, ensuring that React can optimize updates efficiently.

Understanding Keys in React

Keys play a **critical role** in optimizing React's rendering performance and ensuring predictable behavior when working with dynamic lists. React uses keys to identify which elements have changed, been added, or removed during updates, making the reconciliation process efficient. Without keys, React may unnecessarily re-render the entire list, impacting performance. Keys help React minimize DOM updates by reusing existing elements wherever possible and ensuring that updates are applied to the correct list items, especially when the order of elements changes.

To follow best practices, always use **unique and stable identifiers** such as a database `id` or a universally unique identifier (UUID) for keys. Avoid using **array indices** as keys because they can cause unexpected behaviors, particularly when the list is dynamic — such as when items are added, removed, or reordered. For example, when a list relies on array indices, React may lose track of changes and misalign updates, leading to rendering inconsistencies. Proper use of keys ensures smoother performance and a more predictable UI. Listing 6-3 shows how you can avoid common mistakes with keys.

Listing 6-3. Avoiding Common Mistakes with Keys

```
const items = ['Apple', 'Banana', 'Cherry'];
const ItemList = () => {
  return (
    <ul>
      {items.map((item, index) => (
        // Avoid using index as key
        <li key={index}>{item}</li>
      ))}
    </ul>
  );
}
```

If the order of `items` changes or elements are added/removed, using indices can cause unexpected behavior. Always use stable and unique identifiers.

CHAPTER 6   LISTS AND KEYS

Dynamic Lists: Adding, Removing, and Updating Items

Dynamic lists are an integral part of modern web applications where data frequently changes, such as to-do lists, product catalogs, or chat messages. Handling updates, additions, and deletions in these lists requires careful state management to ensure the UI reflects the changes efficiently. React provides the `useState` hook to manage dynamic list states, enabling developers to add, remove, or update items seamlessly while keeping the UI in sync with the underlying data.

When adding an item to a list, it's essential to use **immutable updates**. Instead of modifying the existing array, create a new array using spread syntax (`...`) or methods like `concat()` to ensure React recognizes the change and re-renders the list appropriately. For example, adding a new task to a to-do list involves appending the new task to the existing array without altering it directly.

Similarly, removing an item requires filtering the list based on a condition, such as an index or unique identifier. The `filter()` method allows you to create a new array that excludes the specific item, ensuring the list remains immutable. When updating items, use the `map()` method to iterate over the list, update the matching item, and return a new array with the modified data.

For larger and more complex applications, state management libraries like **Redux** or **Zustand** can provide a more scalable approach for handling dynamic lists. These tools centralize state management and allow components to subscribe to updates, reducing unnecessary re-renders and improving performance.

An example of a dynamic list might involve adding and removing tasks in a to-do application. Each operation—whether adding a new task, removing an existing one, or updating its status—relies on state updates. Proper use of React's tools ensures that dynamic lists remain performant,

CHAPTER 6　LISTS AND KEYS

consistent, and easy to maintain as applications scale. The example in Listing 6-4 illustrates how you can add and remove items from an array of items.

Listing 6-4. Adding and Removing List Items

```
import React, { useState } from 'react';
const TodoApp = () => {
  const [todos, setTodos] = useState(['Learn React', 'Write Code']);

  const addTodo = () => {
    const newTodo = `Task ${todos.length + 1}`;
    setTodos([...todos, newTodo]);
   // Add a new task
  };

  const removeTodo = (index) => {
    setTodos(todos.filter((_, i) => i !== index));
   // Remove a task
  };

  return (
    <div>
      <h2>To-Do List</h2>
      <ul>
        {todos.map((todo, index) => (
          <li key={index}>
            {todo}
            <button onClick={() => removeTodo(index)}>
            Remove</button>
          </li>
        ))}
```

```
      </ul>
      <button onClick={addTodo}>Add Task</button>
    </div>
  );
}

export default TodoApp;
```

Here, the `addTodo` function adds a new task to the list, while the `removeTodo` function deletes a task based on its index.

Nested Lists and Complex Data Structures

Rendering **nested lists** and **complex data structures** is a common requirement in applications that display hierarchical data, such as product categories, menus, or organizational charts. Nested data structures often include items with parent-child relationships, where each parent contains one or more children. In React, this can be achieved using recursive rendering or nested `map()` calls.

When the data is nested, each level of the hierarchy must be iterated over, and components must be created for both parent and child elements. For example, consider a list of categories where each category contains a sublist of items. You can use a recursive approach, where a function calls itself for each nested level, rendering child elements dynamically. Suppose we have a nested data structure of categories, where each category contains subcategories as shown in Listing 6-5, and Figure 6-1 shows the output in the browser.

CHAPTER 6   LISTS AND KEYS

Listing 6-5. Rendering a Nested List

```
import './NestedCategoryList.css';

const categories = [
  {
    name: 'Fruits',
    items: ['Apple', 'Banana', 'Cherry'],
  },
  {
    name: 'Vegetables',
    items: ['Carrot', 'Broccoli', 'Spinach'],
  },
];

const CategoryList = () => {
  return (
    <div className="category-list">
      {categories.map((category) => (
        <div key={category.name} className="category">
          <h3>{category.name}</h3>
          <ul>
            {category.items.map((item) => (
              <li key={item}>{item}</li>
            ))}
          </ul>
        </div>
      ))}
    </div>
  );
};

export default CategoryList;
```

CHAPTER 6   LISTS AND KEYS

Fruits
Apple
Banana
Cherry

Vegetables
Carrot
Broccoli
Spinach

Figure 6-1. *Nested list and complex data structure*

Here, we use a **nested** map() call: the outer map() iterates over the list of categories, and the inner map() generates <li> elements for each item inside the category. Each item and category have a **unique key** to ensure React optimizes the rendering process.

115

CHAPTER 6   LISTS AND KEYS

Recursive Rendering for Deeply Nested Structures

Recursion is a programming technique where a function calls itself to handle repetitive tasks, particularly useful for traversing hierarchical or nested structures. In the context of rendering deeply nested categories, recursion allows us to dynamically process any level of nesting without writing separate code for each level. For instance, in Listing 6-6, the function renders a category and checks for child categories. If child categories exist, the function calls itself to render them, ensuring that every nested level is processed in a consistent manner. This approach is preferred because it simplifies the code and makes it adaptable to varying levels of depth. While recursion can seem complex initially, especially for beginners, it is a powerful and efficient way to manage and render hierarchical data structures. Figure 6-2 shows the output in the browser.

Listing 6-6. Rendering a Recursive Deeply Nested List

```
const nestedCategories = [
  {
    name: 'Electronics',
    subcategories: [
      { name: 'Phones', subcategories: [] },
      { name: 'Laptops', subcategories: [{ name: 'Gaming
      Laptops', subcategories: [] }] },
    ],
  },
  {
    name: 'Clothing',
    subcategories: [
      { name: 'Men', subcategories: [] },
```

```
      { name: 'Women', subcategories: [] },
    ],
  },
];
const RecursiveCategory = ({ categories }) => {
  return (
    <ul>
      {categories.map((category) => (
        <li key={category.name}>
          {category.name}
          {category.subcategories && category.subcategories.
          length > 0 && (
            <RecursiveCategory categories={category.
            subcategories} />
          )}
        </li>
      ))}
    </ul>
  );
}
const App = () => {
  return (
    <div>
      <h2>Categories</h2>
      <RecursiveCategory categories={nestedCategories} />
    </div>
  );
}
```

Categories

Electronics
  Phones
  Laptops
    Gaming Laptops

Clothing
  Men
  Women

Figure 6-2. Rendering deeply nested categories

In this example, the `RecursiveCategory` component calls itself for each nested level of the data. If a category has child categories (`subcategories`), the function recursively renders them as a nested `<ul>` element. This pattern allows you to handle deeply nested or infinite data structures effectively.

Caution Ensure that each nested list has its own unique keys to avoid rendering conflicts.

CHAPTER 6   LISTS AND KEYS

Best Practices for Managing Lists and Keys

1. **Unique Keys**: Always provide unique keys for parent and child elements. This ensures React can track changes efficiently during re-rendering.

2. **Data Consistency**: Ensure the data structure for parent and child elements is consistent to avoid unexpected errors.

3. **Avoid Hardcoding**: Use dynamic iteration (like map()) to avoid hardcoding elements, making your code flexible and maintainable.

4. **Separation of Logic**: Keep recursive rendering logic separate from the main component to ensure readability and reusability.

By leveraging React's dynamic rendering capabilities, you can handle nested data structures with ease, ensuring your components are clean, maintainable, and scalable, even for deeply hierarchical data.

Advanced Techniques: Lazy Rendering and Virtualized Lists

Handling large lists efficiently is crucial for improving the performance and user experience of React applications. When a list contains thousands of items, rendering all elements at once can cause significant delays, slow down page load times, and overwhelm the browser. React offers advanced techniques, such as **lazy loading** and **virtualization**, to address these challenges by optimizing how and when list items are rendered.

CHAPTER 6   LISTS AND KEYS

Lazy Loading in React

Lazy loading defers the loading of components or parts of the application until they are needed. Instead of rendering everything up front, React allows you to split your code into smaller chunks and load components dynamically when required. This reduces the initial bundle size and improves the page load time. React achieves this using the React.lazy method and Suspense. Listing 6-7 demonstrates lazy loading in React.

Listing 6-7. Lazy Loading

```
import React, { Suspense, lazy } from 'react';

// Lazy loaded component
const ProductList = lazy(() => import('./ProductList'));

const App = () => {
  return (
    <div>
      <h1>Welcome to the Store</h1>
      <Suspense fallback={<div>Loading Products...</div>}>
        <ProductList />
      </Suspense>
    </div>
  );
}

export default App;
```

React's React.lazy allows for dynamic importing of the ProductList component, ensuring that it is only fetched when needed. This behavior is complemented by Suspense, which provides a fallback UI—such as a loading spinner—while the lazy-loaded component is being fetched. Together, these features optimize the application's performance by loading resources for ProductList only when the user navigates to that section, reducing initial load times and improving efficiency.

Virtualization of Large Lists

When working with massive datasets, rendering all list items at once is inefficient, as most items are not visible to the user. Virtualization techniques help by rendering only the portion of the list that is currently visible within the viewport. Libraries like react-window and react-virtualized are commonly used for this purpose. In virtualization, items outside the visible area are not rendered to the DOM. This reduces memory consumption and speeds up rendering, resulting in smoother scrolling and improved responsiveness. Listing 6-8 shows a virtualized list with react-window.

Listing 6-8. Virtualized List with react-window

```
import React from 'react';
import { FixedSizeList } from 'react-window';

const items = Array.from({ length: 10000 }, (_, index) =>
`Item ${index + 1}`);

const VirtualizedList = () => {
  return (
    <FixedSizeList
      height={400}    // Height of the container
      width={300}     // Width of the container
      itemSize={35}   // Height of each row
      itemCount={items.length}   // Total number of items
    >
      {({ index, style }) => (
        <div style={style}>{items[index]}</div>
```

```
    )}
  </FixedSizeList>
 );
}

export default VirtualizedList;
```

The FixedSizeList component from react-window allows developers to efficiently render large lists by specifying parameters like height, width, and itemSize to define the viewport and the size of each item. Only the rows currently visible within the viewport are rendered to the DOM, significantly reducing the number of DOM nodes and improving performance. As the list scrolls, items are dynamically rendered, providing a seamless user experience. For instance, if a list contains 10,000 items but only 10 are visible at any time, React will only render those 10 rows, conserving memory and processing power for other parts of the application.

When to Use Lazy Loading and Virtualization

1. Use **lazy loading** when components are large or non-essential, such as modal dialogs, separate pages, or components rendered on demand.

2. Use **virtualization** for rendering long lists, such as product catalogs, user tables, or message threads, where rendering all items simultaneously would cause lag.

By combining these techniques, developers can create highly optimized and scalable React applications capable of handling vast amounts of data while maintaining a smooth user experience.

Example: Product List with Add-to-Cart Functionality

This example in Listing 6-9 demonstrates a product list with dynamic additions and cart functionality.

Listing 6-9. Product List with Add-to-Cart Functionality

```
import React, { useState } from 'react';
import './ProductListAddToCart.css';

const ProductList = () => {
  const [products] = useState([
    { id: 1, name: 'Milk', price: 5 },
    { id: 2, name: 'Egg', price: 8 },
  ]);
  const [cart, setCart] = useState([]);

  const addToCart = (product) => {
    setCart([...cart, product]);
  };

  return (
    <div className="container">
      <div className="products-section">
        <h2>Products</h2>
        <div className="products-grid">
          {products.map((product) => (
            <div key={product.id} className="product-card">
              <h4>{product.name}</h4>
              <p>${product.price}</p>
              <button onClick={() => addToCart(product)}>
              Add</button>
```

CHAPTER 6 LISTS AND KEYS

```
          </div>
        ))}
      </div>
    </div>

    <div className="cart-section">
      <h2>Your Cart</h2>
      {cart.length === 0 ? (
        <p className="empty-cart">Your cart is empty.</p>
      ) : (
        <ul>
          {cart.map((item, index) => (
            <li key={index}>
              <span>{item.name}</span>
              <span>${item.price}</span>
            </li>
          ))}
        </ul>
      )}
    </div>
  </div>
  );
}

export default ProductList;
```

When you run the example in Listing 6-9, the page displays two main sections: Products and Cart. In the Products section, a list of available items (e.g., Laptop, Phone) is displayed, showing their name, price, and an "Add to Cart" button for each. When you click the "Add to Cart" button, the corresponding product is dynamically added to the Cart section on the right. The cart updates instantly without a page refresh, showcasing React's efficient state management.

The Cart section lists all selected products, showing their names and prices. If no items are added, the cart displays an empty state message like "Your cart is empty," ensuring the UI remains clean and user-friendly. Each addition uses React's state management (useState hook) to update the cart in real time. The example also emphasizes the importance of keys for list items to optimize rendering performance. By separating the cart and products visually, the design ensures clarity, allowing users to easily add products and view their cart contents.

This example demonstrates React's core concepts, including dynamic list rendering, state updates, and a responsive user interface, providing a foundation for building interactive ecommerce applications. Figure 6-3 shows the output in the browser.

Figure 6-3. *Output of the product list with Add-to-Cart functionality*

CHAPTER 6   LISTS AND KEYS

Summary

In this chapter, we explored the core concepts of rendering lists and the importance of keys in React applications for efficient updates. We began with the fundamentals of dynamically generating lists using the map() function and emphasized the critical role of unique keys in React's reconciliation process. Through practical examples, you learned how to render lists of both primitive values and objects while following best practices, such as avoiding array indices as keys to prevent unexpected behavior.

We also discussed managing **dynamic lists**, where items can be added, removed, or updated using React's useState hook, ensuring seamless state updates. The chapter introduced techniques for working with **nested and complex data structures**, including recursive rendering for deeply nested lists, allowing you to handle hierarchical data effectively.

On the performance front, we covered advanced techniques such as **lazy loading** and **virtualization**. You learned how lazy loading defers rendering components until needed, improving page load times, and how libraries like react-window optimize list rendering for large datasets by dynamically rendering only visible items.

By implementing these concepts, you are now equipped to build interactive, efficient, and scalable list-based components in React, even for complex applications with vast amounts of data. In the next chapter, we will explore how to break down your user interface into reusable, modular components, a fundamental principle for building scalable and maintainable React applications.

CHAPTER 7

Thinking in Components

React's power lies in its ability to break down complex user interfaces into small, reusable, and modular components. This component-driven architecture helps developers create scalable, maintainable, and flexible applications. In this chapter, we'll learn how to design UIs by "thinking in components," explore best practices for creating modular structures, and implement a practical example that ties these ideas together.

Understanding Components

At its core, a **component** is an independent unit of UI. Each component encapsulates its structure (HTML), behavior (logic), and style (CSS), making it easier to reuse and manage. Whether you are designing a simple button or an entire dashboard, components allow you to divide the interface into smaller pieces that work together seamlessly. Take the **Button** example as shown in Listing 7-1.

Listing 7-1. Button Component

```
function Button(props) {
  return <button>{props.label}</button>;
}
```

This simple Button component accepts a `label` prop, allowing you to reuse it with different text as illustrated in Listing 7-2.

Listing 7-2. Reusable Button Component

```
<Button label="Submit" />
<Button label="Cancel" />
```

Instead of writing repetitive HTML, you build once and reuse everywhere.

Note Components can be either **functional** or **class based**. Functional components are more commonly used in modern React applications due to their simplicity and compatibility with hooks.

Why Adopt a Component-Based Approach?

Thinking in components isn't just a React convention; it's a design philosophy. By adopting this approach, you gain several advantages:

1. **Reusability**: Components are reusable across the application, reducing redundancy and effort. For instance, a Card component can be reused to display products, user profiles, or articles.

2. **Maintainability**: Smaller components are easier to debug, test, and enhance without affecting the rest of the application.

3. **Scalability**: As applications grow, component-driven design ensures that the codebase remains organized and modular.

4. **Separation of Concerns**: Logic, styling, and markup are encapsulated, making components self-contained and easier to reason about.

Tip Treat components like building blocks. Smaller blocks can combine to form complex UIs, just like Lego pieces.

Steps to Think in Components

Breaking down the UI into components requires a systematic approach. Here's a structured way to design applications in React.

Start by examining the UI design (or wireframe) and identifying distinct sections. Each section that serves a specific purpose is a candidate for a component. For example, in a **shopping cart page**, the UI might include

- A **Header** for the app name
- A **Product List** displaying items in the cart
- A **Cart Summary** showing the total price and checkout button

Next, divide the page into small, manageable components. Using the shopping cart as an example, you can create a hierarchy:

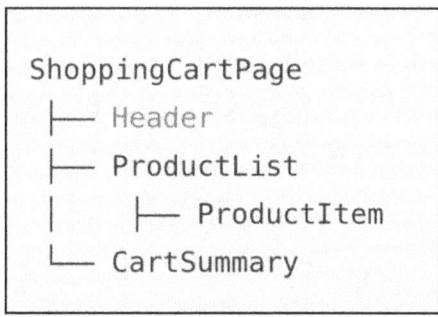

CHAPTER 7   THINKING IN COMPONENTS

At this stage

- `Header` is a stand-alone component displaying navigation.
- `ProductList` holds a list of `ProductItem` components.
- `CartSummary` handles price calculation and checkout actions.

Once components are identified, determine how they interact. Parent components (like `ProductList`) manage the data and pass it down to children (`ProductItem`) through props. Listings 7-3 to 7-5 illustrate `ProductItem`, `ProductList`, and `shoppingCartPage` components, respectively.

Listing 7-3. ProductItem Component

```
const ProductItem = ({ name, price }) => {
  return (
    <div>
      <h4>{name}</h4>
      <p>Price: ${price}</p>
    </div>
  );
}
```

Listing 7-4. ProductList Component

```
const ProductList = ({ products }) => {
  return (
    <div>
      {products.map((product) => (
        <ProductItem key={product.id} name={product.name}
          price={product.price} />
      ))}
```

```
    </div>
  );
}
```

Listing 7-5. ShoppingCartPage Component

```
function ShoppingCartPage() {
  const products = [
    { id: 1, name: 'Laptop', price: 1000 },
    { id: 2, name: 'Phone', price: 500 },
  ];

  return <ProductList products={products} />;
}
```

Here:

- `ProductList` is responsible for rendering a list.

- `ProductItem` is a reusable child that displays individual product details.

- Data flows from the parent (`ShoppingCartPage`) to children via props.

Start by building smaller components, like `ProductItem`, and gradually compose them into larger ones. A common React strategy is **bottom-up development**, where individual components are implemented and integrated into parent components.

Types of Components

React components can be classified into two main types.

Functional Components

Functional components are **JavaScript functions** that take props as input and return **JSX** (JavaScript XML) to render UI elements. Introduced as part of React's modern development approach, functional components are simpler, more concise, and easier to understand compared to class components. They are now the preferred way to build components in React. Listing 7-6 illustrates an example of a functional component.

Listing 7-6. Functional Component

```
function Greeting(props) {
  return <h1>Hello, {props.name}!</h1>;
}
```

Class Components

Class components are **ES6 classes** that extend `React.Component`. They are used to create more complex components that manage their **own state** and include **lifecycle methods**. While functional components are now preferred in modern React development, class components are still essential to understand, especially when working with older React codebases. Listing 7-7 illustrates an example of a class component.

Listing 7-7. Class Component

```
class Greeting extends React.Component {
  render() {
    return <h1>Hello, {this.props.name}!</h1>;
  }
}
```

> **Caution** Functional components are recommended for new projects. Class components are still valid but are less preferred in modern React due to hooks.

Reusability and Composition

Components in React are the building blocks of a user interface. To maximize efficiency, components should be both **reusable** and **composable**. Reusability ensures that a single component can be used multiple times with different data or contexts, reducing redundancy and improving maintainability. To achieve this, components should use **props** to accept dynamic data and avoid hardcoding values within the component itself. For instance, a `Product` component that accepts `name` and `price` as props can display different products without requiring separate implementations. By keeping components generic and stateless, developers can further enhance their flexibility. Stateless components focus on presenting data and avoid managing state, leaving that responsibility to parent components, which pass down data via props. Listing 7-8 illustrates an example of reusability of a `product` component.

Listing 7-8. Component Reusability in React

```
function Product({ name, price }) {
  return (
    <div>
      <h3>{name}</h3>
      <p>Price: ${price}</p>
    </div>
  );
}
```

Chapter 7 Thinking in Components

Composition involves combining smaller components to build complex user interfaces. Instead of creating large, monolithic components, React encourages breaking the UI into smaller, modular components and nesting them together. For example, an application can be composed of a `Header`, `ProductList`, and `CartSummary`, where the `ProductList` itself reuses a `ProductItem` component to display individual products. This modular structure makes the code clean, readable, and easy to maintain while also promoting a clear separation of concerns. Parent components handle state and behavior, while child components focus on presentation. Listing 7-9 illustrates an example of composition in React.

Listing 7-9. Component Composition in React

```
function App() {
  return (
    <div>
      <Header />
      <ProductList />
      <CartSummary />
    </div>
  );
}
```

Tip Aim to create **stateless components** whenever possible. Let parent components handle state and pass it down to child components via props.

Best Practices for Component Design

When designing React components, it is essential to follow best practices to ensure the code remains modular, maintainable, and easy to test. The Single Responsibility Principle states that each component should have one clear purpose, focusing on a specific part of the UI or logic. Avoid overloading components with too many responsibilities; instead, break down large components into smaller, reusable subcomponents that are easier to manage and debug.

Using meaningful names is equally important. Descriptive names like `ProductCard` or `UserProfile` make it clear what the component does, unlike generic names such as `Card` or `Box`, which can cause confusion as the application grows. Additionally, components should implement prop validation using tools like `PropTypes` or `TypeScript` to ensure the correct data types are passed as props. This reduces runtime errors and improves code reliability.

Keeping components small is a good rule of thumb. If a component exceeds 200 lines of code, consider splitting it into smaller, more focused components. This promotes reusability and ensures the code remains clean and readable.

Caution Avoid creating "God components" that handle too much functionality or render an entire page on their own. These components are difficult to test, maintain, and extend, defeating the purpose of React's component-based architecture. By adhering to these best practices, you can design React components that are modular, scalable, and easier to work with across the application lifecycle.

Example: Designing a Shopping Cart Page

Let's design the shopping cart page by breaking it into **reusable components** as shown in Listing 7-10. The application is structured into modular components such as Header, ProductList, and CartSummary, each serving a specific purpose to enhance maintainability and scalability.

The Header displays the title of the page, ProductList dynamically renders a list of products with their details, and CartSummary summarizes the total price with a "Checkout" button. By composing these components together, the UI remains clean, organized, and easy to understand.

Figure 7-1 shows the output of the shopping cart page, demonstrating how the components work together seamlessly to display the products and the cart summary in a well-structured layout. This design reflects the principles of reusability and composition, ensuring a modular and scalable solution.

Header Component

Listing 7-10. Shopping Cart Application

```
import React from "react";
const Header = () => {
  return (
    <header className="shopping-header">
      <h1>Shopping Cart</h1>
    </header>
  );
};
export default Header;
```

Product Component

```
import React from "react";
const Product = ({ name, price }) => {
  return (
    <div>
      <h4>{name}</h4>
      <p>Price: ${price}</p>
    </div>
  );
}
export deafult Product;
```

ProductList Component

```
import React from "react";

const ProductList = ({ products }) => {
  return (
    <div className="product-list-container">
      <h2>Products</h2>
      <ul className="product-list">
        {products.map((product) => (
          <li key={product.id} className="product-item">
            <div>
              <p className="product-name">{product.name}</p>
              <p className="product-price">Price: ${product.
              price}</p>
            </div>
          </li>
        ))}
```

```
      </ul>
    </div>
  );
};

export default ProductList;
```

CartSummary Component

```
import React from "react";
const CartSummary = ({ total }) => {
  return (
    <div className="cart-summary">
      <h2>Cart Summary</h2>
      <p className="cart-total">Total Price: ${total.
      toFixed(2)}</p>
    </div>
  );
};

export default CartSummary;
```

Composing the Page

```
import React from "react";
import Header from "./Header";
import ProductList from "./ProductList";
import CartSummary from "./CartSummary";
import "./ShoppingCart.css"; // Import global styles for this
                                component
```

CHAPTER 7   THINKING IN COMPONENTS

```
const ShoppingCart = () => {
  const products = [
    { id: 1, name: "Laptop", price: 1000 },
    { id: 2, name: "Phone", price: 500 },
  ];

  const total = products.reduce((sum, product) => sum + product.price, 0);

  return (
    <div className="shopping-cart">
      <Header />
      <ProductList products={products} />
      <CartSummary total={total} />
    </div>
  );
};

export default ShoppingCart;
```

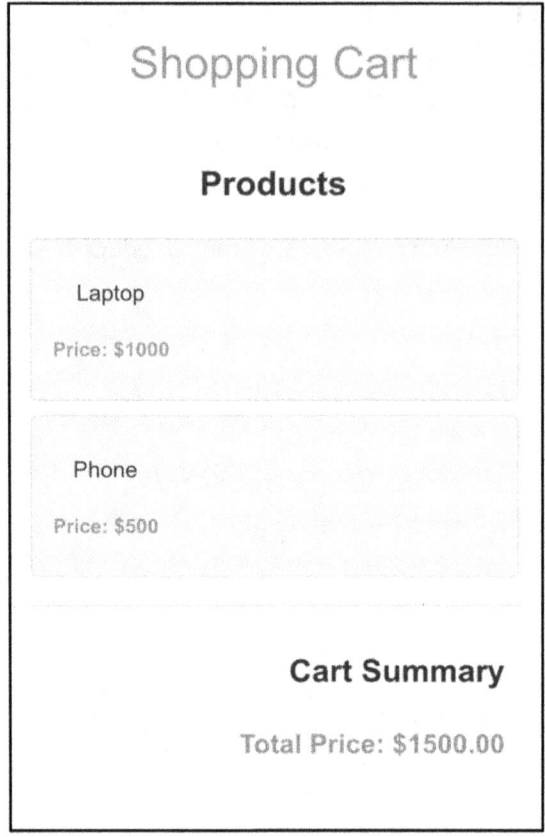

Figure 7-1. Output of the shopping cart page

Common Challenges When Thinking in Components

When designing components in React, developers often encounter several challenges. One common issue is **over-componentization**, where the UI is broken down into too many small components. While modularity is essential, an excessive number of components can make the code difficult to follow, understand, and maintain.

Another challenge is **state management**. Deciding where the state should reside can be tricky, especially in complex applications. The best practice is to **lift the state up** to the nearest common ancestor component that needs to manage or share it. This ensures that child components remain stateless and focus solely on presenting the data.

Lastly, balancing **reusability and specificity** can be difficult. While reusability is important, making components overly generic can complicate their implementation and reduce clarity. Components should be flexible enough to handle variations but not so abstract that they become hard to use or understand. Striking the right balance ensures clean, maintainable, and reusable components without unnecessary complexity.

Summary

In this chapter, we explored the concept of designing applications by **thinking in components**, a core principle in React development. Components are reusable pieces of code that encapsulate UI elements, making applications easier to manage and scale. By breaking the UI into smaller, manageable parts, components improve **reusability**, **maintainability**, and **scalability** of the codebase.

We discussed the essential **steps to thinking in components**, which include analyzing the UI, breaking it down into smaller parts, identifying reusable elements, and defining a clear component hierarchy. The concepts of **reusability** and **composition** were highlighted, emphasizing the importance of using props to pass data, keeping components small and focused, and designing them to be composable.

To ensure clean and efficient designs, we explored **best practices**, such as following the **single responsibility principle** and validating props to maintain code clarity and predictability. Finally, we implemented a **practical example** by building a shopping cart page. This example demonstrated how to create modular, reusable components like `Header`, `ProductList`, and `CartSummary` to construct a complete UI efficiently.

In the next chapter, we will dive into enhancing the visual appearance of components through modern styling techniques and best practices.

CHAPTER 8

Styling Your Application

Styling is a critical aspect of web development, as it determines how your application looks and feels. React provides flexibility in styling, allowing you to choose between traditional CSS, CSS-in-JS libraries, and frameworks like Tailwind or Bootstrap. In this chapter, we will explore various techniques for styling React applications, their pros and cons, and best practices for building a clean, maintainable, and responsive UI.

Importance of Styling in React Applications

Styling in React is more than just making an application look good—it plays a pivotal role in shaping the overall **user experience (UX)** and ensuring accessibility for all users. In modern web development, aesthetics and functionality go hand in hand. A well-designed, visually appealing application can engage users effectively, encourage interaction, and ensure your product stands out from the competition. At the same time, intuitive design and proper styling make navigation seamless, reduce cognitive load, and enable users to complete tasks efficiently.

An essential characteristic of a well-styled React application is its **intuitiveness.** Intuitive styling ensures that users can interact with your application effortlessly, where design choices align naturally with

CHAPTER 8   STYLING YOUR APPLICATION

user expectations. For instance, buttons are visibly clickable, links are highlighted appropriately, and form inputs have clear focus indicators. Users should never be left guessing where to click or how to navigate the application.

Additionally, well-executed styling enhances the **visual appeal** of the application, keeping users engaged. Carefully chosen color palettes, font styles, and spacing create a harmonious look and feel, making your app not only functional but also pleasant to use. When aesthetics aligns with branding and content, it evokes a stronger emotional connection with users, boosting retention and satisfaction.

Another critical factor is **responsiveness**. In today's digital landscape, where users access applications from a wide range of devices—from desktops and tablets to smartphones—styling must adapt seamlessly to varying screen sizes and resolutions. Responsive design techniques, such as flexible grids, CSS media queries, and relative units (like percentages and rem), ensure that your app maintains usability and visual consistency across all devices. React applications often leverage libraries like **styled-components**, **CSS-in-JS**, or frameworks like **Bootstrap** and **Tailwind CSS** to achieve responsiveness effortlessly.

It's important to note that styling also directly influences **accessibility**. A well-styled application considers users with visual impairments or other disabilities, ensuring they can interact with the content effectively. Prioritizing **contrast ratios** for text and background colors is vital to meet **Web Content Accessibility Guidelines (WCAG)** standards, making content readable for all users, including those with low vision. Using semantic HTML elements, appropriate ARIA roles, and visible focus states for keyboard navigation further enhances accessibility, enabling an inclusive experience.

Ultimately, styling in React applications should strike a balance between form and function. While aesthetics creates visual appeal, the purpose of styling is to ensure clarity, usability, and accessibility for every

CHAPTER 8 STYLING YOUR APPLICATION

user interacting with the app. By combining responsive techniques, accessibility best practices, and modern styling tools, developers can create engaging, user-friendly, and inclusive interfaces that elevate the overall quality of their applications.

Adding Styles Using Traditional CSS

One of the simplest and most widely understood methods for styling React applications is **traditional CSS**, which involves linking external stylesheets to components. By leveraging this approach, developers can apply familiar CSS techniques without introducing additional complexity or dependencies. Traditional CSS is ideal for developers transitioning from conventional web development to React because it aligns closely with how styles are managed in static HTML applications.

To implement traditional CSS, you first define styles in a .css file and then import that file into your React component. The styles are applied using class names, just as you would in standard HTML. Listing 8-1 demonstrates this approach effectively.

Listing 8-1. Using a CSS File

```
/* App.css */
.header {
  font-size: 2rem;
  color: blue;
}
```

In your component, import the CSS file and apply the class name to the desired element:

```
// App.js
import './App.css';

const Header = () => {
  return <h1 className="header">Welcome to My App</h1>;
}

export default Header;
```

Here, the header class from the CSS file is applied to the <h1> tag, styling it with a font size of 2rem and a blue color. This method keeps the styling and logic neatly separated, providing clarity to developers and reducing code clutter within the component.

Pros of Using Traditional CSS

Traditional CSS has several advantages, particularly for developers who are already proficient with standard CSS techniques. The first major benefit is its **simplicity**—no additional tools, libraries, or configurations are needed beyond linking the stylesheet. Developers can maintain a clear separation of concerns by keeping styles in a centralized file, making the codebase clean and easy to understand. This method is also ideal for small projects where managing styles does not require advanced techniques like CSS-in-JS or scoped styles.

Cons of Using Traditional CSS

While traditional CSS offers simplicity, it does come with limitations, especially in large-scale applications. One significant challenge is the risk of **class name collisions**. When multiple components share the same class names, unintended style overrides can occur, leading to inconsistent UI behavior. For example, using generic names like `title` or `button` across components can create conflicts, as the styles may unintentionally bleed into unrelated elements.

Inline Styling in React

Inline styling in React provides a straightforward way to apply styles directly to an element using the style attribute. Unlike traditional CSS, inline styles in React are defined as **JavaScript objects**, where style properties are written in camelCase instead of the usual kebab-case. This makes it convenient to dynamically update styles based on logic or user interactions within a component. In Listing 8-2, a simple button is styled using inline styles.

Listing 8-2. Inline Style in React

```
const Button = () => {
  return (
    <button
      style={{
        backgroundColor: 'blue',
        color: 'white',
        padding: '10px',
        borderRadius: '5px',
      }}
    >
      Click Me
    </button>
  );
}
```

Here, the `style` attribute accepts a JavaScript object where properties like `backgroundColor`, `padding`, and `borderRadius` are defined in camelCase format. The resulting button appears with a blue background, white text, and rounded corners.

Pros of Inline Styling

One of the biggest advantages of inline styling is that **styles are scoped to the specific component**. This eliminates the risk of class name collisions and makes the styling explicit and localized to the element. Inline styling is also particularly useful for **dynamic styling**, where styles need to change based on certain conditions or user interactions. For instance, you can easily toggle the button's background color based on a state variable as shown in Listing 8-3.

Listing 8-3. Dynamic Style in React

```
function DynamicButton() {
  const [isClicked, setIsClicked] = React.useState(false);

  return (
    <button
      style={{
        backgroundColor: isClicked ? 'green' : 'red',
        color: 'white',
        padding: '10px',
        borderRadius: '5px',
      }}
      onClick={() => setIsClicked(!isClicked)}
    >
```

```
      {isClicked ? 'Clicked' : 'Click Me'}
    </button>
  );
}
```

Here, the background color dynamically changes to green when the button is clicked and returns to red otherwise. Inline styling makes it intuitive to manage such interactive styles without relying on external stylesheets.

Cons of Inline Styling

Despite its simplicity and dynamic capabilities, inline styling has notable limitations. One of the main drawbacks is the **lack of reusability**. Since inline styles are defined directly within components, they cannot be shared across multiple elements or components, leading to code duplication and redundancy.

Additionally, inline styles can quickly become **hard to maintain** in larger applications. As the number of style properties increases, the inline style object can clutter your component, making the code less readable. This is particularly problematic when dealing with complex UIs that require extensive styling.

CSS Modules

CSS Modules are a powerful approach to styling components in React, enabling scoped and modular styles without the risk of class name collisions. With CSS Modules, each .css or .module.css file generates unique class names that apply only to the component where they are imported, providing a clean and maintainable way to style applications.

CHAPTER 8   STYLING YOUR APPLICATION

How CSS Modules Work

A CSS Module file is defined with the `.module.css` extension. When the styles are imported into a React component, they are automatically transformed into **unique class names** by the build tool (e.g., Webpack). These class names ensure that styles remain scoped to the component, preventing conflicts with other stylesheets. The example in Listing 8-4 demonstrates how CSS Modules are implemented in a React project.

Listing 8-4. Using CSS Modules

```css
/* Button.module.css */
.button {
  background-color: blue;
  color: white;
  padding: 10px;
  border-radius: 5px;
  font-size: 16px;
  cursor: pointer;
}
```

Importing and Using the Module in a Component:

```js
// Button.js
import React from 'react';
import styles from './Button.module.css';

function Button() {
  return <button className={styles.button}>Click Me</button>;
}

export default Button;
```

In this example, the button class defined in Button.module.css is imported into the Button component as an object (styles.button). When the component is rendered, React generates a unique class name (e.g., Button_button__3Kj4b), which ensures the style applies only to this specific component.

Pros of CSS Modules

One of the main advantages of CSS Modules is that they **scope styles locally** to the components, ensuring a modular and conflict-free approach to styling. This is particularly beneficial in large-scale applications where multiple developers might work on various components. By scoping styles, you eliminate the need to follow strict class naming conventions to avoid clashes.

Furthermore, CSS Modules enable you to **write clean and semantic CSS** without worrying about manually generating unique class names. This helps maintain a clean separation of styles and logic, adhering to good coding practices. Another notable advantage is that CSS Modules integrate seamlessly with popular build tools like **Create React App** and **Webpack**. Most modern React setups come preconfigured to support CSS Modules, so minimal effort is required to get started.

Cons of CSS Modules

Despite their benefits, CSS Modules do require a build setup that supports them, such as Webpack or Vite. For developers unfamiliar with these tools, configuring the project to enable CSS Modules might present a slight learning curve. Additionally, while CSS Modules excel at scoping styles, they can become verbose when used extensively, especially in components with dynamic class names or large style objects.

CHAPTER 8   STYLING YOUR APPLICATION

CSS-in-JS Libraries

CSS-in-JS libraries are a modern approach to styling React applications, where styles are written directly in JavaScript code. These libraries, such as **styled-components** and **emotion**, enable you to define component-level styles using JavaScript syntax. Unlike traditional CSS or CSS Modules, CSS-in-JS tightly integrates styling with logic, allowing for dynamic and context-aware styling.

CSS-in-JS libraries allow you to define styles as JavaScript variables or template literals, which are then injected into the DOM as inline styles or scoped class names. This approach eliminates the need for external CSS files and provides a seamless styling solution within your components. The example in Listing 8-5 demonstrates the use of **styled-components**, one of the most popular CSS-in-JS libraries.

Listing 8-5. Using Styled Components

```
import styled from 'styled-components';

const Button = styled.button`
  background-color: blue;
  color: white;
  padding: 10px;
  border-radius: 5px;
  font-size: 16px;
  cursor: pointer;

  &:hover {
    background-color: darkblue;
  }
`;
```

CHAPTER 8   STYLING YOUR APPLICATION

```
const App = () => {
  return <Button>Click Me</Button>;
}

export default App;
```

In this example, the Button component is styled directly within the JavaScript file using `styled.button`. The styles are defined as template literals and include CSS features such as pseudo-classes (e.g., &:hover) for dynamic behaviors. When the component is rendered, a unique class name is automatically generated for the Button, ensuring the styles remain scoped and conflict-free.

The primary benefit of CSS-in-JS libraries is the ability to **combine styles with logic** seamlessly. By embedding styles within the component file, you ensure that styling logic stays closely tied to the component's behavior and structure. This is especially useful for projects that require highly dynamic styles, such as themes or conditional styling based on component states.

Dynamic Styling

With CSS-in-JS, you can dynamically change styles based on props, states, or themes. For instance, Listing 8-6 demonstrates dynamic styling using CSS-in-JS.

Listing 8-6. Dynamic Styled Components

```
const Button = styled.button`
  background-color: ${(props) => (props.primary ? 'blue' : 'gray')};
  color: white;
  padding: 10px;
`;
```

```
function App() {
  return (
    <>
      <Button primary>Primary</Button>
      <Button>Secondary</Button>
    </>
  );
}
```

Here, the primary prop determines the background color of the button dynamically, enabling component-level customization.

Theming Support

Libraries like **styled-components** and **emotion** provide built-in support for theming, making it easy to manage global styles and themes across your application. You can define a theme and pass it to components using a ThemeProvider as mentioned in Listing 8-7.

Listing 8-7. Theming Using ThemeProvider

```
import { ThemeProvider } from 'styled-components';

const theme = {
  colors: {
    primary: 'blue',
    secondary: 'gray',
  },
};

const Button = styled.button`
  background-color: ${(props) => props.theme.colors.primary};
  color: white;
  padding: 10px;
`;
```

CHAPTER 8   STYLING YOUR APPLICATION

```
const App = () => {
  return (
    <ThemeProvider theme={theme}>
      <Button>Click Me</Button>
    </ThemeProvider>
  );
}
```

    This approach centralizes your styles and makes them reusable across components, which is particularly beneficial for applications requiring light/dark modes or consistent design systems. CSS-in-JS automatically generates unique class names for components, ensuring that styles do not clash with other parts of the application. This eliminates the need for naming conventions or tools like CSS Modules.

Using Preprocessors (SCSS/SASS)

Preprocessors like **SASS** (Syntactically Awesome Style Sheets) and its more commonly used extension **SCSS** provide an enhanced way to write CSS, adding features that make styles more powerful, maintainable, and reusable. By extending the capabilities of traditional CSS, preprocessors streamline styling workflows, particularly for large projects with complex design requirements.

    While CSS works well for basic styling, it lacks features like variables, nesting, mixins, and functions that make styles easier to manage. SCSS and SASS fill this gap, enabling you to write cleaner and more organized styles. SCSS syntax closely resembles traditional CSS, making it easier for developers to transition, while SASS offers a more concise, indentation-based syntax.

CHAPTER 8   STYLING YOUR APPLICATION

Features of SCSS/SASS

Variables: Variables allow you to define reusable values, such as colors, fonts, or spacing, making it easy to maintain consistency across your application as shown in Listing 8-8.

Listing 8-8. Reusable Variables in SCSS

```
// styles.scss
$primary-color: blue;
$padding: 10px;

.button {
  background-color: $primary-color;
  color: white;
  padding: $padding;
  border-radius: 5px;
}
```

Here, the $primary-color and $padding variables are reused to ensure uniform styling for buttons. Changing a single variable updates all instances where it is used, reducing redundancy.

Nesting: SCSS allows you to nest styles within parent selectors, reflecting the structure of your HTML and reducing repetitive code as shown in Listing 8-9.

Listing 8-9. Nesting in SCSS

```
// styles.scss
.navbar {
  background-color: blue;

  ul {
    list-style: none;
```

```
    li {
      display: inline-block;

      a {
        text-decoration: none;
        color: white;

        &:hover {
          color: yellow;
        }
      }
    }
  }
}
```

The nested syntax improves readability and eliminates the need for repeatedly typing parent class names. In this example, the hover state for the anchor <a> element is neatly nested within the .navbar class structure.

Mixins: Mixins allow you to define reusable blocks of styles that can be included in multiple selectors. They support dynamic inputs, making them highly versatile for repetitive tasks as shown in Listing 8-10.

Listing 8-10. Mixins in SCSS

```
// styles.scss
@mixin button-style($bg-color) {
  background-color: $bg-color;
  color: white;
  padding: 10px;
  border-radius: 5px;
}

.primary-button {
  @include button-style(blue);
}
```

```
.secondary-button {
  @include button-style(gray);
}
```

Here, the @mixin directive defines a reusable style for buttons, and @include applies the mixin to individual components with dynamic background colors.

Functions and Operations: SCSS supports mathematical operations and functions for creating dynamic styles, such as adjusting colors, margins, or sizes as shown in Listing 8-11.

Listing 8-11. Functions and Operations in SCSS

```
$base-size: 16px;

.header {
  font-size: $base-size * 2; // 32px
}
.button {
  background-color: lighten(blue, 10%);
}
```

Functions like lighten() and mathematical calculations simplify tasks that would otherwise require manual adjustments in traditional CSS.

How to Use SCSS/SASS in React

To integrate SCSS/SASS in a React project, you need to configure a preprocessor using tools like **node-sass** or **sass**. Install SASS via npm, rename your CSS files with a .scss extension (e.g., styles.scss), and import the SCSS file into your React component as shown in Listing 8-12.

Listing 8-12. Install SASS

```
npm install sass
// Button.jsx
import './styles.scss';

const Button = () => {
  return <button className="button">Click Me</button>;
}
export default Button;
```

When the project compiles, the SCSS file will be transformed into standard CSS and injected into the DOM.

Styling with Frameworks (Bootstrap, Tailwind)

CSS frameworks such as **Bootstrap** and **Tailwind CSS** offer prebuilt styles and utility classes that streamline the process of creating visually appealing and consistent user interfaces. These frameworks save time by providing ready-to-use components, such as buttons, forms, and grids, eliminating the need to write extensive custom CSS from scratch.

Bootstrap, one of the most popular frameworks, follows a component-based approach and comes with predefined styles for components like navigation bars, modals, and cards. Developers can quickly integrate these components into their React applications to ensure a clean and polished UI. For example, a Bootstrap button can be created by adding class names like `btn` and `btn-primary` as shown in Listing 8-13.

Listing 8-13. Integrate Bootstrap Classes

```
const BootstrapButton = () => {
  return <button className="btn btn-primary">Click Me</button>;
}
```

Tailwind CSS, on the other hand, takes a utility-first approach, allowing developers to apply styles directly to elements using small, composable classes. Instead of relying on prestyled components, Tailwind gives developers full control over the design while maintaining consistency. For instance, a button styled using Tailwind might look like Listing 8-14.

Listing 8-14. Integrate Tailwind Classes

```
const TailwindButton = () => {
  return (
    <button className="bg-blue-500 text-white py-2 px-4
    rounded">
      Click Me
    </button>
  );
}
```

The major advantage of frameworks like Tailwind CSS is their **customizability** and **flexibility**. Utility classes enable fine-grained styling without writing custom CSS, making it possible to build unique designs quickly. However, excessive use of utility classes can lead to bloated HTML and reduce code readability if not managed properly.

CSS frameworks come with both advantages and challenges that developers must carefully consider. One of the key benefits is **speed**—prebuilt styles and utility classes significantly reduce development time, allowing developers to quickly prototype and implement UI designs without starting from scratch. Frameworks also promote **consistency** by enforcing a uniform design across the application, ensuring a cohesive look and feel. Additionally, frameworks like Tailwind CSS and Bootstrap offer **customization** options. Tailwind's utility classes provide fine-grained control over styles, while Bootstrap's theming capabilities allow developers to adapt the default styles to meet project-specific requirements.

However, there are some drawbacks to using frameworks. One major concern is **code bloat**, as overusing utility classes or relying too heavily on prebuilt components can clutter the HTML, making the codebase harder to read and maintain. Furthermore, frameworks can lead to **generic designs**, especially when developers fail to customize the default styles. This can result in applications that look similar to others, lacking uniqueness and brand identity. To overcome these challenges, developers should strike a balance by using frameworks thoughtfully, combining their strengths with custom styles for better performance and a distinctive user interface.

Responsive Design Techniques

Responsive design is critical to ensuring that modern applications adapt seamlessly to various screen sizes and devices, providing a consistent user experience across desktops, tablets, and smartphones. In React applications, **media queries** are a popular technique to handle responsive behavior. By defining styles that adjust dynamically based on screen dimensions, developers can control elements like padding, margins, and layouts.

For example, consider a container element that changes its padding based on screen size. Using **CSS media queries**, you can implement the code as shown in Listings 8-15 and 8-16.

Listing 8-15. Sample Style.css

```css
.container {
  padding: 20px;
  background-color: lightgray;
  text-align: center;
}
@media (max-width: 768px) {
  .container {
    padding: 10px;
    background-color: lightblue;
  }
}
```

Listing 8-16. Sample Container File

```
import './styles.css';

const Container = () => {
  return <div className="container">Responsive Container</div>;
}
export default Container;
```

In this example, when the screen width is reduced to 768px or smaller, the container's padding is reduced to 10px, and its background color changes to light blue. This ensures that the content remains visually appealing and readable on smaller devices.

Responsive Frameworks like **Bootstrap** or **Tailwind CSS** offer predefined grid systems and utility classes that simplify responsive development. For instance, Bootstrap provides a grid layout that allows developers to create flexible and responsive components quickly as illustrated in Listing 8-17. To use Bootstrap's grid, structure your layout using col classes.

Listing 8-17. Responsive Grid with Bootstrap

```
import 'bootstrap/dist/css/bootstrap.min.css';

const ResponsiveGrid = () => {
  return (
    <div className="container">
      <div className="row">
        <div className="col-md-6 col-sm-12">Column 1</div>
        <div className="col-md-6 col-sm-12">Column 2</div>
      </div>
    </div>
  );
}

export default ResponsiveGrid;
```

In this example, the grid system ensures that the two columns appear side by side on medium-sized screens (using `col-md-6`) and stack vertically on smaller screens (using `col-sm-12`). For more utility-driven frameworks like **Tailwind CSS**, responsiveness can be achieved using utility classes as illustrated in Listing 8-18.

Listing 8-18. Responsive Button with Tailwind CSS

```
const ResponsiveButton = () => {
  return (
    <button className="bg-blue-500 text-white px-4 py-2 rounded
    md:px-6 md:py-3">
      Responsive Button
    </button>
  );
}

export default ResponsiveButton;
```

Here, Tailwind classes like md:px-6 and md:py-3 ensure that the button padding increases on medium-sized screens and larger. To ensure a truly responsive design, always test your application on multiple devices, screen sizes, and orientations. Browser developer tools, like Chrome DevTools, offer responsive mode for quick validation and fine-tuning. Combining traditional **media queries** with frameworks like Bootstrap or Tailwind and modern tools ensures your application provides a seamless and intuitive experience across all platforms.

Best Practices for Styling

When it comes to styling React applications, following best practices ensures maintainable, scalable, and accessible code. First, it is crucial to **organize your styles** effectively. Separate global styles, component-specific styles, and utility styles into their respective files or modules to avoid clutter and improve maintainability. This organization helps maintain clarity as your application grows. To promote consistency across your design, focus on **reusing styles** by leveraging variables, mixins, or reusable classes, particularly when using preprocessors like SASS or frameworks like Tailwind CSS.

While inline styles can be useful for quick fixes or dynamic styling, it is recommended to **avoid inline styles** for large-scale applications. External stylesheets, CSS Modules, or CSS-in-JS libraries like styled-components are better alternatives, as they improve readability and simplify updates. Adopting a **naming convention** such as BEM (Block Element Modifier) further enhances maintainability by providing a structured approach to naming classes, making it easier to understand relationships between elements.

Accessibility testing should be an integral part of your styling process. Ensure your styles accommodate **keyboard navigation** and screen readers, with a focus on sufficient contrast ratios, clear focus states, and responsive font sizes for readability. Neglecting accessibility can alienate users with disabilities, compromising the overall user experience. Finally, avoid overusing **global styles**. While global styles are necessary for base resets or common utilities, excessive use can lead to unintended side effects, making debugging and updates more complex.

By following these best practices, you can ensure a well-organized, maintainable, and inclusive styling approach that aligns with modern development standards.

Summary

In this chapter, we explored a range of styling techniques to enhance React applications, ensuring they are visually appealing, maintainable, and responsive. We began with **traditional CSS**, where external stylesheets are linked to components, offering simplicity and familiarity for developers. Moving forward, we introduced **CSS Modules**, which allow styles to be scoped locally to components, preventing class name collisions in large applications. We also delved into **CSS-in-JS libraries** like `styled-components` that enable writing styles directly in JavaScript, promoting dynamic styling and greater flexibility.

Additionally, we covered **framework-based styling** using tools like Bootstrap and Tailwind CSS, which provide prebuilt styles and utility classes to speed up development. These frameworks ensure consistency and responsiveness but require careful handling to avoid bloated HTML and overly generic designs. To address modern design challenges, we explored **responsive design techniques**, including media queries and responsive frameworks, which ensure applications adapt seamlessly to various screen sizes and devices. Lastly, we emphasized **best practices for styling**, such as organizing styles, reusing code, following conventions like BEM, and testing for accessibility to ensure an inclusive user experience.

CHAPTER 8   STYLING YOUR APPLICATION

In the next chapter, we will dive into **lifecycle methods and Hooks** in React. You will learn how React components manage their lifecycle stages, from mounting to unmounting, and how Hooks like `useEffect`, `useState`, and `useContext` allow functional components to handle state, side effects, and logic efficiently. Mastering these concepts will enable you to build dynamic, reactive, and efficient applications.

CHAPTER 9

Lifecycle Methods and Hooks

React components follow a well-defined lifecycle, progressing through distinct phases from their creation to removal from the DOM. Understanding this lifecycle is crucial for managing state, handling side effects, and ensuring efficient performance in dynamic applications.

Class components traditionally relied on lifecycle methods like componentDidMount, componentDidUpdate, and componentWillUnmount to interact with these phases. However, the introduction of React Hooks, such as useEffect and useState, transformed functional components, enabling them to manage state and lifecycle events more intuitively and with less complexity.

This chapter explores the component lifecycle's key phases—mounting, updating, and unmounting—alongside their corresponding lifecycle methods and hooks. Through practical examples, advanced techniques, and best practices, you will learn how to leverage these tools to create clean, efficient, and responsive applications. Whether you're working with class components or functional components, mastering these concepts is fundamental to writing modern React applications.

CHAPTER 9   LIFECYCLE METHODS AND HOOKS

Understanding the Component Lifecycle

React components follow a structured lifecycle that governs their behavior from creation to removal. This lifecycle is divided into three key phases: **mounting**, **updating**, and **unmounting**. Understanding and managing these phases allow developers to handle tasks like state initialization, side effects, DOM updates, and resource cleanup efficiently.

- **Mounting Phase**: This phase begins when a component is created and inserted into the DOM. It is ideal for tasks such as setting up initial state or fetching data. For example:

  - In class components, use the `componentDidMount` method to fetch API data after the component is rendered.

  - In functional components, use the `useEffect` hook with an empty dependency array `[]` for similar tasks.

- **Updating Phase**: This phase occurs when a component's state or props change, triggering a re-render. Developers use this phase to update the DOM or respond to user interactions.

  - Use `componentDidUpdate` in class components to handle updates or the `useEffect` hook with dependencies in functional components.

  - For performance optimization, the `shouldComponentUpdate` method allows you to control unnecessary re-renders.

CHAPTER 9   LIFECYCLE METHODS AND HOOKS

- **Unmounting Phase**: This final phase removes the component from the DOM. Developers must clean up resources like event listeners, timers, or subscriptions to prevent memory leaks.

  - In class components, use the `componentWillUnmount` method.
  - In functional components, implement the cleanup function within the `useEffect` hook.

React also provides an **Error-Handling Phase** through the `componentDidCatch` method to gracefully manage errors during rendering or lifecycle events by logging errors or displaying fallback UIs.

By leveraging lifecycle methods and hooks effectively, developers can optimize performance, manage resources efficiently, and ensure data consistency in React applications.

Lifecycle Methods in Class Components

Lifecycle methods in React are exclusive to **class components** and allow developers to hook into specific phases of a component's lifecycle. These methods are crucial for handling tasks such as data fetching, optimizing performance, and cleaning up resources. The lifecycle is divided into three main phases: **mounting**, **updating**, and **unmounting**.

Mounting Phase

The mounting phase occurs when a component is created and inserted into the DOM as illustrated in Listing 9-1.

169

1. constructor: This is the first method called when the component is created. It is used for initializing the state and binding methods. Avoid calling setState here, as it is meant for the initial setup only.

2. componentDidMount: Called immediately after the component has been rendered into the DOM. It is commonly used for tasks like fetching data, starting subscriptions, or performing DOM operations.

Listing 9-1. Mounting and Fetching Data

```
class DataFetcher extends React.Component {
  constructor(props) {
    super(props);
    this.state = { data: null };
  }

  componentDidMount() {
    fetch('https://jsonplaceholder.typicode.com/posts')
      .then((response) => response.json())
      .then((data) => this.setState({ data }));
  }

  render() {
    return <div>{this.state.data ? 'Data Loaded' :
    'Loading...'}</div>;
  }
}
```

Caution Avoid calling setState in constructor. Use it in componentDidMount for state updates after the initial render.

CHAPTER 9   LIFECYCLE METHODS AND HOOKS

Updating Phase

The updating phase occurs when a component re-renders due to changes in its state or props as illustrated in Listing 9-2.

1. shouldComponentUpdate: This method allows you to control whether the component re-renders. By returning false, you can prevent unnecessary renders and optimize performance.

2. componentDidUpdate: Called after the component has been updated in the DOM. This is useful for performing actions in response to state or prop changes, such as fetching new data or updating the DOM.

Unmounting Phase

The unmounting phase occurs when a component is removed from the DOM.

1. componentWillUnmount: This method is used to perform cleanup tasks, such as removing timers, event listeners, or unsubscribing from services. Proper cleanup ensures that resources are released and prevents memory leaks.

Listing 9-2. Cleanup in componentWillUnmount

```
class Timer extends React.Component {
  componentDidMount() {
    this.timerID = setInterval(() => console.
    log('Tick'), 1000);
  }
```

```
  componentWillUnmount() {
    clearInterval(this.timerID);
  }
  render() {
    return <div>Timer Running</div>;
  }
}
```

Tip Always clean up timers, event listeners, or subscriptions in `componentWillUnmount` to avoid memory leaks.

Hooks for Functional Components

React introduced **Hooks** in version 16.8, revolutionizing functional components by enabling them to use **state** and **lifecycle features** previously exclusive to class components. Hooks allow developers to write cleaner, more concise code while avoiding the complexities of classes. The most used hooks include `useState` for managing state and `useEffect` for handling side effects.

Using useEffect for Side Effects

The useEffect hook consolidates the functionality of `componentDidMount`, `componentDidUpdate`, and `componentWillUnmount` into a single method. It allows functional components to handle side effects like **data fetching**, **DOM updates**, or **subscriptions**.

CHAPTER 9 LIFECYCLE METHODS AND HOOKS

The **syntax** for useEffect includes a function that performs the side effect and an optional **cleanup function** returned from it. A dependency array determines when the effect should rerun. If the dependency array is empty, the effect runs only once after the initial render as described in Listings 9-3 and 9-4.

Listing 9-3. UseEffect Syntax

```
useEffect(() => {
  // Perform side effect
  return () => {
    // Cleanup
  };
}, [dependencies]);
```

Listing 9-4. Data Fetching with useEffect

```
const DataFetcher = () => {
  const [data, setData] = React.useState(null);

  React.useEffect(() => {
    fetch('https://jsonplaceholder.typicode.com/posts')
      .then((response) => response.json())
      .then((data) => setData(data));
  }, []); // Empty dependency array ensures this runs once

  return <div>{data ? 'Data Loaded' : 'Loading...'}</div>;
}
```

The useState hook is used to manage the data state in functional components, providing a simple way to initialize and update state values. The useEffect hook is responsible for fetching data when the component mounts, as indicated by the empty dependency array, which ensures the effect runs only once after the initial render. This approach effectively replaces the `componentDidMount` lifecycle method used in class components, making the logic cleaner, more readable, and easier to manage. By consolidating state and side-effect logic into functional components, hooks simplify React development without sacrificing functionality.

Managing State with useState

The `useState` hook introduces **state management** to functional components, allowing them to hold and update local state. Unlike class components where `this.setState` is used, `useState` provides a simpler way to declare state variables and update them as described in Listings 9-5 and 9-6.

Listing 9-5. UseState Syntax

```
const [state, setState] = useState(initialValue);
```

The `state` holds the current value of the state, while the `setState` function is responsible for updating the state and triggering a re-render of the component. This ensures that any changes to the state are immediately reflected in the UI, keeping the component in sync with its data.

Listing 9-6. Counter Component Using useState

```
const Counter = () => {
  const [count, setCount] = React.useState(0);

  return (
    <div>
      <p>Count: {count}</p>
      <button onClick={() => setCount(count + 1)}>
      Increment</button>
    </div>
  );
}
```

The `useState` hook initializes the `count` state with an initial value of 0, providing a simple way to manage local state in functional components. The `setCount` function is used to increment the count whenever the button is clicked, updating the state and triggering a re-render. This approach replaces the use of `this.state` and `this.setState` in class components, making state management more straightforward and easier to implement.

Advanced Hooks for Lifecycle Scenarios

React provides advanced hooks like `useRef` and `useLayoutEffect` to handle more complex lifecycle scenarios in functional components. These hooks offer powerful capabilities for managing mutable references and synchronizing logic after DOM updates.

The `useRef` hook is used to create a mutable reference that persists across re-renders. Unlike state variables, updating a `useRef` value does not trigger a re-render, making it useful for accessing DOM elements or maintaining values without causing unnecessary updates.

The `useLayoutEffect` hook, on the other hand, runs synchronously after DOM updates but before the browser paints the screen. It is particularly useful for tasks like measuring DOM elements or synchronizing scroll positions since it ensures that the DOM is updated before the effect runs. However, developers should use `useLayoutEffect` sparingly, as it can block rendering and impact performance if overused. The example in Listing 9-7 demonstrates the use of `useRef` to scroll an input field into view when the component mounts.

Listing 9-7. Scroll to Input

```
const ScrollToInput = () => {
  const inputRef = React.useRef(null);

  React.useEffect(() => {
    inputRef.current.scrollIntoView({ behavior: 'smooth' });
  }, []);

  return <input ref={inputRef} />;
}
```

Here, `useRef` creates a reference to the input field, and the `useEffect` hook scrolls it into view when the component renders. This approach avoids triggering additional re-renders and efficiently interacts with the DOM.

Caution Use `useLayoutEffect` only when necessary, such as for measuring elements or synchronizing the DOM, because it runs synchronously and can delay rendering. For most side effects, `useEffect` remains the preferred choice.

By combining hooks like `useRef` and `useLayoutEffect`, developers can handle advanced lifecycle scenarios, achieving greater control over the behavior of functional components while maintaining clean and efficient code.

Example: A Timer Component with Cleanup

In this example illustrated in Listing 9-8, we build a **Timer component** using React hooks that dynamically updates the current time every second. This demonstrates how to use the `useEffect` hook for side effects and

CHAPTER 9   LIFECYCLE METHODS AND HOOKS

the **cleanup function** to prevent resource leaks. The output of the Timer component, as displayed in Figure 9-1, shows the current time dynamically updating every second.

Listing 9-8. Timer Component with Hooks

```
const Timer = () => {
  const [time, setTime] = React.useState(new Date());

  React.useEffect(() => {
    // Start a timer that updates the state every second
    const timerID = setInterval(() => setTime(new Date()), 1000);

    // Cleanup function to clear the interval when the component unmounts
    return () => clearInterval(timerID);
  }, []); // Empty dependency array ensures this runs only once

  return <h1>{time.toLocaleTimeString()}</h1>;
}
```

Figure 9-1. *Timer component showing current time dynamically*

In this example, we create a Timer component using React hooks to dynamically display the current time and update it every second. The component demonstrates the use of the `useState` hook for state management and the `useEffect` hook to handle side effects, along with a cleanup function to prevent resource leaks.

The `useState` hook initializes a state variable called `time` with the current date and time using `new Date()`. This state will be responsible for holding the current time, which needs to update at regular intervals. To achieve this, the `useEffect` hook sets up a timer using `setInterval`, which updates the `time` state every second by calling the `setTime` function with the updated value. The `useEffect` hook ensures that this side effect runs only once when the component mounts, as indicated by the empty dependency array `[]`.

One crucial aspect of this implementation is the cleanup function returned by `useEffect`. React automatically invokes this cleanup function when the component unmounts, ensuring that the timer created with `setInterval` is cleared using `clearInterval(timerID)`. This cleanup is critical because failing to clear the timer would allow it to continue running in the background, even after the component is no longer part of the DOM. Such lingering intervals can lead to memory leaks, unnecessary performance overhead, or unexpected behavior, especially when components remount multiple times.

The `time` state, which updates every second, is displayed using the `toLocaleTimeString()` method. This method formats the `Date` object into a readable time string, such as "10:45:20 AM." The formatted value is rendered within an `<h1>` element, and the UI seamlessly updates every second as the state changes.

By combining `useState` and `useEffect`, this Timer component replaces the traditional class component lifecycle methods like `componentDidMount` for setting up the timer and `componentWillUnmount` for cleanup. This approach makes the code cleaner and easier to maintain.

Overall, this example illustrates how functional components with hooks can handle dynamic updates and resource cleanup efficiently, ensuring optimal performance and preventing memory leaks.

Common Challenges and Solutions

When working with React components and hooks, developers often encounter common challenges that can impact application performance and behavior. One frequent issue is memory leaks, which occur when resources like timers, subscriptions, or event listeners are not cleaned up properly. The solution is to ensure that all side effects are cleaned up using the cleanup function in `useEffect` or the `componentWillUnmount` method in class components. Proper cleanup prevents lingering operations that could slow down or crash the application.

Another challenge is infinite loops in `useEffect`, which typically happen when dependencies in the effect's dependency array are not correctly defined. If a variable that changes frequently is included unnecessarily or omitted when needed, the effect will keep re-running indefinitely. The solution is to carefully manage the dependency array to include only the necessary variables, ensuring that the effect runs predictably and avoids unintended behavior.

Lastly, mixed logic in hooks can make code harder to read and maintain. Combining unrelated logic within a single `useEffect` hook can lead to confusion and reduced reusability. The recommended solution is to separate concerns by using multiple `useEffect` hooks. Each hook should handle a specific piece of logic, such as data fetching, event listeners, or cleanup. This approach promotes cleaner, modular code that is easier to understand and debug.

CHAPTER 9   LIFECYCLE METHODS AND HOOKS

Best Practices for Lifecycle Management

Effective lifecycle management ensures that React components remain efficient, maintainable, and free of resource leaks. To achieve this, it is important to keep **effects focused** by using separate useEffect hooks for different pieces of logic. Splitting logic into multiple hooks improves code clarity and modularity. Additionally, always use **cleanup functions** within useEffect to avoid resource leaks, such as uncleaned timers, event listeners, or subscriptions, which can lead to memory issues.

When working with dependencies in useEffect, carefully add only the variables that trigger necessary updates. Incorrect or excessive dependencies can cause unnecessary re-renders or infinite loops, so optimizing the dependency array is crucial.

Thorough testing is another key practice for lifecycle management. Simulating various lifecycle scenarios in unit tests ensures that effects, state updates, and cleanup logic work as expected under different conditions. Finally, while useLayoutEffect can be useful for synchronizing DOM updates, it should be used sparingly. Prefer useEffect for most side effects, as useLayoutEffect blocks rendering and can negatively impact performance if overused.

By following these best practices, developers can manage component lifecycles efficiently, write clean and predictable code, and optimize application performance.

Summary

In this chapter, we explored the core concepts of managing the component lifecycle in both class components and functional components. We began by understanding **lifecycle methods** in class components, such as componentDidMount, componentDidUpdate, and componentWillUnmount,

CHAPTER 9   LIFECYCLE METHODS AND HOOKS

which allow developers to perform side effects like data fetching, DOM updates, and resource cleanup at different phases of a component's existence.

We then introduced **React Hooks**, particularly useState and useEffect, which enable functional components to replicate the behavior of lifecycle methods. The useState hook allowed us to manage state in functional components, while useEffect consolidated lifecycle logic, providing a cleaner and more concise way to handle side effects and cleanup. Advanced hooks like useRef and useLayoutEffect were also discussed, showcasing their importance in managing references and synchronous DOM updates.

To reinforce these concepts, we implemented a **practical example** of a timer component that dynamically updates the current time. This example demonstrated the use of useEffect to set up and clean up an interval, ensuring proper resource management and preventing memory leaks.

Finally, we highlighted **best practices** for lifecycle management, emphasizing focused effects, proper cleanup, dependency optimization, and avoiding unnecessary use of useLayoutEffect. These practices help ensure clean, efficient, and maintainable React components.

In the next chapter, we will explore state management techniques that simplify data sharing across components and enhance the scalability of React applications.

CHAPTER 10

Managing State with Context and Redux

State management is a fundamental concept in React applications, ensuring that components stay in sync and reflect the current data efficiently. As applications grow in complexity, managing state across multiple components can become challenging. React offers two primary tools to address this problem: the **React Context API** for lightweight state sharing and **Redux Toolkit** for more robust, centralized state management. This chapter introduces both tools, explores their differences, and walks through a practical implementation using Redux Toolkit.

Understanding State Management in React

State management refers to the process of handling and sharing the state of an application across its components. In modern web applications, managing state is crucial for ensuring that user interactions and dynamic data updates are handled seamlessly. At its core, state represents the data that determines the behavior and appearance of an application. For example, this could include user preferences, the contents of a shopping cart, or the current page in a multistep form. In simpler applications, managing state at the component level using tools like React's useState hook can suffice. However, as applications grow in complexity, challenges

CHAPTER 10   MANAGING STATE WITH CONTEXT AND REDUX

such as synchronizing state across multiple components, handling nested component hierarchies, and preserving state during navigation or page reloads often arise.

One of the primary issues in larger applications is "**prop drilling**," where state and its update logic must be passed through several layers of components. This not only increases the coupling between components but also makes the code more challenging to maintain and refactor. For instance, consider an ecommerce application where the shopping cart state is needed in multiple components, such as the product listing, cart summary, and checkout form. Managing such shared state using only local state would lead to deeply nested props and redundant code.

To address these challenges, global state management tools such as the **React Context API** and **Redux Toolkit** offer robust solutions. These tools enable developers to manage the state at a centralized location, making it accessible to any component that requires it. Beyond simplifying state sharing, these tools also bring added benefits such as easier debugging, better scalability, and more predictable behavior. By centralizing state management, developers can create applications that are not only easier to maintain but also more resilient to changes and feature additions.

React Context API

The **React Context API** is a built-in solution that allows developers to share state across components without manually passing props. Context provides a way to "broadcast" data to child components, simplifying the process of managing global state. Context is a mechanism in React that enables components to share values like themes, user data, or application settings without explicitly passing props. It consists of three main parts: `createContext`, `Provider`, and `useContext`.

CHAPTER 10 MANAGING STATE WITH CONTEXT AND REDUX

To create context, use the `createContext` method, which returns a **Provider** and a **Consumer**. The `Provider` wraps components to provide data, while `useContext` allows child components to access the shared data. The example in Listing 10-1 shows how to use Context with `useContext` Hook.

Listing 10-1. Using Context with useContext Hook

```jsx
// ThemeProvider.jsx
import React, { createContext, useContext, useState } from 'react';

const ThemeContext = createContext();

const ThemeProvider = ({ children }) => {
  const [theme, setTheme] = useState('light');
  return (
    <ThemeContext.Provider value={{ theme, setTheme }}>
      {children}
    </ThemeContext.Provider>
  );
}

const ThemedButton = () => {
  const { theme, setTheme } = useContext(ThemeContext);
  return (
    <button onClick={() => setTheme(theme === 'light' ? 'dark' : 'light')}>
      Current Theme: {theme}
    </button>
  );
}
```

```
const App = () => {
  return (
    <ThemeProvider>
      <ThemedButton />
    </ThemeProvider>
  );
}
```

In this example, the `ThemeContext` is created using the `createContext` method, which sets up a context for sharing data like the current theme state (light or dark) across multiple components. The `ThemeProvider` component wraps the child components with the `ThemeContext.Provider` and provides the theme state (`theme`) and an updater function (`setTheme`) as the context value. By doing so, any child component within the provider can access and modify the shared state without the need to pass props explicitly through multiple levels, solving the problem of **prop drilling**.

The `useContext` hook simplifies accessing the context in child components. In the `ThemedButton` component, we use `useContext(ThemeContext)` to directly retrieve the theme value and the `setTheme` function. When the button is clicked, the `setTheme` function toggles the theme state between "light" and "dark." React automatically re-renders all components consuming the context when the state updates, ensuring the UI reflects the current theme seamlessly.

This approach showcases the **power of React Context** for global state management without external libraries, making it ideal for scenarios like theming, user authentication, or sharing simple application-wide data. By wrapping components in a context provider and accessing shared state using the `useContext` hook, developers can create cleaner, more maintainable code without unnecessary prop-passing.

Introduction to Redux Toolkit

Redux Toolkit is the official, modernized toolset for **Redux**, simplifying state management with minimal boilerplate. Unlike vanilla Redux, Redux Toolkit streamlines common tasks like creating reducers, managing actions, and setting up the store.

Redux Toolkit is a collection of utilities that help manage global state efficiently. It provides abstractions like `createSlice` for reducers and actions, `configureStore` for creating the store, and hooks like `useSelector` and `useDispatch` for connecting state to components.

Core Features of Redux Toolkit

1. `createSlice`: Combines reducers and actions into a single function
2. `configureStore`: Simplifies store creation with built-in middleware
3. `createAsyncThunk`: Manages asynchronous operations like API calls

Redux Toolkit simplifies state management in React applications by reducing boilerplate code and providing modern utilities to manage global state effectively. The setup involves a few key steps, including installation, slice creation, store configuration, and integrating the store into the React app. Let's break this down step by step.

Step 1: Install Redux Toolkit and React-Redux

The first step is to install the required dependencies as shown in Listing 10-2. Redux Toolkit provides the core features for state management, while react-redux allows React components to connect to the Redux store. Run the command in Listing 10-2.

CHAPTER 10 MANAGING STATE WITH CONTEXT AND REDUX

Listing 10-2. Install Dependencies

`npm install @reduxjs/toolkit react-redux`

This command installs both the Redux Toolkit and react-redux libraries, which are essential for connecting the store to the React app.

Step 2: Create a Slice

A **slice** represents a logical piece of the application's state as illustrated in Listing 10-3, combining the state structure, reducer logic, and action creators into a single, manageable unit. Redux Toolkit's `createSlice` simplifies this process.

Listing 10-3. Creating a Slice

```
import { createSlice } from '@reduxjs/toolkit';
const initialState = {
  cart: [],
};
const cartSlice = createSlice({
  name: 'cart', // Slice name
  initialState, // Initial state
  reducers: {
    addItem: (state, action) => {
      state.cart.push(action.payload); // Add item to cart
    },
    removeItem: (state, action) => {
      state.cart = state.cart.filter((item) => item.id !==
      action.payload.id); // Remove item
    },
  },
});
```

```
// Export actions and reducer
export const { addItem, removeItem } = cartSlice.actions;
export default cartSlice.reducer;
```

In this example, the `createSlice` function simplifies state management by generating the state, actions, and reducer logic all in one place. The `initialState` defines the default structure of the slice, where the `cart` is initialized as an empty array to represent an empty shopping cart. The `reducers` field contains the logic to manipulate the state. Specifically, the `addItem` reducer pushes a new item into the `cart` array, effectively adding it to the state. Similarly, the `removeItem` reducer filters the `cart` array to remove an item that matches the given `id`, ensuring that items are removed efficiently. Finally, the actions (`addItem` and `removeItem`) and the reducer are exported. The actions allow components to trigger state updates, while the reducer integrates seamlessly into the Redux store for global state management. This approach makes the state logic concise, reusable, and easy to maintain.

Step 3: Configure the Store

The **store** is where the global state is managed. Redux Toolkit provides the `configureStore` function, which simplifies creating the store and includes default middleware for development as illustrated in Listing 10-4.

Listing 10-4. Configuring the Store

```
import { configureStore } from '@reduxjs/toolkit';
import cartReducer from './cartSlice';

const store = configureStore({
  reducer: {
    cart: cartReducer, // Add the cart slice to the store
  },
});

export default store;
```

The `configureStore` function simplifies the process of combining reducers for all slices in a Redux application. In this example, the `cartReducer`, which was exported from the `cartSlice`, is integrated into the store and assigned to the `cart` key. This allows the `cart` slice to manage its corresponding piece of the application state. The configured store is then exported so it can be provided to the React application, enabling components to access and interact with the global state seamlessly.

Step 4: Provide the Store to the React App

To make the Redux store available to all components in the React application, the store is passed to the `Provider` component from the react-redux library. The Provider wraps the root component of the app, allowing child components to access the global state as shown in Listing 10-5.

Listing 10-5. Providing the Store to the App

```
import React from 'react';
import { Provider } from 'react-redux';
import store from './store';
import App from './App';
function Root() {
  return (
    <Provider store={store}>
      <App />
    </Provider>
  );
}
export default Root;
```

The `Provider` component wraps the root `App` component and takes the Redux store as a prop. This setup ensures that the store is made available to all components within the application. By doing so, components can access the global state using the `useSelector` hook and dispatch actions to update the state using the `useDispatch` hook, enabling seamless state management throughout the application.

Connecting Redux Toolkit with React Components

Redux Toolkit integrates seamlessly with React through the `react-redux` library. It offers hooks like `useSelector` to access state and `useDispatch` to trigger actions, and the `createSlice` function combines the reducer logic and actions in one place as illustrated in Listing 10-6.

Listing 10-6. Counter Slice

```
import { createSlice, configureStore } from '@reduxjs/toolkit';
import { Provider, useSelector, useDispatch } from 'react-redux';

// Define a slice
const counterSlice = createSlice({
  name: 'counter',
  initialState: { value: 0 },
  reducers: {
    increment: (state) => { state.value += 1; },
    decrement: (state) => { state.value -= 1; },
  },
});

// Configure store
const store = configureStore({ reducer: { counter: counterSlice.reducer } });
```

```
// Counter component
const Counter = () => {
  const count = useSelector((state) => state.counter.value);
  const dispatch = useDispatch();
  return (
    <div>
      <button onClick={() => dispatch(counterSlice.actions.
      decrement())}>-</button>
      <span>{count}</span>
      <button onClick={() => dispatch(counterSlice.actions.
      increment())}>+</button>
    </div>
  );
}
// App component
const App = () => {
  return (
    <Provider store={store}>
      <Counter />
    </Provider>
  );
}
```

In this example, the `createSlice` function is used to define the state and actions, such as `increment` and `decrement`, for managing the application's state in a structured manner. The `useSelector` hook allows the component to retrieve the current state value from the Redux store, ensuring the component stays updated with the latest state. Meanwhile, the `useDispatch` hook provides a way to dispatch actions, such as triggering `increment` or `decrement`, to update the state. Together, these hooks seamlessly connect the component to the Redux store, enabling efficient state management and reactivity.

CHAPTER 10 MANAGING STATE WITH CONTEXT AND REDUX

Comparing Context API and Redux Toolkit

While both the Context API and Redux Toolkit can manage global state, they serve different purposes. The **Context API** is ideal for simple use cases like themes, authentication, or small apps. On the other hand, **Redux Toolkit** is better suited for complex applications that require structured state management, advanced debugging, and middleware support. Figure 10-1 shows the comparison in terms of setup complexity, debugging tools, boilerplate code, and use cases.

Feature	Context API	Redux Toolkit
Setup Complexity	Low	Moderate
Boilerplate Code	Minimal	More structured
Debugging Tools	Limited	Extensive (Redux DevTools)
Best Use Case	Simple apps, local state	Complex apps, global state

Figure 10-1. Comparison of Context API and Redux Toolkit

Best Practices for State Management

Effective state management is essential for building scalable and maintainable React applications. The React Context API is an excellent choice for lightweight state needs, such as theming, authentication, or sharing user preferences across components. It allows for seamless global state sharing without the complexity of Redux, making it ideal for small- to medium-sized features. However, for larger applications with complex state requirements, the Redux Toolkit is highly recommended. Its structured approach, reduced boilerplate, and features like `createSlice` and `createAsyncThunk` simplify managing reducers and asynchronous logic, making it a powerful tool for enterprise-level applications.

To optimize performance, it is important to keep the state normalized, ensuring related data is stored in a single source of truth rather than duplicating it across the state. This avoids redundancy and makes updates more efficient. Additionally, splitting the state into logical slices—where each slice represents a distinct domain or feature, such as `cart`, `user`, or `products`—keeps reducers modular and easy to manage. When fetching data or syncing state with APIs, always use hooks like `useEffect` or subscriptions to ensure the state remains consistent with the server. Following these best practices ensures that your state management strategy is efficient, maintainable, and well suited for both simple and complex applications.

Example: Building a Shopping Cart with Redux Toolkit

In this practical example, we will create a fully functional shopping cart application that uses **Redux Toolkit** to manage the state of the cart. The cart will support actions to add, remove, and update items, while the user interface will reflect these changes dynamically. Redux Toolkit simplifies state management by combining state, actions, and reducers into slices, allowing for clean and organized code. Let's walk through the example step by step, demonstrating how the cart state is managed efficiently with Redux Toolkit and how it interacts with React components.

Step 1: Define the Cart Slice

Using `createSlice` from Redux Toolkit, we define a slice of state to manage the shopping cart. This slice will include an `initialState` and reducers for actions like `addItem`, `removeItem`, and `updateItemQuantity` as illustrated in Listing 10-7.

Listing 10-7. Creating a Slice

```
import { createSlice } from '@reduxjs/toolkit';
const initialState = {
  cart: [],
};
const cartSlice = createSlice({
  name: 'cart',
  initialState,
  reducers: {
    addItem: (state, action) => {
      state.cart.push(action.payload); // Add new item
    },
    removeItem: (state, action) => {
      state.cart = state.cart.filter((item) => item.id !==
      action.payload.id); // Remove item by ID
    },
    updateItemQuantity: (state, action) => {
      const item = state.cart.find((item) => item.id ===
      action.payload.id);
      if (item) {
        item.quantity = action.payload.quantity; // Update
        quantity
      }
    },
  },
});
export const { addItem, removeItem, updateItemQuantity } =
cartSlice.actions;
export default cartSlice.reducer;
```

Here, the `createSlice` function defines the cart's state and actions. The `addItem` reducer adds a new item to the cart, `removeItem` removes an item based on its unique ID, and `updateItemQuantity` updates the quantity of an existing item. These actions will later be dispatched by components to modify the state.

Step 2: Configure the Store

We configure the Redux store and add the `cartSlice` reducer as shown in Listing 10-8.

Listing 10-8. Configuring the Store

```
import { configureStore } from '@reduxjs/toolkit';
import cartReducer from './cartSlice';

const store = configureStore({
  reducer: {
    cart: cartReducer,
  },
});

export default store;
```

The `configureStore` function combines the reducers and sets up the Redux store. Here, the `cartReducer` manages the cart-related state and integrates seamlessly into the global store.

Step 3: Provide the Store to the Application

The Redux store is provided to the React application using the Provider component from react-redux as shown in Listing 10-9.

CHAPTER 10   MANAGING STATE WITH CONTEXT AND REDUX

Listing 10-9. Providing the Store to the App

```
import React from 'react';
import { Provider } from 'react-redux';
import store from './store';
import App from './App';

const Root = () => {
  return (
    <Provider store={store}>
      <App />
    </Provider>
  );
}

export default Root;
```

The `Provider` wraps the root `App` component, passing the store as a prop. This ensures that all components in the application can access the Redux state and dispatch actions.

Step 4: Build the Shopping Cart Component

The shopping cart component interacts with the Redux store to display cart items, and it uses `useSelector` to access the state and `useDispatch` to dispatch actions as shown in Listing 10-10. The output of the shopping cart component is shown in Figure 10-2, demonstrating how items are displayed along with controls for updating and removing them.

Listing 10-10. Shopping Cart Component

```
import React from "react";
import { useSelector, useDispatch } from "react-redux";
import { addItem, removeItem, updateItemQuantity } from "../../
```

197

```
store/cartSlice";
import "./ShoppingCart.css";

const ShoppingCart = () => {
  const cart = useSelector((state) => state.cart.cart);
  const dispatch = useDispatch();

  const handleAddItem = () => {
    const newItem = { id: Date.now(), name: "New Product",
    quantity: 1 };
    dispatch(addItem(newItem));
  };

  const handleRemoveItem = (id) => {
    dispatch(removeItem({ id }));
  };

  const handleUpdateQuantity = (id, quantity) => {
    dispatch(updateItemQuantity({ id, quantity }));
  };

  return (
    <div className="shopping-cart">
      <h1>Shopping Cart</h1>
      <button className="add-item" onClick={handleAddItem}>
        Add Item
      </button>
      <ul className="cart-list">
        {cart.map((item) => (
          <li key={item.id} className="cart-item">
            <div className="item-info">
              <div className="item-name">{item.name}</div>
              <div className="item-quantity">Quantity: {item.
              quantity}</div>
```

```
            </div>
            <div className="item-actions">
              <button
                className="update-button"
                onClick={() => handleUpdateQuantity(item.id,
                item.quantity + 1)}
              >
                Increase
              </button>
              <button
                className="remove-button"
                onClick={() => handleRemoveItem(item.id)}
              >
                Remove
              </button>
            </div>
          </li>
        ))}
      </ul>
    </div>
  );
};

export default ShoppingCart;
```

CHAPTER 10 MANAGING STATE WITH CONTEXT AND REDUX

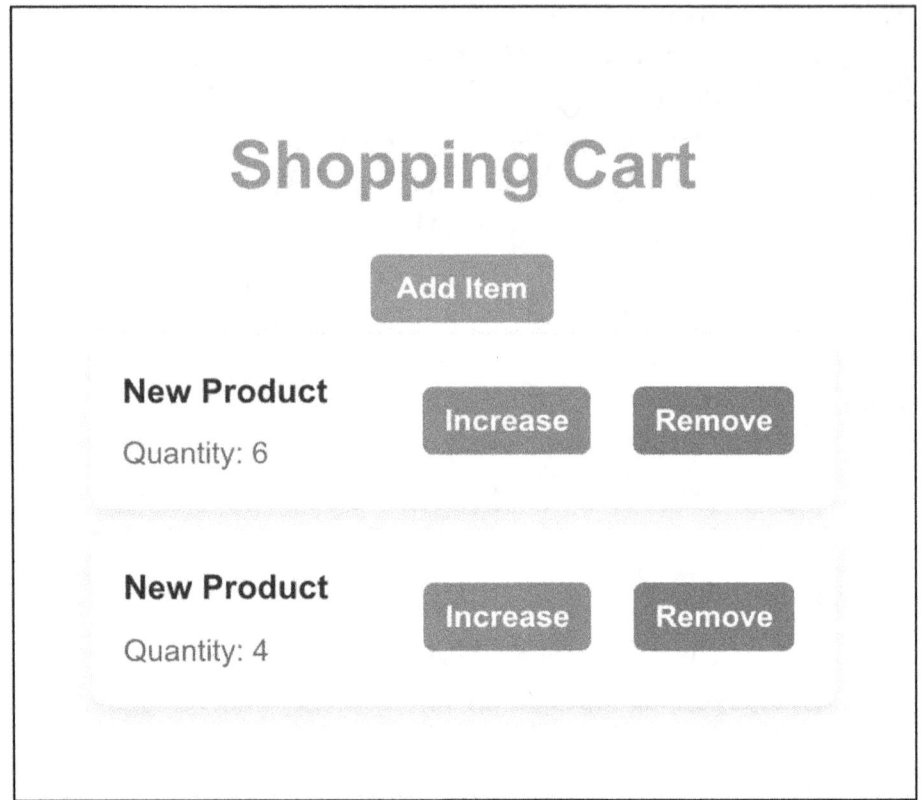

Figure 10-2. Shopping cart component with Redux state management

The useSelector hook is a critical tool for accessing the current state managed by Redux. In this example, it retrieves the cart state, enabling the component to dynamically render a list of items in the shopping cart. The useDispatch hook complements this by providing a mechanism to dispatch actions that update the state. For instance, the handleAddItem function leverages useDispatch to add a new item to the cart, handleRemoveItem removes an item based on its unique ID, and handleUpdateQuantity modifies the quantity of an existing item in the cart. Together, these hooks enable seamless interaction between the component and the Redux store. Additionally, the `cart.map` function iterates over the cart array, rendering each item along with buttons to trigger the respective actions (e.g., remove or update quantity). This integration ensures the UI stays responsive and reflects the latest state changes effectively.

This example demonstrates the power and simplicity of Redux Toolkit for managing application state. By organizing state into slices and connecting them with React components using hooks like `useSelector` and `useDispatch`, Redux Toolkit eliminates boilerplate code and provides a clean, structured approach to state management. The shopping cart example illustrates how Redux Toolkit makes it easy to build scalable and maintainable React applications.

Summary

In this chapter, we explored state management in React using the **React Context API** and **Redux Toolkit**, two versatile tools that address the challenges of managing local and global state. The Context API provides a lightweight solution for simple data sharing across components, eliminating the need for prop drilling. For more complex applications, Redux Toolkit stands out as a robust and efficient framework, simplifying state management with tools like `createSlice`, `configureStore`, and hooks such as `useSelector` and `useDispatch`.

We demonstrated the setup of Redux Toolkit, including creating slices, configuring the Redux store, and connecting the store to React components using the `Provider` component. Through a practical example of building a **shopping cart**, we showcased how Redux Toolkit efficiently handles state updates with actions to add, remove, and update items in the cart, ensuring a responsive and consistent UI.

CHAPTER 10   MANAGING STATE WITH CONTEXT AND REDUX

Additionally, best practices were discussed, including keeping state normalized, splitting it into logical slices, and selecting the right state management tool for the application's complexity. These guidelines ensure maintainable and scalable React applications.

In the next chapter, we will focus on managing user input in forms, implementing validation logic, and ensuring a seamless user experience with controlled components and libraries like Formik and React Hook Form.

CHAPTER 11

Form Handling and Validation

Forms are the primary way users interact with web applications. They enable data collection for purposes like user authentication, product search, and order submission. In React, form handling can be simplified by using **controlled** and **uncontrolled** components. This chapter will cover both approaches, delve into **validation techniques**, explore third-party libraries, and implement a practical checkout form example.

Controlled vs. Uncontrolled Components

Controlled Components

Controlled components are a core concept in React that simplify the process of managing form data. These components rely exclusively on React state to manage and control the values of form inputs. In this approach, every input field is bound to a piece of state in the component, and any changes to the input value are handled by an event, such as onChange, that updates the corresponding state variable. This ensures that React is always in control of the data displayed in the form, providing a seamless way to synchronize the user interface (UI) with the application's state.

CHAPTER 11　FORM HANDLING AND VALIDATION

One of the primary advantages of controlled components is their ability to make validation straightforward. Since the input values are managed by React state, developers can easily incorporate validation logic within the same `onChange` or `onSubmit` handlers. For instance, you can immediately check if an email is valid as the user types or prevent submission if required fields are left empty. Another significant benefit is the complete synchronization between the UI and the application state. This synchronization not only ensures consistency but also allows developers to prefill forms with data or reset them programmatically by simply modifying the state. Controlled components are particularly useful in complex forms where real-time feedback, such as error messages or dynamic input validation, is essential. Their declarative nature aligns perfectly with React's design philosophy, making form management both predictable and efficient as illustrated in Listing 11-1.

Listing 11-1. Controlled Component

```
const ControlledExample = () => {
  const [username, setUsername] = React.useState("");

  const handleChange = (e) => {
    setUsername(e.target.value);
  };

  return (
    <form>
      <label>
        Username:
        <input type="text" value={username}
          onChange={handleChange} />
      </label>
      <p>Typed Username: {username}</p>
    </form>
  );
}
```

CHAPTER 11 FORM HANDLING AND VALIDATION

This example demonstrates the essence of a controlled component in React. The username state is tied directly to the value of the input field, and any changes made by the user are handled via the onChange event, which updates the state with the new value. This setup ensures that React has full control over the form data, allowing the application state and UI to stay perfectly synchronized. Additionally, since the state drives the component, developers can easily manipulate the form programmatically or validate the input data during the user's interaction. This makes controlled components highly suitable for scenarios requiring dynamic form updates or real-time validation.

Uncontrolled Components

In uncontrolled components, the form element's state is not managed by React but by the DOM itself. This approach utilizes React's ref to directly interact with the DOM elements to retrieve their current values. Since React does not maintain the input values in its state, uncontrolled components are well suited for scenarios where minimal interaction with form data is needed, such as simple, one-time data collection forms. This approach also reduces the overhead of state management, making it a lightweight option for specific use cases as shown in Listing 11-2.

Listing 11-2. Uncontrolled Component

```
const UncontrolledExample = () => {
  const inputRef = React.useRef();

  const handleSubmit = (e) => {
    e.preventDefault();
    alert(`Input value: ${inputRef.current.value}`);
  };
```

```
  return (
    <form onSubmit={handleSubmit}>
      <label>
        Username:
        <input type="text" ref={inputRef} />
      </label>
      <button type="submit">Submit</button>
    </form>
  );
}
```

This example illustrates how uncontrolled components function by using the `ref` attribute to directly access the value of the DOM element. Unlike controlled components, the input's value is not stored in React's state but is retrieved directly when needed. This approach is simple and avoids the need for continuous state updates, making it ideal for forms that do not require real-time validation or dynamic behavior. However, it limits the flexibility and control provided by React over form inputs.

Handling User Input

React simplifies the process of managing user input by leveraging event handling. Events like `onChange`, `onSubmit`, and `onClick` enable developers to create dynamic, interactive forms that respond to user actions. These events are an integral part of form handling in React, allowing developers to capture and process user input in real time. Understanding how React handles events is key to building robust and responsive applications.

React uses a synthetic event system that wraps native **DOM** events. This system provides a consistent interface across different browsers, ensuring a seamless developer experience. Event handlers in React are written as functions that take an event object as their argument. This object contains all the details about the event, such as the **target element**, **input value**, and **event type**.

OnChange Event

The onChange event is triggered whenever the value of an input element changes. This event is commonly used in **controlled components** to update the state with the latest user input as illustrated in Listing 11-3.

Listing 11-3. Basic Input Handling

```
const InputExample = () => {
  const [text, setText] = React.useState("");

  const handleChange = (e) => {
    setText(e.target.value); // Update the state with the
    input's value
  };

  return (
    <form>
      <label>
        Enter Text:
        <input type="text" value={text}
        onChange={handleChange} />
      </label>
      <p>You typed: {text}</p>
    </form>
  );
}
```

The onChange event is used to detect changes in the input field, allowing developers to handle user input dynamically. In the example, the handleChange function is triggered whenever the input value changes. This function captures the new value from the event object and updates the text state with it. By tying the input's value attribute to the text state,

CHAPTER 11   FORM HANDLING AND VALIDATION

React ensures that the UI reflects the most recent input in real time. This synchronization between the input field and the state makes the form responsive and interactive, providing immediate feedback to the user as they type.

OnSubmit Event

The onSubmit event is fired when a form is submitted. React allows developers to prevent the default form submission behavior (reloading the page) and handle the submission programmatically as shown in Listing 11-4.

Listing 11-4. Handling Form Submission

```
const FormSubmitExample = () => {
  const [email, setEmail] = React.useState("");

  const handleSubmit = (e) => {
    e.preventDefault(); // Prevent the default form submission
    alert(`Email submitted: ${email}`);
  };

  return (
    <form onSubmit={handleSubmit}>
      <label>
        Email:
        <input
          type="email"
          value={email}
          onChange={(e) => setEmail(e.target.value)}
        />
      </label>
```

CHAPTER 11   FORM HANDLING AND VALIDATION

```
    <button type="submit">Submit</button>
  </form>
 );
}
```

The onSubmit event is bound to the <form> element, enabling React to handle form submissions programmatically. In the example, the handleSubmit function is triggered when the form is submitted. This function prevents the browser's default behavior, such as reloading the page, by calling e.preventDefault(). Instead, it processes the form data in a controlled manner. Additionally, the input field's value is dynamically managed using the onChange handler, ensuring that the state stays updated with the user's input in real time. This combination allows for a seamless and efficient form submission process.

Combined Event

React enables the combination of multiple events to create complex, interactive forms. For example, you can use onBlur to validate input when the user leaves a field or onFocus to provide feedback when a user focuses on an input as illustrated in Listing 11-5.

Listing 11-5. Using onBlur and onFocus for Validation and Feedback

```
const BlurFocusValidationExample = () => {
  const [username, setUsername] = React.useState("");
  const [error, setError] = React.useState("");
  const [focusMessage, setFocusMessage] = React.useState("");

  const handleBlur = () => {
    if (username.trim() === "") {
      setError("Username cannot be empty.");
```

```
    } else {
      setError("");
    }
  };

  const handleFocus = () => {
    setFocusMessage("Enter a valid username (e.g., at least 3
    characters).");
  };

  return (
    <form>
      <label>
        Username:
        <input
          type="text"
          value={username}
          onChange={(e) => setUsername(e.target.value)}
          onBlur={handleBlur}
          onFocus={handleFocus}
        />
      </label>
      {focusMessage && <p style={{ color: "blue"
      }}>{focusMessage}</p>}
      {error && <p style={{ color: "red" }}>{error}</p>}
    </form>
  );
}
```

In this example, the onBlur event is used to validate the input when the user moves focus away from the input field, displaying an error message if the field is empty. Additionally, the onFocus event provides feedback to the user when they focus on the input field by displaying a helpful message to guide their input. This approach illustrates how combining multiple events can enhance the user experience by simultaneously offering contextual feedback and validation.

Event Object

The event object in React provides detailed information about the triggered event, as shown in Listing 11-6, including

- target: The element that triggered the event
- type: The type of event (e.g., click, change)
- preventDefault: A method to prevent the default browser behavior

Listing 11-6. Accessing Event Properties

```
const EventObjectExample = () => {
  const handleClick = (e) => {
    console.log(`Event Type: ${e.type}`);
    console.log(`Target Value: ${e.target.value}`);
  };

  return (
    <button onClick={handleClick} value="Button Clicked">
      Click Me
    </button>
  );
}
```

The e.type property provides information about the type of event that was triggered, such as a click or change event. Meanwhile, the e.target.value property retrieves the current value of the element that initiated the event, allowing developers to access and utilize the user's input or interaction within the event handler.

CHAPTER 11   FORM HANDLING AND VALIDATION

Form Validation

Client-Side Validation

Form validation is an essential step in ensuring that user inputs meet the required criteria before submission. In React, client-side validation can be effectively implemented using state management and simple conditional checks as shown in Listing 11-7. By validating inputs on the client side, developers can provide immediate feedback to users, improving the overall user experience while reducing unnecessary server requests caused by invalid submissions.

Validation logic is typically incorporated into onChange, onBlur, or onSubmit event handlers. For instance, as users type into a form field, you can validate their input in real time and display appropriate error messages. Alternatively, you can validate the form only when the user attempts to submit it, ensuring that all fields meet the necessary requirements.

Listing 11-7. Basic Validation

```
const BasicValidation = () => {
  const [username, setUsername] = React.useState("");
  const [error, setError] = React.useState("");

  const validate = () => {
    if (username.length < 3) {
      setError("Username must be at least 3 characters long.");
      return false;
    }
    setError("");
    return true;
  };
```

```
  const handleSubmit = (e) => {
    e.preventDefault();
    if (validate()) {
      alert("Form submitted successfully!");
    }
  };

  return (
    <form onSubmit={handleSubmit}>
      <label>
        Username:
        <input
          type="text"
          value={username}
          onChange={(e) => setUsername(e.target.value)}
        />
      </label>
      {error && <p style={{ color: "red" }}>{error}</p>}
      <button type="submit">Submit</button>
    </form>
  );
}
```

The handleChange function is responsible for updating the name state whenever the user types into the input field, ensuring that the application keeps track of the latest input in real time. The handleSubmit function is executed when the form is submitted and checks whether the name field is empty. If the validation fails, such as when the field is left blank, an error message is displayed to the user, and the form submission is halted. On the other hand, if the validation passes, the error message is cleared, and the form data is successfully processed. This example highlights how React's state management can be effectively leveraged to implement form validation logic. Client-side validation plays a vital role in improving user experience by providing immediate feedback and reducing the burden on the server by preventing invalid submissions early.

Real-Time Validation

Real-time validation is a user-friendly feature that provides immediate feedback as users type into input fields. By leveraging React's ability to update state dynamically, developers can validate user input and display the results in real time, creating a more interactive and engaging user experience. This approach helps users correct errors or improve their input as they type, reducing the likelihood of invalid form submissions and improving overall usability as illustrated in Listing 11-8.

Listing 11-8. Password Strength Meter

```
const PasswordStrength = () => {
  const [password, setPassword] = React.useState("");
  const [strength, setStrength] = React.useState("");

  const handleChange = (e) => {
    const value = e.target.value;
    setPassword(value);

    if (value.length < 6) {
      setStrength("Weak");
    } else if (value.length < 10) {
      setStrength("Moderate");
    } else {
      setStrength("Strong");
    }
  };
```

CHAPTER 11   FORM HANDLING AND VALIDATION

```
  return (
    <form>
      <label>
        Password:
        <input type="password" value={password}
        onChange={handleChange} />
      </label>
      <p>Strength: {strength}</p>
    </form>
  );
}
```

The example demonstrates how to implement real-time validation using a password strength meter. The `handleChange` function updates the `password` state whenever the user types into the password field. Simultaneously, it evaluates the strength of the entered password based on its length and updates the `strength` state accordingly. If the password length is less than six characters, the strength is classified as "Weak." For lengths between six and ten characters, it is classified as "Moderate," and for passwords longer than ten characters, the strength is deemed "Strong."

The feedback is displayed immediately beneath the input field, providing users with a clear indication of their password's strength as they type. This real-time feedback not only enhances the user experience but also guides users toward creating stronger passwords, ensuring better security. Such interactive validation features are increasingly expected in modern applications and can be easily implemented using React's state management capabilities. In the next section, we will explore how to handle more complex validation requirements using third-party libraries.

CHAPTER 11   FORM HANDLING AND VALIDATION

Using Third-Party Libraries
Formik

Formik is a powerful library that simplifies form handling and validation in React applications. It provides a declarative API that minimizes boilerplate code and allows developers to focus on their application logic rather than managing form state manually. One of the standout features of Formik is its ability to integrate seamlessly with validation libraries like Yup, making it easy to enforce validation rules and display error messages. This combination provides a structured and efficient way to handle complex forms with minimal effort.

In the example below, Formik is used to create a form with an `email` input field. The `initialValues` prop initializes the form state, setting the default value for the email field to an empty string. The `onSubmit` function processes the form data when the user submits the form. Validation rules are defined using Yup, which ensures that the email field must contain a valid email address and cannot be left empty. Formik's `<Field>` component automatically binds the input field to the form state, reducing the need for explicit `onChange` handlers. Additionally, the `<ErrorMessage>` component displays validation error messages dynamically, providing immediate feedback to the user as shown in Listing 11-9. The corresponding output is shown in Figure 11-1.

Listing 11-9. Formik Integration with Yup

```
import { Formik, Form, Field, ErrorMessage } from "formik";
import * as Yup from "yup";

const FormikExample = () => {
  const validationSchema = Yup.object({
    email: Yup.string().email("Invalid email").
    required("Required"),
  });
```

CHAPTER 11 FORM HANDLING AND VALIDATION

```
  return (
    <Formik
      initialValues={{ email: "" }}
      validationSchema={validationSchema}
      onSubmit={(values) => console.log(values)}
    >
      <Form>
        <label>Email:</label>
        <Field type="email" name="email" />
        <ErrorMessage name="email" component="div" style={{
        color: "red" }} />
        <button type="submit">Submit</button>
      </Form>
    </Formik>
  );
}
Export default FormikExample;
```

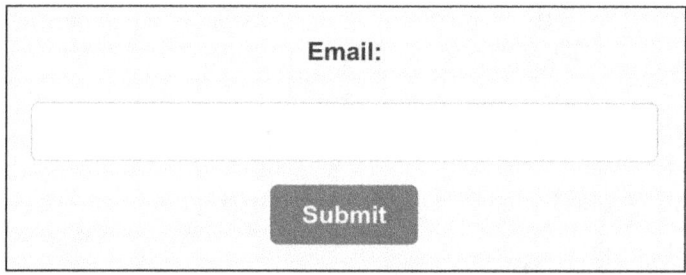

Figure 11-1. *Formik integration with Yup*

In this example, Formik's declarative approach simplifies form management by automatically handling state updates, validation, and error display. The validationSchema defined using Yup enforces two key rules: the email must be valid, and the field must not be empty. Formik's <Field> component binds the email input to its internal state, while the

`<ErrorMessage>` component displays error messages dynamically if the validation fails. When the user submits the form, the `onSubmit` function logs the form values to the console.

This example demonstrates how Formik and Yup work together to streamline form handling and validation. By reducing boilerplate code and centralizing validation logic, Formik makes it easier to build robust and maintainable forms in React applications. This approach not only saves development time but also enhances the user experience with real-time validation and error feedback.

React Hook Form

React Hook Form is a lightweight and performant library for managing forms in React. Unlike Formik, it leverages uncontrolled components, which rely on the DOM to manage form values. This approach reduces the need for React state updates, minimizing re-renders and improving performance, especially for large or complex forms. React Hook Form is highly flexible, providing powerful utilities for validation, error handling, and integration with third-party libraries, making it a great choice for efficient form handling as shown in Listing 11-10.

Listing 11-10. Using React Hook Form for Email Validation

```
import { useForm } from "react-hook-form";
const HookFormExample = () => {
  const {
    register,
    handleSubmit,
    formState: { errors }, // Correct way to access errors in v7+
  } = useForm();

  const onSubmit = (data) => console.log(data);
```

```
  return (
    <form onSubmit={handleSubmit(onSubmit)}
    className="hook-form">
      <label>Email:</label>
      <input
        type="email"
        {...register("email", { required: "Required" })}
        // Updated syntax
      />
      {errors.email && <p className="error-message">{errors.
      email.message}</p>}

      <button type="submit">Submit</button>
    </form>
  );
}

export default HookFormExample;
```

In the example, the `useForm` hook provides essential tools such as `register`, `handleSubmit`, and `errors`. The `register` function binds the input field to React Hook Form, enabling validation rules to be applied directly. Here, the email field is marked as required, and if the user attempts to submit the form without providing a value, an error message is displayed dynamically. The `handleSubmit` function wraps the submission logic and ensures that validation is performed before the `onSubmit` function is called. This seamless integration of validation and submission logic reduces boilerplate code and provides a clean, declarative approach to form handling. Additionally, the `errors` object dynamically tracks validation issues, making it easy to provide real-time feedback to users. This approach demonstrates how React Hook Form streamlines form handling and validation, offering a lightweight and efficient solution for managing forms in React applications.

CHAPTER 11 FORM HANDLING AND VALIDATION

Example: Checkout Form

The checkout form is designed to streamline the process of collecting customer details while ensuring the data is valid and ready for submission. This form will collect the user's name, email, and shipping address, performing both basic and asynchronous validations to provide immediate feedback. Once all inputs are validated, the form will handle submission by making an API call to store or process the provided information, simulating a real-world ecommerce workflow. This example incorporates key features of form handling and validation to create a robust and user-friendly checkout experience as illustrated in Listing 11-11. The output of the checkout form is shown in Figure 11-2.

Listing 11-11. Checkout Form

```
import React from "react";
import "./CheckoutForm.css"; // Import external CSS for styling

const CheckoutForm = () => {
  // State to store form data
  const [formData, setFormData] = React.useState({
    name: "",
    email: "",
    address: "",
  });

  // State to store validation errors
  const [errors, setErrors] = React.useState({});

  // Validation function to check required fields
  const validate = () => {
    const newErrors = {};
    if (!formData.name.trim()) newErrors.name = "Name is required";
```

CHAPTER 11 FORM HANDLING AND VALIDATION

```
  if (!formData.email.includes("@")) newErrors.email =
  "Invalid email format";
  if (!formData.address.trim()) newErrors.address = "Address
  is required";
  setErrors(newErrors);

  // Return true if no errors exist
  return Object.keys(newErrors).length === 0;
};

// Handles form submission
const handleSubmit = (e) => {
  e.preventDefault();
  if (validate()) {
    console.log("Form submitted:", formData);
  }
};

// Handles changes to input fields and updates state
const handleChange = (e) => {
  setFormData({ ...formData, [e.target.name]: e.target.
  value });
};

return (
  <div className="checkout-container">
    <form onSubmit={handleSubmit} className="checkout-form">
      {/* Name Field */}
      <label>Name:</label>
      <input
        type="text"
        name="name"
        value={formData.name}
```

```jsx
      onChange={handleChange}
      placeholder="Enter your name"
    />
    {errors.name && <p className="error-message">{errors.name}</p>}

    {/* Email Field */}
    <label>Email:</label>
    <input
      type="email"
      name="email"
      value={formData.email}
      onChange={handleChange}
      placeholder="Enter your email"
    />
    {errors.email && <p className="error-message">{errors.email}</p>}

    {/* Address Field */}
    <label>Address:</label>
    <textarea
      name="address"
      value={formData.address}
      onChange={handleChange}
      placeholder="Enter your address"
    />
    {errors.address && <p className="error-message">{errors.address}</p>}

    {/* Submit Button */}
    <button type="submit">Checkout</button>
```

CHAPTER 11 FORM HANDLING AND VALIDATION

```
      </form>
    </div>
  );
};

export default CheckoutForm;
```

Figure 11-2. Checkout form with form handling and validation

This checkout form demonstrates a comprehensive implementation of form handling, validation, and submission in a React application. The formData state is used to manage the input values for the name, email, and address fields, while the errors state tracks validation messages for each field, ensuring users receive immediate feedback when they enter invalid or incomplete information. Basic validation is handled through the validate function, which checks whether all fields are filled and whether the email input follows a valid format using a regular expression. Validation errors are displayed dynamically next to the relevant fields using conditional rendering, enhancing the user experience.

CHAPTER 11   FORM HANDLING AND VALIDATION

The form also incorporates asynchronous validation and submission. The `handleSubmit` function validates the inputs first and prevents submission if errors are detected. Once the inputs are validated, the function performs an API call to a simulated endpoint (https://api.example.com/checkout) to process the form data. Upon successful submission, a success message is displayed to inform the user. If the submission fails, an error message alerts the user of the issue, ensuring clear communication at every step. Additionally, the `isSubmitting` state is used to disable the submit button and provide feedback to the user during the API call, preventing duplicate submissions and enhancing usability. This well-rounded implementation illustrates best practices for handling forms in React, combining real-time validation, asynchronous operations, and user-friendly feedback.

Summary

This chapter provided a comprehensive exploration of form handling and validation in React, addressing a wide range of techniques and tools to manage user input effectively. We began by examining the differences between controlled and uncontrolled components, highlighting how controlled components rely on React state for input management, while uncontrolled components leverage the DOM for simpler use cases. Next, we delved into real-time validation techniques that provide instant feedback as users type, ensuring a smoother and more interactive user experience.

The chapter also covered asynchronous validation and the use of third-party libraries such as Formik and React Hook Form. Formik simplifies form state management and integrates seamlessly with validation libraries like Yup for schema-based validation. React Hook Form, on the other hand, utilizes uncontrolled inputs to enhance performance by minimizing re-renders. These libraries were demonstrated through practical examples, showcasing how to implement efficient and user-friendly forms in React applications.

To solidify these concepts, we built a fully functional checkout form app. This example integrated state management, validation, error handling, and API calls, demonstrating how to apply these techniques in a real-world context. The form incorporated both basic and asynchronous validation, offering immediate feedback and ensuring data integrity before submission. Together, these examples provided a solid foundation for handling forms and validations in modern React applications.

In the next chapter, we will explore **routing and navigation**, where we will learn how to implement dynamic navigation, nested routes, and more using React Router, enabling seamless transitions and improved user experience in single-page applications.

CHAPTER 12

Routing and Navigation

Routing is one of the most fundamental aspects of single-page applications (SPAs) like those built with React. Unlike traditional multipage applications, SPAs dynamically update the content of a single HTML page based on the URL, eliminating the need for full page reloads. This approach creates a smoother and faster user experience. In React, routing is achieved using specialized libraries like **React Router**, which provide powerful tools to handle navigation and manage different views or pages.

This chapter delves into the key concepts of React Router, the most widely used library for implementing routing in React applications. We will cover topics such as route definitions, dynamic routing, nested routes, protected routes, and programmatic navigation. By the end of this chapter, you will have a clear understanding of how to create a structured and intuitive navigation flow in your applications. Additionally, we will demonstrate how to apply these concepts by implementing routing and navigation features in a **blog** app, enabling users to move seamlessly between the app's pages, such as the home page, blog post page, and the dashboard page.

CHAPTER 12   ROUTING AND NAVIGATION

Understanding Routing in SPAs

Routing is a critical feature in single-page applications (SPAs), enabling smooth transitions between different views or pages within the same application. Unlike traditional multipage applications where navigation requires fetching a new page from the server, SPAs handle routing on the client side. This means that the URL changes dynamically without requiring a full page reload. Instead, React updates the content displayed on the screen based on the current URL, making the navigation experience seamless and efficient.

How SPAs Handle Routing

In SPAs, routing is managed entirely by the front-end application. When a user navigates to a different route, the SPA intercepts the request and dynamically updates the view without involving the server. For example, when a user clicks a link to view a product details page, the application updates the content to show the product information while keeping the rest of the application, such as the navigation bar, intact. This approach provides several key advantages:

1. **Faster Navigation**: Since SPAs only update the necessary parts of the application, the navigation process is much faster compared to traditional applications where the entire page is reloaded.

2. **A Smoother User Experience**: The lack of full page reloads creates a more fluid and responsive experience for users, mimicking the feel of a native application.

3. **Reduced Server Load**: By handling most of the rendering on the client side, SPAs minimize the load on the server, as fewer requests are made to fetch HTML pages.

To facilitate routing in React, developers rely on React Router, the most popular and widely used library for handling navigation in React applications. React Router offers a declarative approach to defining routes, allowing developers to specify which component should be rendered for each URL. It efficiently handles dynamic routing by mapping the URL to the corresponding component or view, enabling developers to build scalable and maintainable applications.

With React Router, you can define **nested routes**, **dynamic parameters**, **protected routes**, and more, providing all the tools necessary to create a robust navigation system. Its declarative nature and rich feature set make it an essential tool for building modern SPAs. In the following sections, we will explore these features in detail and demonstrate how to implement them in our blog application.

Setting Up React Router

Setting up React Router is the first step toward enabling routing and navigation in your React application. React Router provides a powerful, declarative API to define and manage routes, making it an essential tool for building single-page applications (SPAs). This section explains how to install React Router, configure it in your application, and set up basic routing.

To begin, you need to install the `react-router-dom` package, which is specifically designed for web-based React applications. This package includes all the necessary components and utilities for client-side routing. Refer to Listing 12-1 for the installation command.

Listing 12-1. Installation Command

```
npm install react-router-dom
```

This command adds the React Router library to your project, allowing you to use features like `BrowserRouter`, `Routes`, and `Route` for defining navigation paths.

Once installed, React Router requires you to wrap your application with the `BrowserRouter` component. This component enables React Router to listen to changes in the browser's URL and render the appropriate components dynamically. Refer to Listing 12-2 for an example configuration.

Listing 12-2. Example Configuration

```
import { BrowserRouter, Routes, Route } from "react-router-dom";

function Home() {
  return <h1>Welcome to the Home Page</h1>;
}

function About() {
  return <h1>About Us</h1>;
}

const App = () => {
  return (
    <BrowserRouter>
      <Routes>
        <Route path="/" element={<Home />} />
        <Route path="/about" element={<About />} />
      </Routes>
    </BrowserRouter>
  );
}

export default App;
```

The `BrowserRouter` component serves as a high-level wrapper that allows React Router to interact with the browser's history API, ensuring the application can properly respond to URL changes. By wrapping the application with `BrowserRouter`, you enable React Router to manage navigation and render the appropriate components based on the current URL. Within the `BrowserRouter`, the `Routes` component acts as a container for all defined routes in the application. It replaces the older `Switch` component from earlier versions of React Router and provides a more intuitive way to organize and manage routing logic. Each `Route` defined inside the `Routes` component specifies a `path` and the corresponding component to render.

For instance, navigating to / renders the `Home` component displaying "Welcome to the Home Page.", while navigating to /about renders the `About` component displaying "About Us." This declarative approach to routing ensures that the structure of the routes is clearly defined directly in the JSX, making the logic easy to understand and maintain. React Router's declarative nature not only simplifies the routing process but also enhances the readability and scalability of the codebase.

Core Concepts of React Router

React Router provides a robust and flexible way to manage navigation and routing in React applications. Understanding its core concepts is essential for creating efficient and user-friendly navigation experiences. This section covers the fundamentals, including route matching and navigating between pages, highlighting how React Router handles these tasks declaratively and programmatically.

CHAPTER 12   ROUTING AND NAVIGATION

Route Matching

React Router uses route matching to determine which component to render based on the current URL in the browser. It compares the URL path to the path property of each Route component and renders the associated component if a match is found. React Router supports both static and dynamic routes, enabling developers to create flexible and scalable navigation. **Dynamic Routes** allow you to handle dynamic segments within the URL. These segments are defined using a colon (:), followed by a parameter name. For example, refer to Listing 12-3 for a dynamic route.

Listing 12-3. Dynamic Route

```
<Route path="/product/:id" element={<ProductDetails />} />
```

In this example, :id represents a dynamic parameter that can hold any value (e.g., /product/1, /product/42). The dynamic value is accessible within the ProductDetails component using the useParams hook. Refer to Listing 12-4 for an example.

Listing 12-4. Accessing Dynamic Parameters with useParams

```
import { useParams } from "react-router-dom";
const ProductDetails = () => {
  const { id } = useParams();
  return <h1>Product ID: {id}</h1>;
}
export default ProductDetails
```

This approach enables you to create pages that dynamically adapt based on the provided URL parameters. For instance, in a product-based application, the ProductDetails component can fetch and display data for a specific product using the id parameter, providing a highly flexible and user-specific navigation experience.

CHAPTER 12   ROUTING AND NAVIGATION

Navigating Between Pages

Navigation in React Router can be achieved both declaratively and programmatically. These methods provide flexibility in designing user flows for single-page applications (SPAs).

The <Link> component is used for **declarative navigation**. It allows users to navigate between pages without triggering a full page reload. For example, refer to Listing 12-5.

Listing 12-5. Declarative Navigation with <Link>

```
<Link to="/about">About</Link>
```

When users click this link, the URL changes to /about, and React Router dynamically renders the About component without refreshing the page. This method is simple, efficient, and ideal for navigation elements like menus and links.

React Router also supports **programmatic navigation** using the useNavigate hook. This is useful when navigation needs to be triggered based on an event, such as a button click or form submission. See Listing 12-6 for an example.

Listing 12-6. Programmatic Navigation with useNavigate

```
import { useNavigate } from "react-router-dom";
const Home = () => {
  const navigate = useNavigate();
  return <button onClick={() => navigate("/about")}>Go to
  About</button>;
}
export default Home;
```

In this example, clicking the button programmatically navigates the user to the /about page, rendering the About component. React Router's core concepts of route matching and navigation empower developers to create dynamic and interactive single-page applications. The ability to define dynamic routes simplifies the handling of parameters within URLs, while the flexibility of declarative and programmatic navigation enhances user experience. Together, these tools provide a solid foundation for building modern React applications with efficient and intuitive navigation. In the next section, we will explore advanced routing features such as nested routes and protected routes to further enhance your application's navigation logic.

Nested Routes

Nested routes are a powerful feature in React Router that allow developers to structure related views within a parent-child hierarchy. They enable you to define routes that are part of a larger section of your application, such as a dashboard with multiple subsections. This approach enhances the organization and scalability of your application's routing logic, making it easier to manage and navigate between related components.

To define nested routes, you can nest <Route> components within a parent route. This creates a hierarchy where child routes are rendered as part of the parent component's structure. For example, refer to Listing 12-7.

Listing 12-7. Dynamic Route

```
<Route path="/dashboard" element={<Dashboard />}>
  <Route path="analytics" element={<Analytics />} />
  <Route path="settings" element={<Settings />} />
</Route>
```

CHAPTER 12   ROUTING AND NAVIGATION

In this configuration

- Navigating to /dashboard renders the Dashboard component.

- Navigating to /dashboard/analytics renders the Analytics component within the Dashboard layout.

- Navigating to /dashboard/settings renders the Settings component, also within the Dashboard layout.

This setup is ideal for applications with complex structures, such as admin panels or user dashboards, where multiple subsections need to be displayed within a common parent layout. It enhances the organization and scalability of your routing logic by grouping related routes together.

To render these nested routes, the parent component must include the <Outlet> component provided by React Router. The <Outlet> acts as a placeholder that is replaced by the child route's component when the route matches. See Listing 12-8 for an example.

Listing 12-8. Rendering Nested Routes with <Outlet>

```
const Dashboard = () => {
  return (
    <div>
      <h1>Dashboard</h1>
      <Outlet />
    </div>
  );
}
```

In this example

- The Dashboard component always displays the heading "Dashboard."
- The <Outlet> dynamically renders the matching child component, such as Analytics or Settings, depending on the URL.

This approach enables developers to build sophisticated routing systems with ease. For example, a dashboard page can display shared navigation elements and dynamically load the relevant content for each subsection (e.g., analytics, settings) without reloading the page.

Protected Routes

Protected routes are an essential feature in applications where certain pages or sections should only be accessible to authenticated users. For instance, in an ecommerce application, user profiles, order histories, or admin panels may need to be restricted based on the user's authentication status. React Router allows you to implement such access control seamlessly using custom components and conditional rendering.

A protected route acts as a wrapper around the component you want to secure. It checks whether the user is authenticated and, based on the authentication status, either renders the protected component or redirects the user to a login page. Refer to Listing 12-9.

Listing 12-9. Protected Route Component

```
const ProtectedRoute = ({ element, isAuthenticated }) => {
  return isAuthenticated ? element : <Navigate to="/login" />;
}
```

In this component, the `isAuthenticated` prop acts as a boolean indicator to determine whether the user is logged in. If `isAuthenticated` is `true`, the component passed via the `element` prop is rendered, granting access to the protected content. However, if `isAuthenticated` is `false`, the user is redirected to the `/login` page using the `Navigate` component, ensuring that only authenticated users can access the specified route. This logic provides a secure and straightforward way to manage protected routes in React applications.

You can use the `ProtectedRoute` component to secure specific routes. For instance, to protect a user profile page, refer to Listing 12-10.

Listing 12-10. Securing a Route with ProtectedRoute

```
<Route
  path="/profile"
  element={<ProtectedRoute isAuthenticated={isLoggedIn}
  element={<Profile />} />}
/>
```

In this example, the `/profile` route is configured to be accessible only if the `isLoggedIn` value is true. If the user is not authenticated (i.e., `isLoggedIn` is `false`), any attempt to access the `/profile` route will automatically redirect them to the `/login` page. This ensures that only authorized users can view the profile page, while unauthenticated users are directed to log in before gaining access.

Lazy Loading Routes

Lazy loading is an optimization technique that significantly improves the performance of React applications by splitting the application into smaller chunks and loading them only when required. This technique is especially useful for large applications with many routes, as it prevents users from having to download unnecessary components up front. Instead, the browser fetches the specific route's component only when the user navigates to it, reducing the initial load time and enhancing the overall user experience.

Lazy loading significantly enhances the performance of an application by ensuring that only the components necessary for the current view are loaded. In traditional React setups, all components are typically bundled together, resulting in larger bundle sizes and slower load times. Lazy loading addresses these issues by reducing the initial load time, as only the essential components are loaded when the application starts. Additionally, it improves performance by fetching other components on demand as users navigate through the application, making the loading process more efficient. This approach also optimizes resource usage, as unused routes and components are not fetched until required, ensuring that resources are allocated effectively, and unnecessary data transfer is minimized.

React provides the `lazy` function to define components that should be loaded on demand. When combined with the `Suspense` component, lazy loading becomes seamless experience. Refer to Listing 12-11.

Listing 12-11. Lazy Loading a Route

```
import { lazy, Suspense } from "react";
const ProductDetails = lazy(() => import("./ProductDetails"));
const App = () => {
  return (
    <Suspense fallback={<div>Loading...</div>}>
      <Routes>
        <Route path="/product/:id"
          element={<ProductDetails />} />
      </Routes>
    </Suspense>
  );
}
```

The `lazy` function dynamically imports the specified component, allowing it to be loaded only when needed. In this example, the `ProductDetails` component is imported dynamically when the user navigates to the `/product/:id` route. This approach reduces the size of the initial JavaScript bundle, improving the application's performance. The Suspense component acts as a fallback mechanism for lazy-loaded components. While the `ProductDetails` component is being fetched, the content specified in the `fallback` prop, such as `<div>Loading...</div>`, is displayed to the user. Once the component is fully loaded, it replaces the fallback content seamlessly. Additionally, the lazy-loaded `ProductDetails` component is integrated into the routing structure using the `element` property of the `Route` component, ensuring that the routing logic remains clear and easy to manage. This combination of `lazy`, `Suspense`, and React Router ensures efficient and user-friendly dynamic loading of routes.

Error Handling

Error handling is an essential aspect of building robust web applications. React Router provides built-in mechanisms to handle errors such as unmatched routes and lazy loading failures. By incorporating error handling, you ensure that your application gracefully manages unexpected scenarios and provides users with clear feedback when something goes wrong.

A common use case for error handling in React Router is defining a fallback route for unmatched paths. When users navigate to a route that doesn't exist in your application, you can display a custom **404 page** to inform them that the requested page could not be found. This is achieved using the wildcard route (*), which acts as a catch-all for any undefined paths. Refer to Listing 12-12.

CHAPTER 12 ROUTING AND NAVIGATION

Listing 12-12. Defining a 404 Page

```
import { BrowserRouter, Routes, Route } from "react-router-dom";

const NotFound = () => {
  return <h1>404 - Page Not Found</h1>;
}

const App = () => {
  return (
    <BrowserRouter>
      <Routes>
        <Route path="/" element={<h1>Home Page</h1>} />
        <Route path="/about" element={<h1>About Page</h1>} />
        <Route path="*" element={<NotFound />} />
      </Routes>
    </BrowserRouter>
  );
}

export default App;
```

The wildcard route, defined with path="*", matches any URL that does not correspond to the previously defined routes in your application. It is typically placed at the end of the Routes component to serve as a fallback for unmatched paths. The NotFound component is used to display a custom 404 page, which can include a message or design to inform users that the requested page is not available. This component can also include helpful navigation links to guide users back to the home page or other valid sections of the site. By integrating the wildcard route, your application gracefully handles all unmatched paths, ensuring a seamless and user-friendly experience for your audience.

In addition to handling unmatched routes, React provides the Suspense component for managing errors during lazy loading. For instance, if a component fails to load due to a network issue, the Suspense component can display a fallback message or implement retry logic as discussed in the "Lazy Loading Route" section.

By incorporating a well-designed 404 page for unmatched routes and managing errors effectively in lazy-loaded components, your application can gracefully handle unexpected scenarios while maintaining a polished and professional appearance.

Example: Simple Blog Navigation with React Router

To bring together all the concepts discussed in this chapter, we will implement a practical example of a **blog application**. This app will demonstrate routing and navigation using React Router while incorporating advanced concepts like dynamic routes, lazy loading, protected routes, and error handling. The application will include several key pages: a **home page (/)**, a **blog post details page (/blog/:id)**, a **protected dashboard page (/dashboard)** for authenticated users, and a **404 error page for unmatched routes**.

The application's routing structure integrates lazy loading, route protection, and error handling. See Listing 12-13 for an overview.

Listing 12-13. Defining Routes

```
//BlogApp.js
import React, { lazy, Suspense } from "react";
import { Routes, Route, Navigate } from "react-router-dom";

const HomePage = lazy(() => import("./Home"));
const BlogPost = lazy(() => import("./BlogPost"));
```

CHAPTER 12 ROUTING AND NAVIGATION

```
const Dashboard = lazy(() => import("./Dashboard"));
const NotFound = lazy(() => import("./NotFound"));

function ProtectedRoute({ element, isAuthenticated }) {
  return isAuthenticated ? element : <Navigate to=".." />;
  // Navigate back
}

const BlogApp = () => {
  const isAuthenticated = false; // Simulated authentication status

  return (
    <Suspense fallback={<div>Loading...</div>}>
      <Routes>
        <Route path="/" element={<HomePage />} /> {/* Matches /example/17 */}
        <Route path="blog/:id" element={<BlogPost />} /> {/* Matches /example/17/blog/:id */}
        <Route path="dashboard" element={<ProtectedRoute isAuthenticated={isAuthenticated} element={<Dashboard />} />} /> {/* Matches /example/17/dashboard */}
        <Route path="*" element={<NotFound />} /> {/* Matches /example/17/* */}
      </Routes>
    </Suspense>
  );
};

export default BlogApp;
```

Page Implementations

1. **Home Page**: Displays a list of products with links to individual product details. See Listing 12-14.

Listing 12-14. Home Page Implementation

```
import React from "react";
import { Link } from "react-router-dom";

const Home = () => {
  const posts = [
    { id: 1, title: "Understanding React Hooks" },
    { id: 2, title: "Introduction to JavaScript ES6
    Features" },
  ];

  return (
    <div>
      <h1>Welcome to My Blog</h1>
      <ul>
        {posts.map((post) => (
          <li key={post.id}>
            <Link to={`blog/${post.id}`}>{post.title}</Link>
            {/* Relative path */}
          </li>
        ))}
      </ul>
    </div>
  );
};

export default Home;
```

2. **Blog Post Page**: Displays product-specific information using dynamic routing. See Listing 12-15.

Listing 12-15. Blog Post Page Implementation

```
import { useParams } from "react-router-dom";
const BlogPost = () => {
  const { id } = useParams();
  return <h1>Blog Post Content for ID: {id}</h1>;
}
export default BlogPost;
```

3. **Protected Dashboard Page**: A protected route accessible only to authenticated users. See Listing 12-16.

Listing 12-16. Dashboard Page Implementation

```
const Dashboard = () => {
  return <h1>Dashboard: Only Accessible to Logged-in Users</h1>;
}
export default Dashboard;
```

4. **404 Page:** Handles unmatched routes with a custom message. See Listing 12-17.

Listing 12-17. 404 Page Implementation

```
const NotFound = () => {
  return <h1>404 - Page Not Found</h1>;
}
export default NotFound;
```

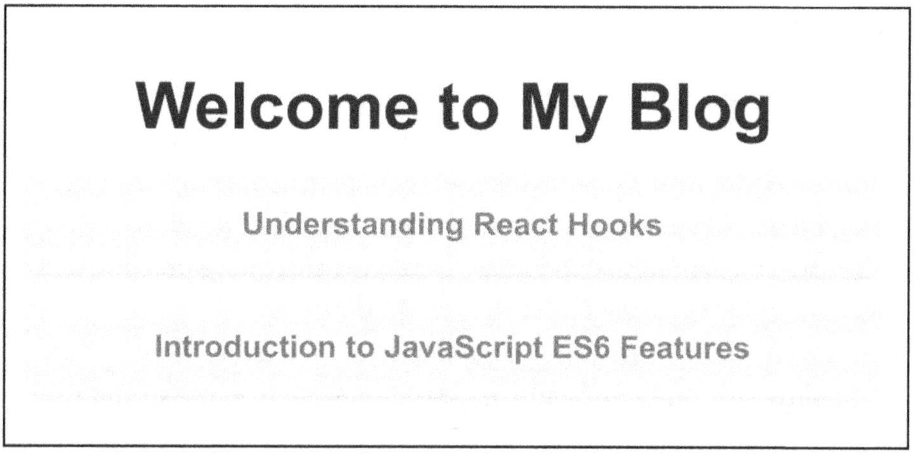

CHAPTER 12   ROUTING AND NAVIGATION

> # Welcome to My Blog
>
> Understanding React Hooks
>
> Introduction to JavaScript ES6 Features

Figure 12-1. *Blog application using React Router*

The **blog app** includes several advanced features that demonstrate the effective use of React Router. The `/dashboard` route is protected using the `ProtectedRoute` component, ensuring that only authenticated users can access it, thereby safeguarding restricted sections of the application. All pages are lazy loaded using React's `lazy` and `Suspense` functions, optimizing performance by loading only the necessary components when needed. The `/blog/:id` route showcases dynamic routing, leveraging route parameters to fetch and display blog-specific content dynamically. For error handling, a wildcard route (`*`) is implemented to handle unmatched paths gracefully, redirecting users to the custom `NotFound` page.

The app's flow is designed to provide a **seamless user experience**. Users can navigate to `/` to view the **home page**, which displays a list of blog posts. Clicking a blog post directs them to the `/blog/:id` page, where they can see the details of the selected article. The `/dashboard` page, accessible only to **authenticated users**, provides a protected view for managing content. Additionally, entering an `invalid` URL redirects users to the **404 page**, ensuring that all paths are handled appropriately. This complete flow demonstrates a practical implementation of **React Router's features** in a real-world **blogging application**.

245

CHAPTER 12 ROUTING AND NAVIGATION

Summary

Routing and navigation are fundamental aspects of creating seamless and user-friendly single-page applications (SPAs). In this chapter, we delved into the essential features of React Router, including dynamic routing, nested routes, lazy loading, protected routes, and error handling. Each concept was explained with practical examples and integrated into a blog application to demonstrate their real-world usage.

Dynamic routing enabled the application to fetch and display data based on route parameters, while nested routes allowed the structuring of related views within a parent-child hierarchy. Lazy loading improved performance by splitting the application into smaller chunks and loading routes only when necessary. Protected routes ensured that sensitive sections of the application, such as the dashboard page, were accessible only to authenticated users. Error handling, implemented via a custom 404 page, provided a user-friendly way to manage unmatched paths.

These routing principles were consolidated in the blog app, where users could navigate between the home, blog post, and dashboard pages. By combining all the discussed concepts, the app delivered a smooth navigation experience and demonstrated the scalability of React Router's features. As we move to the next chapter, we will focus on **optimizing performance**, a crucial step in enhancing the efficiency and responsiveness of our React applications.

CHAPTER 13

Optimizing Performance

Performance optimization is a critical aspect of modern web application development, especially as applications grow in complexity and scale. In React, delivering a smooth and responsive user experience involves addressing challenges like reducing unnecessary re-renders, optimizing state and prop management, and minimizing the app's bundle size. Poorly optimized applications can lead to sluggish performance, impacting user satisfaction and retention.

This chapter delves into best practices and techniques for optimizing React applications. We will explore concepts like **memoization** to prevent redundant computations, lazy loading to improve initial load times, and effective use of developer tools like **React Profiler**. Each technique will be illustrated with practical examples, ensuring you can apply these strategies to real-world scenarios.

Understanding React's Rendering Behavior

React uses a virtual DOM as an abstraction layer to optimize updates to the real DOM. The virtual DOM keeps a lightweight in-memory representation of the actual DOM and applies a process called **"reconciliation"** to determine the minimal set of changes needed to update the real

DOM. When the state or props of a component change, React compares the current virtual DOM with the previous version to identify differences, known as the "**diffing**" process. Only the nodes that have changed are updated in the real DOM, significantly improving efficiency.

However, unnecessary renders can occur if React re-renders components that have not experienced any meaningful changes. This can lead to wasted computational resources and slower application performance. For example, if a parent component re-renders unnecessarily, all its child components will also re-render, even if their props or state have not changed. Understanding and controlling React's rendering behavior is critical to improving performance.

Performance bottlenecks in React applications often manifest as laggy interactions, slow page transitions, or high CPU and memory usage. These issues can degrade user experience, especially in large-scale applications.

Symptoms of Bottlenecks

- **Laggy Interactions**: Clicking buttons, typing into inputs, or other UI interactions feel delayed or unresponsive.

- **Slow Page Transitions**: Navigation between views or pages takes noticeably longer.

- **High CPU or Memory Usage:** The application consumes excessive resources, impacting performance on less powerful devices.

Tools for Identifying Bottlenecks

- **React Developer Tools**: This browser extension provides insights into React components, their props, state, and rendering behavior. It allows you to visualize component hierarchies and detect components that are rendering more frequently than necessary.

- **Chrome DevTools Profiler**: This tool enables you to record the performance of your application and analyze rendering timelines. It can pinpoint components or operations consuming excessive resources.

By combining these tools, you can systematically identify and address performance bottlenecks in your application.

Preventing Unnecessary Re-renders

Unnecessary re-renders in React can lead to performance bottlenecks, especially in components that handle large datasets or complex UI structures. To mitigate this, React provides tools like `React.memo`, `useCallback`, and `useMemo` to optimize rendering behavior.

React.memo

React.memo is a higher-order component (HOC) that prevents a functional component from re-rendering if its props have not changed. It works by memoizing the rendered output of the component and reusing it for subsequent renders, provided the props remain unchanged as shown in Listing 13-1.

Listing 13-1. Memoizing a Functional Component

```
const ProductCard = React.memo(({ product }) => {
  console.log("Rendering ProductCard");
  return <div>{product.name}</div>;
});

const ProductList = ({ products }) => {
  return (
    <div>
      {products.map((product) => (
        <ProductCard key={product.id} product={product} />
      ))}
    </div>
  );
}
```

In this example, the ProductCard component is wrapped with React.memo. This ensures that it re-renders only when the product prop changes. For instance, if the products array remains the same between renders, ProductCard will not re-render unnecessarily.

React.memo should be used when dealing with components that have stable props, meaning they render the same output for the same input values. This optimization is particularly beneficial for preventing unnecessary re-renders, thereby improving performance. However, React.memo should be applied selectively, especially to components with significant rendering costs, as overusing it may introduce unnecessary complexity without providing substantial benefits.

useCallback and useMemo

React's useCallback and useMemo hooks provide finer control over memoization in functional components. The useCallback hook is used to memoize callback functions, preventing their unnecessary re-creation

CHAPTER 13 OPTIMIZING PERFORMANCE

and improving performance in components that rely on stable function references. On the other hand, the useMemo hook is designed to memoize computed values, helping to avoid expensive recalculations by caching the result of a computation unless its dependencies change. These hooks enhance efficiency by reducing redundant processing and optimizing rendering performance in React applications as illustrated in Listing 13-2.

Listing 13-2. Memoizing Callback Functions Using useCallback and Memoizing Computer Values Using useMemo

```
// useCallback
const ProductList = ({ products }) => {
  const renderProduct = useCallback(
    (product) => <ProductCard key={product.id}
    product={product} />,
    []
  );

  return <div>{products.map(renderProduct)}</div>;
};

// useMemo
const ExpensiveCalculationComponent = ({ items }) => {
  const totalValue = useMemo(() => {
    console.log("Computing total value...");
    return items.reduce((sum, item) => sum + item.price, 0);
  }, [items]);

  return <div>Total: ${totalValue}</div>;
};
```

In this example, the useCallback hook memoizes the renderProduct function, ensuring it is not recreated on every render unless the products array changes. This reduces the computational overhead, particularly

CHAPTER 13   OPTIMIZING PERFORMANCE

when passing callback functions to child components, and in the other case, `useMemo` ensures that the total value is only recomputed when items change, avoiding unnecessary recalculations and improving performance.

By combining `React.memo`, `useCallback`, and `useMemo`, you can effectively prevent unnecessary re-renders in your React application. However, overusing these tools can lead to increased code complexity and even degrade performance in some scenarios. It's important to profile your application using tools like React Developer Tools and apply these optimizations judiciously to achieve the best results.

Code Splitting and Lazy Loading

Code splitting and **lazy loading** are essential techniques for improving React application performance by reducing the initial load time. Instead of downloading the entire application up front, these strategies break large JavaScript bundles into smaller, manageable chunks that are loaded only when needed.

This approach mitigates the performance impact of large JavaScript files, ensuring that only the necessary components are fetched dynamically. As a result, the application becomes more responsive, enhances user experience, and efficiently utilizes resources.

React supports code splitting using dynamic `import()` statements. This functionality enables developers to load components or modules on demand, seamlessly integrating with routing and other features. The `React.lazy` function simplifies the process by allowing components to be dynamically loaded and rendered only when they are needed. The example in Listing 13-3 demonstrates how to implement lazy loading and code splitting for a product details page.

Listing 13-3. Implementing Lazy Loading with React Router

```
import { lazy, Suspense } from "react";
// Lazy-loaded component
const ProductDetails = lazy(() => import("./ProductDetails"));
const App = () => {
  return (
    <Suspense fallback={<div>Loading...</div>}>
      <Routes>
{/* Route with lazy-loaded component */}
<Route path="/product/:id" element={<ProductDetails />} />
      </Routes>
    </Suspense>
  );
}
```

In Listing 13-3, the `lazy` function dynamically imports the `ProductDetails` component. This ensures that the component is loaded only when the user navigates to the `/product/:id` route. The `Suspense` component provides a fallback UI (in this case, a `Loading...` message) while the dynamically imported component is being fetched. Once the component is loaded, it replaces the fallback content seamlessly.

By incorporating code splitting and lazy loading into your React application, you can significantly enhance its performance. These techniques reduce the amount of JavaScript required at the initial load and improve the user experience, especially for large-scale applications with multiple routes and components. The approach illustrated is a cornerstone of modern performance optimization in React applications.

CHAPTER 13   OPTIMIZING PERFORMANCE

Optimizing State Management

Efficient state management is essential to ensure that your React applications remain performant and scalable as they grow. Poorly designed state structures can lead to unnecessary re-renders, deeply nested state dependencies, and hard-to-maintain code. This section explores techniques to optimize state management using both local state and global state libraries like **Redux**.

Avoiding Deeply Nested State

Deeply nested state structures can introduce unnecessary complexity and lead to performance issues due to frequent re-renders triggered by small updates. Keeping state as flat as possible and localizing it where appropriate can improve performance and maintainability. For example:

- **Local State:** When a state is only relevant to a specific component, use `useState` or `useReducer` to manage it locally instead of elevating it unnecessarily.

- **Context API:** Avoid overusing React's Context API for frequently changing data, as it can propagate re-renders across the component tree. Reserve it for static or rarely changing values, such as themes or localization settings.

Using Selectors in Redux

Selectors are a powerful way to optimize state management in Redux. By using libraries like reselect, you can memoize derived state and avoid recalculating values unnecessarily. This is particularly useful when you need to compute expensive operations or extract portions of the state tree. Listing 13-4 shows the illustration.

Listing 13-4. Memoizing State Using Selectors

```
import { useSelector } from "react-redux";
import { createSelector } from "reselect";

// Base selector to get cart items
const selectCartItems = (state) => state.cart.items;

// Memoized selector to calculate total price
const selectTotalPrice = createSelector(
  [selectCartItems],
  (items) => items.reduce((total, item) => total + item.price, 0)
);

// Usage in a component
const CartSummary = () => {
  const totalPrice = useSelector(selectTotalPrice);
  return <h1>Total Price: ${totalPrice}</h1>;
};

export default CartSummary;
```

In this example, `selectCartItems` retrieves the raw cart items from the Redux state, while `selectTotalPrice` uses `createSelector` to memoize the derived total price. This ensures that the total price is only recalculated when the cart items change, preventing unnecessary computations and re-renders.

Optimizing Large Lists

Handling large datasets efficiently is crucial for maintaining a smooth user experience in React applications. Rendering large lists without optimization can result in performance bottlenecks, such as slow rendering, high memory usage, and degraded user interactions. **Virtualization** is a powerful technique for improving the performance of applications that need to display extensive lists.

Virtualization

Virtualization involves rendering only the visible portion of a list while keeping the rest of the items hidden until they come into view. This drastically reduces the number of DOM nodes created and manipulated, which in turn enhances the application's performance. React libraries like `react-window` and `react-virtualized` provide robust solutions for implementing virtualization in React applications.

Listing 13-5. Efficient List Rendering Using Virtualization

```
import { FixedSizeList } from "react-window";

const Row = ({ index, style, data }) => (
  <div style={style}>{data[index].name}</div>
);

const ProductList = ({ products }) => (
  <FixedSizeList
    height={400} // Height of the container
    width={300}  // Width of the container
    itemCount={products.length} // Total items in the list
    itemSize={35} // Height of each item in the list
    itemData={products} // Pass products as data
  >
    {Row}
  </FixedSizeList>
);

export default ProductList;
```

In this example, the `FixedSizeList` component from `react-window` is utilized to create a scrollable list efficiently, as shown in Listing 13-5. The `height` and `width` properties define the visible dimensions of the list container, ensuring that only a portion of the list is rendered at any given time. The `itemCount` property specifies the total number of items in the dataset, while the `itemSize` property determines the height of each individual list item. To render visible items dynamically, a function is passed as a child to the `FixedSizeList` component. This function leverages the `style` prop to position each rendered item correctly within the container, ensuring smooth scrolling and optimal performance.

Optimizing Images and Media

Optimizing images and media is crucial for enhancing the performance of web applications, as media files often contribute significantly to the total page size. Proper optimization ensures faster load times and a better user experience, especially on slower networks.

Lazy Loading Images

Lazy loading is an effective technique for deferring the loading of images until they are needed, such as when they come into the user's viewport. This reduces the initial load time by only loading visible media and fetching other assets on demand. In HTML, this can be achieved using the `loading="lazy"` attribute, as shown in Listing 13-6.

Listing 13-6. Lazy Loading an Image

```
<img src="example.jpg" loading="lazy" alt="Example" />
```

CHAPTER 13　OPTIMIZING PERFORMANCE

In this example, the `loading="lazy"` attribute instructs the browser to delay loading the image until it becomes visible, thereby saving bandwidth and improving the time-to-interactive metric.

Responsive Images

To optimize images for different devices and screen sizes, developers can use the `<picture>` element. This allows the browser to select the most appropriate image based on the user's device resolution and screen size. Consider Listing 13-7, which demonstrates this approach.

Listing 13-7. Responsive Image Setup

```
<picture>
  <source srcSet="image-large.jpg" media="(min-width: 1024px)" />
  <img src="image-small.jpg" alt="Example" />
</picture>
```

In this example, the `<picture>` element specifies a large image for devices with a screen width of at least 1024 pixels and a smaller image as a fallback for other devices. This setup ensures that users with larger screens receive higher-resolution images, while smaller devices conserve bandwidth by loading appropriately scaled-down versions.

By combining lazy loading and responsive design techniques, developers can significantly enhance the performance and usability of their applications. These practices not only improve load times but also contribute to a more polished and professional user experience across diverse devices and network conditions.

CHAPTER 13   OPTIMIZING PERFORMANCE

Network Performance

Optimizing network performance is essential to creating fast and responsive web applications. One way to achieve this is by implementing efficient data fetching and caching mechanisms. React Query is a powerful library that simplifies data management, allowing developers to fetch, cache, and synchronize server state in React applications with minimal effort.

Caching with React Query

React Query handles data fetching and caching seamlessly, reducing redundant API calls and improving the application's responsiveness. It automatically updates the cache when the underlying data changes, ensuring that users always see the latest information without unnecessary network requests. The example in Listing 13-8 illustrates the basic usage of React Query for data fetching and caching.

Listing 13-8. Fetching and Caching with React Query

```
import { useQuery } from "react-query";

const fetchProducts = async () => {
  const res = await fetch("/api/products");
  if (!res.ok) {
    throw new Error("Failed to fetch products");
  }
  return res.json();
};

const ProductList = () => {
  const { data, isLoading, isError, error } =
  useQuery("products", fetchProducts);
```

```
  if (isLoading) return <div>Loading...</div>;
  if (isError) return <div>Error: {error.message}</div>;

  return (
    <div>
      {(data ?? []).map((product) => ( <div key={product.
      id}>{product.name}</div> ))}
    </div>
  );
}
export default ProductList;
```

In this example, the `useQuery` hook is used to fetch and cache the product data from the `/api/products` endpoint. The `fetchProducts` function defines the asynchronous fetch operation, ensuring error handling by checking `res.ok` and throwing an error if the request fails. The `useQuery` hook not only handles the request and manages caching but also provides `isLoading` and `isError` flags to manage different UI states. This ensures that users see a loading indicator while the data is being fetched and an appropriate error message if the request fails. Additionally, the `data ?? []` fallback ensures that the application does not crash due to an unexpected response format.

React Query's caching mechanism significantly enhances network performance by storing API results and serving cached data when the same request is made, thereby reducing latency and bandwidth usage. It also supports advanced features such as automatic retries for failed requests, background refetching to keep data fresh, pagination, and infinite scrolling. These features make React Query a powerful and versatile choice for managing server state in modern React applications.

CHAPTER 13 OPTIMIZING PERFORMANCE

Prefetching Data

Prefetching data is an advanced technique that further optimizes network performance by proactively fetching data before it is needed. This approach reduces latency and ensures smoother navigation, particularly in scenarios where users are likely to visit specific pages or interact with certain components. By preloading data in the background, you can significantly enhance the user experience by minimizing wait times for critical information.

React Query's useQueryClient hook provides a prefetchQuery method, enabling developers to fetch and cache data ahead of time. This can be particularly useful for scenarios where user actions, such as hovering over a link or button, indicate an intent to navigate to a specific route. The example in Listing 13-9 demonstrates how to implement prefetching in a product listing component.

Listing 13-9. Prefetching Data with React Query

```
import { useQueryClient } from "react-query";
import { Link } from "react-router-dom";

const fetchProductDetails = async (productId) => {
  const res = await fetch(`/api/product/${productId}`);
  if (!res.ok) {
    throw new Error("Failed to fetch product details");
  }
  return res.json();
};

const ProductList = () => {
  const queryClient = useQueryClient();
```

```
  const handleMouseEnter = (productId) => {
    queryClient.prefetchQuery(["product-details", productId],
    () => fetchProductDetails(productId));
  };

  return (
    <div onMouseEnter={() => handleMouseEnter(1)}>
      <Link to="/product/1">Product 1</Link>
    </div>
  );
};

export default ProductList;
```

In this example, the `useQueryClient` hook is used to access the React Query client instance. The `handleMouseEnter` function is triggered when the user hovers over the `<div>` containing the product link. This function dynamically calls `prefetchQuery`, using a **unique query key** (`["product-details", productId]`) to **cache product-specific data**. It invokes the `fetchProductDetails` function, which fetches the product details based on the given `productId`.

By storing the fetched data in the cache, the application **instantly displays preloaded data** when the user navigates to the `/product/1` route, reducing network requests and improving performance. This optimization is especially useful for **faster page transitions and better user experience**.

Summary

This chapter delved into the critical aspects of optimizing React applications for performance. By understanding React's rendering behavior and employing techniques such as preventing unnecessary re-renders with

React.memo, useCallback, and useMemo, we explored ways to enhance efficiency. The use of advanced features like lazy loading and code splitting showcased how to reduce initial load times and improve resource utilization. Techniques for managing large datasets with virtualization and optimizing state management through libraries like reselect highlighted the importance of scalability.

For media, strategies like lazy loading images and leveraging the `<picture>` element for responsive images ensured efficient rendering across devices. Network performance was addressed through caching data with React Query and prefetching to provide smoother navigation. These optimizations were applied holistically in the sample examples, demonstrating their practical impact in real-world scenarios. By adhering to best practices, such as profiling before optimizing and leveraging modern tools, developers can create highly responsive and scalable React applications.

The next chapter will focus on ensuring application quality and reliability through rigorous testing methodologies and tools tailored for React applications.

CHAPTER 14

Testing Your Application

Testing is a cornerstone of modern application development, ensuring that your React application functions as intended and remains robust as it scales. With React's dynamic nature and modular architecture, testing becomes even more critical to maintain reliability, prevent regressions, and build confidence in the codebase. This chapter introduces you to the core levels of testing—unit, integration, and end to end—while providing practical guidance on leveraging powerful tools like **Jest**, **React Testing Library**, and **Cypress** to achieve comprehensive coverage. Through practical examples, you will gain the expertise needed to create a structured and reliable testing suite.

Why Testing Matters

Testing is not just about finding bugs; it's about ensuring that your application consistently delivers a seamless user experience. One of the key advantages of a robust testing strategy is **reliability**—verifying that your app behaves as expected under various conditions. Testing also aids in **regression prevention**, identifying issues that may arise when new changes are introduced to the codebase. For developers, a well-tested application fosters an **improved development workflow**, enabling confident refactoring and optimization without fear of breaking existing features.

CHAPTER 14   TESTING YOUR APPLICATION

The Testing Pyramid

To structure your testing approach effectively, consider the **testing pyramid**, which emphasizes the importance of balancing different test types for optimal results:

1. **Unit Tests (Base)**: These tests focus on individual functions, components, or modules in isolation, verifying their behavior in controlled environments. Unit tests form the foundation of the pyramid due to their simplicity, speed, and ease of maintenance.

2. **Integration Tests**: These tests evaluate how different components or modules interact with each other, ensuring seamless collaboration between various parts of the application. Integration tests are essential for identifying issues that might not surface in isolated unit tests.

3. **End-to-End (E2E) Tests**: Positioned at the top of the pyramid, these tests simulate real-world scenarios from the user's perspective, covering the entire application flow. While more resource-intensive, E2E tests are invaluable for validating the overall user experience and functionality.

By understanding the testing pyramid and prioritizing different test types appropriately, you can achieve a balanced and efficient testing strategy for your React applications. In the following sections, we will delve deeper into these testing levels, exploring practical tools and techniques to implement them effectively.

CHAPTER 14   TESTING YOUR APPLICATION

Setting Up a Testing Environment

Before diving into testing your React applications, it's essential to set up a robust testing environment equipped with the right tools. This involves installing and configuring libraries and frameworks that support different types of testing. By doing so, you ensure a smooth workflow for writing and running tests across all levels—unit, integration, and end to end.

To begin, install the following key tools to cover various testing requirements:

1. **Jest**: A versatile testing framework designed for JavaScript, Jest excels in writing and executing unit and integration tests with minimal setup.

2. **React Testing Library**: A library specifically for testing React components, it encourages writing tests focused on user interactions and outcomes rather than implementation details.

3. **Cypress**: A powerful tool for end-to-end testing, Cypress enables developers to simulate user flows and verify the application's behavior in real-world scenarios.

Listing 14-1. Installing Jest, React Testing Library, and Cypress

```
npm install --save-dev jest @testing-library/react
@testing-library/jest-dom cypress
```

The command shown in Listing 14-1 adds Jest, React Testing Library, and Cypress as development dependencies, ensuring they do not bloat your production build.

CHAPTER 14   TESTING YOUR APPLICATION

Configuring Jest

Most modern React setups, such as those created with **Create React App** or **Vite**, come with Jest preconfigured, making it easier to get started. However, if you're working on a custom setup, you might need to configure Jest manually. To streamline the testing process, you can define a test script in your package.json file as follows:

```
"scripts": {
  "test": "jest"
}
```

This configuration enables you to run your tests conveniently using the npm test command. Jest's zero-config approach simplifies the process, allowing you to focus on writing effective tests rather than worrying about configuration.

Configuring React Testing Library

React Testing Library works seamlessly with Jest. To enhance your testing capabilities, install the additional package @testing-library/jest-dom, which provides custom matchers like toBeInTheDocument() and toHaveTextContent(). Once installed, you can include the following setup in your setupTests.js file (if it exists in your project):

```
import '@testing-library/jest-dom';
```

This ensures that all your tests can use the custom matchers provided by React Testing Library.

Configuring Cypress

For Cypress, some minimal configuration may be required to specify test folders and customize behavior. By default, Cypress scans the cypress/integration folder for test files. You can update the `cypress.json` configuration file for additional settings, like the base URL of your app:

```
{
  "baseUrl": "http://localhost:3000",
  "viewportWidth": 1280,
  "viewportHeight": 720
}
```

To run Cypress tests, execute the following command:

```
npx cypress open
```

This opens the Cypress test runner, allowing you to select and run your end-to-end test cases.

Unit Testing

Unit testing is a fundamental practice in software development that focuses on verifying individual pieces of functionality in isolation. Using Jest, a popular JavaScript testing framework, we can create fast and reliable tests to ensure that specific functions, utilities, or React components work as expected.

Unit tests are designed to validate the smallest testable parts of an application, such as utility functions or components. By testing these units in isolation, we can catch bugs early in the development process and build a robust foundation for our application. Utility functions are common candidates for unit testing because they encapsulate reusable logic. Let's look at an example of testing a simple function.

Listing 14-2. Unit Testing a Utility Function with Jest

```
// utils.jsx
export function add(a, b) {
  return a + b;
}
// utils.test.js
import { add } from './utils';

test('adds two numbers correctly', () => {
  expect(add(2, 3)).toBe(5);
});
```

In Listing 14-2, the test validates that the add function works as intended by checking that the sum of 2 and 3 equals 5. This ensures the utility is performing its basic operation correctly. Similarly, react components can also be tested to ensure they render the expected output based on their props and state. Let's examine an example.

Listing 14-3. Unit Testing a React Component Using React Testing Library

```
// Greeting.jsx
const Greeting = ({ name }) => {
  return <h1>Hello, {name}!</h1>;
}

export default Greeting;
// Greeting.test.js
import { render, screen } from '@testing-library/react';
import Greeting from './Greeting';
```

```
test('renders greeting message', () => {
  render(<Greeting name="John" />);
  expect(screen.getByText('Hello, John!')).toBeInTheDocument();
});
```

In Listing 14-3, the `Greeting` component is rendered with the name prop set to "John." The `screen.getByText` function is used to locate the expected text, and the `toBeInTheDocument` matcher verifies that the element containing the greeting message is present in the rendered output.

Integration Testing

Integration testing ensures that multiple components or modules within an application work cohesively. Unlike unit tests, which focus on isolated parts of the code, integration tests evaluate the interaction between components, helping developers catch issues that arise when modules are combined. These tests are particularly valuable for verifying complex user flows and state changes in React applications.

In the example in Listing 14-4, the Counter component consists of a button that increments a displayed count when clicked.

Listing 14-4. Integration Test for Counter Component

```
// Counter.jsx
const Counter = () => {
  const [count, setCount] = React.useState(0);

  return (
    <div>
      <p>Count: {count}</p>
      <button onClick={() => setCount(count +
      1)}>Increment</button>
```

```
    </div>
  );
}

export default Counter;

// Counter.test.js

import { render, screen, fireEvent } from '@testing-library/react';
import Counter from './Counter';

test('increments count on button click', () => {
  render(<Counter />);
  const button = screen.getByText('Increment');
  fireEvent.click(button);
  expect(screen.getByText('Count: 1')).toBeInTheDocument();
});
```

In Listing 14-4, the integration test verifies that the Counter component behaves as expected when interacting with the button. The render method mounts the component in a simulated DOM environment provided by React Testing Library. The screen.getByText function identifies the "Increment" button, while the fireEvent.click function simulates a user clicking the button. After the click event, the test confirms that the displayed text updates to "Count: 1" by checking its presence in the document using the toBeInTheDocument matcher.

End-to-End Testing

End-to-end (E2E) testing plays a critical role in ensuring that your application behaves as expected under real-world conditions. Unlike unit or integration tests, which focus on specific components or interactions,

CHAPTER 14   TESTING YOUR APPLICATION

E2E tests simulate complete user workflows, including navigation, interactions, and data flows. These tests validate the application's overall functionality and user experience.

E2E tests simulate real-world scenarios from the perspective of the user, ensuring that the entire application, from front end to back end, functions correctly. For example, E2E tests can verify that a user can log in, browse products, add items to a cart, and complete a checkout process without encountering errors.

Cypress is a popular tool for E2E testing in modern web applications due to its robust API and intuitive interface. Setting it up involves the following steps:

1. **Install Cypress**

   Use the following command to add Cypress to your project as a development dependency:

   ```
   npm install --save-dev cypress
   ```

2. **Open Cypress**

   Launch Cypress using the command:

   ```
   npx cypress open
   ```

   This opens the Cypress Test Runner, where you can manage and execute tests.

3. **Add Test Files**

   Create test files in the `cypress/integration` directory. For example, you can add a file named `navigation.spec.js` for testing navigation.

The example in Listing 14-5 demonstrates how to use Cypress to test navigation to a product details page.

Listing 14-5. Cypress Test for Navigation

```
// cypress/integration/navigation.spec.js

describe('Navigation', () => {
  it('should navigate to the product details page', () => {
    cy.visit('/'); // Visit the home page
    cy.get('a[href="/product/1"]').click(); // Click the product link
    cy.url().should('include', '/product/1'); // Verify URL has changed
    cy.contains('Product Details').should('be.visible');
    // Confirm the product details page is displayed
  });
});
```

In Listing 14-5, Cypress simulates a user visiting the home page and clicking a link to navigate to a product details page. The `cy.visit` function loads the application, while the `cy.get` function identifies the anchor tag corresponding to the product details page. The `cy.url` assertion ensures that the URL updates as expected, and `cy.contains` verifies that the target page's content is displayed correctly. This test not only checks navigation but also ensures the page content is rendered as expected.

Snapshot Testing

Snapshot testing is a technique used to ensure that a component's rendered output remains consistent over time. It captures the current output of a component and compares it to a previously stored "snapshot." If any changes are detected, the test will fail, alerting developers to review and update the snapshot if the changes are intentional.

Snapshot testing is particularly useful for

- **Detecting Unexpected Changes**: Prevents unintended modifications to a component's structure or styling
- **Documenting Components**: Provides a clear reference for what a component's output should look like at a given state
- **Quick Validation**: Enables developers to test visual components without writing extensive assertions

Consider a simple button component that renders a label passed via props.

Listing 14-6. Snapshot Testing a Button Component

```
// Button.jsx
const Button = ({ label }) => {
  return <button>{label}</button>;
}
export default Button;

// Button.test.js
import React from 'react';
import renderer from 'react-test-renderer';
import Button from './Button';

describe('Button Snapshot Test', () => {
  it('matches the snapshot', () => {
    const tree = renderer.create(<Button label="Click Me" />).
    toJSON();
    expect(tree).toMatchSnapshot();
  });
});
```

In Listing 14-6, the renderer module from the react-test-renderer library is used to create a serialized representation of the Button component's output. The toJSON() method converts the rendered output into a JSON format suitable for snapshot testing.

How Snapshot Testing Works

1. **Initial Test Run**: During the first test run, Jest generates a snapshot file and stores it in a __snapshots__ directory.

2. **Subsequent Runs**: In subsequent runs, the current output of the component is compared to the stored snapshot.

3. **Pass/Fail Logic**

   - If the output matches the stored snapshot, the test passes.

   - If differences are detected, the test fails, prompting the developer to either update the snapshot (if changes are intentional) or fix the component.

Mocking and Stubbing

Mocking and stubbing are critical techniques in testing to isolate components and ensure predictable behavior during tests. They enable you to simulate dependencies, such as **API calls** or **third-party libraries**, without relying on real implementations. This is especially useful when testing React components that fetch data from external sources or rely on complex dependencies.

CHAPTER 14   TESTING YOUR APPLICATION

Mocking API Calls

Mocking API calls prevents the need for actual server interactions during tests, making the tests faster, more reliable, and independent of network conditions. In this example, the jest-fetch-mock library is used to mock the behavior of the fetch API for a React component that retrieves a list of products. First, install jest-fetch-mock if not already installed:

npm install --save-dev jest-fetch-mock

Listing 14-7. Mocking API Calls for a Product List

```
// ProductList.jsx
import React, { useEffect, useState } from 'react';

const ProductList = () => {
  const [products, setProducts] = useState([]);

  useEffect(() => {
    fetch('/api/products')
      .then((res) => res.json())
      .then((data) => setProducts(data));
  }, []);

  return (
    <div>
      <h1>Product List</h1>
      <ul>
        {products.map((product) => (
          <li key={product.id}>{product.name}</li>
        ))}
      </ul>
    </div>
  );
}
```

277

CHAPTER 14 TESTING YOUR APPLICATION

```
export default ProductList;

// ProductList.test.js
import { render, screen, waitFor } from '@testing-
library/react';
import ProductList from './ProductList';

// Enable fetch mocks
global.fetch = jest.fn();

beforeEach(() => {
  fetch.mockClear();
});

test('displays products fetched from API', async () => {
  fetch.mockResolvedValueOnce({
    json: async () => [{ id: 1, name: 'Product 1' }]
  });

  render(<ProductList />);

  await waitFor(() => {
    expect(screen.getByText('Product 1')).toBeInTheDocument();
  });
});
```

The explanation of Listing 14-7 highlights the key steps involved in mocking an API call within a test. Instead of using `fetchMock.enableMocks()`, this example **directly mocks fetch using Jest's built-in** `jest.fn()`, eliminating the need for additional dependencies.

To maintain test isolation, `fetch.mockClear()` is called before each test to reset any previous mock data. The `fetch.mockResolvedValueOnce()` function is then used to simulate an API call by returning a mock JSON response containing a product list.

Within the test, the `ProductList` component is rendered in a controlled environment, allowing for validation of its behavior. The `waitFor` function ensures that assertions, such as verifying the presence of the product name in the DOM, are executed only after the component has completed rendering with the fetched data.

This approach provides a **lightweight and easy-to-follow method for testing API calls**, making it more accessible for beginners while still effectively verifying that the ProductList component correctly fetches and displays data from the mocked API.

Summary

Testing is a cornerstone of maintaining high-quality applications, ensuring reliability and confidence during development and scaling. In this chapter, we explored the three primary levels of testing: **unit tests** for validating individual components or functions, **integration tests** to verify component interactions, and **end-to-end (E2E) tests** to simulate user flows across the application.

We demonstrated unit testing with **Jest** and **React Testing Library**, focusing on isolated functionality and rendering. Integration tests showcased workflows like counter updates and data interactions, ensuring seamless behavior between components. For E2E tests, **Cypress** was used to simulate real-world scenarios such as navigating the product details page. Snapshot testing added another layer by capturing component outputs for future comparisons, while mocking and stubbing allowed testing of API calls without hitting live servers.

Applying these testing strategies ensures it remains robust, reliable, and scalable while maintaining a seamless user experience. This comprehensive approach to testing not only detects issues early but also streamlines the development process by providing confidence in the application's stability.

The next chapter will focus on **securing your React application**, discussing strategies for handling vulnerabilities, protecting user data, and adhering to industry standards for a secure development lifecycle.

CHAPTER 15

Security Best Practices

In today's digital landscape, ensuring the security of your web application is more than just a best practice—it is a necessity. React applications, like any other web apps, are potential targets for various security vulnerabilities, and the consequences of neglecting these risks can range from data breaches to loss of user trust. Developers must adopt a proactive approach to mitigate threats and protect sensitive information.

Common security concerns include **Cross-Site Scripting (XSS)**, where attackers inject malicious scripts into your application, and **Cross-Site Request Forgery (CSRF)**, which tricks users into performing unintended actions. Additionally, insecure API endpoints can become gateways for attackers to exploit vulnerabilities. This chapter identifies these risks and delves into best practices to mitigate them, empowering you to build secure and resilient React applications. By the end of this chapter, you will have a comprehensive understanding of how to secure your application against modern threats and ensure a safe experience for your users.

CHAPTER 15   SECURITY BEST PRACTICES

Common Security Risks in React Applications

Securing a React application requires understanding the common vulnerabilities that malicious actors exploit. Below are key security risks every developer should be aware of, along with their potential impacts.

Cross-Site Scripting (XSS)

Cross-Site Scripting (XSS) occurs when attackers inject malicious scripts into your application, often through input fields or external data sources. These scripts can execute in the user's browser, bypassing the security model of your application.

The consequences of XSS attacks include stealing user data (e.g., cookies or session tokens), hijacking user sessions, and potentially compromising the user's device or account. For instance, an attacker might embed a malicious script that sends the user's session token to a remote server, allowing unauthorized access to their account.

Cross-Site Request Forgery (CSRF)

Cross-Site Request Forgery (CSRF) tricks authenticated users into performing unintended actions on your application. This often occurs when attackers send unauthorized requests using the user's credentials without their knowledge.

CSRF attacks can result in unauthorized transactions, changes to account settings, or other actions that exploit the user's logged-in state. For example, a CSRF attack might use the user's authentication token to initiate a bank transfer without their consent.

Sensitive Data Exposure

Sensitive Data Exposure occurs when applications fail to adequately protect data such as passwords, API tokens, or personally identifiable information (PII). Improper encryption, storing data in plaintext, and exposing sensitive information in logs are common causes.

The exposure of sensitive data can lead to identity theft, unauthorized access to accounts, and large-scale data breaches. For example, if an application stores passwords in plaintext and its database is compromised, attackers gain direct access to user accounts.

Insecure API Endpoints

APIs that lack proper authentication, authorization, or input validation are a prime target for attackers. This includes APIs that allow unrestricted access to sensitive operations or fail to sanitize input data.

Exploiting insecure API endpoints can enable attackers to manipulate back-end systems, access sensitive data, or even take control of your application. For instance, an endpoint that doesn't validate input might allow an attacker to inject malicious SQL queries into the database.

By recognizing and addressing these vulnerabilities, you can proactively safeguard your application and user data against common threats. In the next section, we will explore practical techniques to mitigate these risks effectively.

Securing React Components

Securing your React components is a critical step in safeguarding your application from security vulnerabilities like Cross-Site Scripting (XSS). This section discusses two essential practices: sanitizing user inputs and escaping output, with examples illustrating their implementation.

CHAPTER 15 SECURITY BEST PRACTICES

Sanitizing User Inputs

User inputs are a common entry point for XSS attacks. To prevent attackers from injecting malicious scripts, it is crucial to sanitize all user-provided data before rendering it in your application. React discourages using dangerouslySetInnerHTML due to the inherent risks. If you must use it, ensure proper sanitization of the input content. Figure 15-1 illustrates the output of the sample example we used to demonstrate the Sanitization concept.

Listing 15-1. Input Sanitization Using DOMPurify

```
import React from "react";
import DOMPurify from "dompurify";

const SafeComponent = ({ content }) => {
  const sanitizedContent = DOMPurify.sanitize(content);
  return <div dangerouslySetInnerHTML={{ __html: sanitizedContent }} />;
};

const App = () => {
  const unsafeHTML = `<h1>Hello World</h1><script>alert('XSS Attack!');</script>`;

  return (
    <div>
      <h2>Sanitized Content:</h2>
      <SafeComponent content={unsafeHTML} />
    </div>
  );
};

export default App;
```

CHAPTER 15 SECURITY BEST PRACTICES

```
Sanitized Content:

Hello World
```

Figure 15-1. Sanitized component content using DOMPurify

In Listing 15-1, the DOMPurify.sanitize function ensures that the content prop is sanitized before being injected into dangerouslySetInnerHTML, preventing malicious scripts such as embedded <script> tags from executing in the browser. By using DOMPurify, we add a crucial layer of security when rendering dynamic HTML, allowing safe elements while stripping out potentially harmful ones. For example, if the content includes <h1>Hello World</h1><script>alert('XSS Attack!');</script>, the <h1>Hello World</h1> part will be rendered, while the <script>alert('XSS Attack!');</script> part will be removed by DOMPurify, preventing any potential XSS attack. This approach is essential for mitigating Cross-Site Scripting (XSS) attacks in React applications while still allowing controlled HTML rendering.

Escaping Output

React automatically escapes special characters in dynamic content, mitigating the risk of XSS attacks. However, you should still ensure that data rendered in your application is trusted and sanitized when necessary. Figure 15-2 illustrates the output of the sample example we used to demonstrate the escaping output concept.

Listing 15-2. Escaping Output in React

```
import React from "react";

const SafeOutput = ({ message }) => {
  return <p>{message}</p>;
};

const App = () => {
  return (
    <div>
      <h2>React Escaping Example</h2>
      <SafeOutput message={"Hello <script>alert('XSS')
      </script>"} />
    </div>
  );
};

export default App;
```

React Escaping Example

Hello <script>alert('XSS')</script>

Figure 15-2. *Escaping React example*

Listing 15-2 highlights React's built-in escaping mechanism, ensuring that dynamic content is safely rendered inside a <p> tag. React automatically escapes special characters like <, >, and &, preventing them from being interpreted as HTML or JavaScript. For example, if the message prop contains `<script>alert('XSS')</script>`, React treats it as plaintext, displaying it exactly as written without executing the script. This built-in security feature mitigates XSS vulnerabilities while allowing safe rendering of user-generated content.

By combining input sanitization in Listing 15-1 with React's escaping output in Listing 15-2, you can effectively safeguard your components from malicious scripts and ensure that dynamic content is handled securely. In the next section, we will delve into securing API communication in React applications.

Authentication and Authorization

Proper implementation of authentication and authorization mechanisms is critical for ensuring that only legitimate users can access your application and that they are restricted to actions they are authorized to perform. This section highlights secure authentication practices and the importance of **Role-Based Access Control** (RBAC).

Secure Authentication

Authentication is the first line of defense in securing your application. Using robust methods like **OAuth** or **JSON Web Tokens (JWT)** is highly recommended to verify user identity. Additionally, storing sensitive information like tokens securely can prevent them from being exploited.

Best Practices for Secure Authentication:

- Use `HttpOnly` cookies to store authentication tokens. These cookies are not accessible via JavaScript, preventing XSS attacks from exposing sensitive data.

- Avoid storing tokens in localStorage or sessionStorage, as these are more vulnerable to being accessed by malicious scripts.

- Implement secure session management to protect user sessions from hijacking.

Listing 15-3 shows a short example demonstrating authentication using **HttpOnly cookies**.

Listing 15-3. Implementing Role-Based Access Control

```
// Login request that sends credentials and stores token
securely in HttpOnly cookie

fetch("/api/login", {
  method: "POST",
  credentials: "include", // Ensures cookies are sent with
  the request
  headers: { "Content-Type": "application/json" },
  body: JSON.stringify({ username: "admin", password:
  "password" }),
});
```

In Listing 15-3, tokens are handled securely and not exposed to potential XSS attacks. Secure authentication mechanisms are critical for protecting user data and preventing session hijacking.

Role-Based Access Control (RBAC)

RBAC is an essential mechanism for restricting access to specific parts of your application based on user roles. For instance, administrators may have access to management panels, while regular users may not. Figure 15-3 shows the output of the sample example we used to demonstrate the RBAC implementation.

Listing 15-4. Implementing Role-Based Access Control

```jsx
// RBACExample.jsx
import React from "react";

// AdminPanel Component
const AdminPanel = ({ user }) => {
  if (!user || user?.role !== "admin") {
    return <p style={{ color: "red", fontWeight: "bold"
    }}>Access Denied</p>;
  }

  return <div style={{ padding: "10px", border: "1px solid
  black" }}>
    <h2>Admin Panel</h2>
    <p>Welcome, {user.name}! You have administrator access.</p>
  </div>;
};

// App Component
const App = () => {
  const adminUser = { name: "Alice", role: "admin" };
  const regularUser = { name: "Bob", role: "user" };
  const guestUser = null; // Handles case where no user is
  logged in

  return (
    <div style={{ fontFamily: "Arial, sans-serif", padding:
    "20px" }}>
      <h1>Role-Based Access Control (RBAC) Example</h1>

      <h3>Admin User:</h3>
      <AdminPanel user={adminUser} /> {/* Displays Admin
      Panel */}
```

CHAPTER 15 SECURITY BEST PRACTICES

```
      <h3>Regular User:</h3>
      <AdminPanel user={regularUser} /> {/* Displays "Access
      Denied" */}

      <h3>Guest (No User Logged In):</h3>
      <AdminPanel user={guestUser} /> {/* Also Displays "Access
      Denied" */}
    </div>
  );
};

export default App;
```

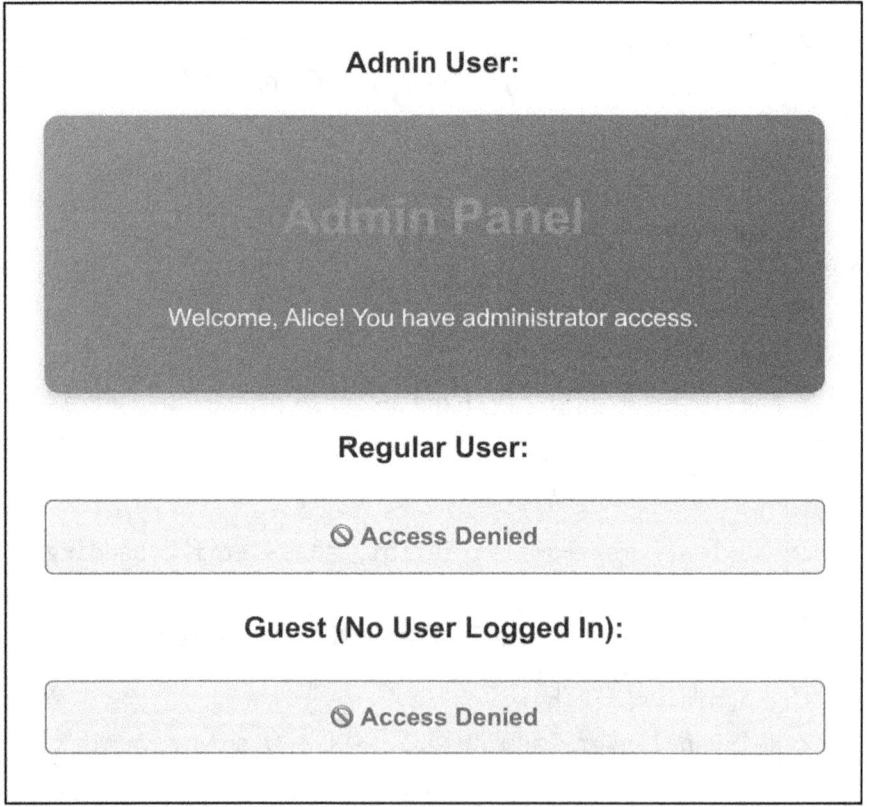

Figure 15-3. *Role-Based Access Control*

In Listing 15-4, the `AdminPanel` component verifies the `role` property of the `user` object to enforce **Role-Based Access Control (RBAC)**. If the user is either `null`, `undefined`, or does not have the "admin" role, the component displays a styled `"Access Denied"` message in red for better visibility. Otherwise, it renders a structured admin panel, welcoming the authorized user by name. This approach ensures that **unauthorized users cannot access sensitive sections** of the application while maintaining **scalability** for additional roles and permissions in the future.

By combining secure authentication methods with RBAC in Listings 15-3 and 15-4, you can protect sensitive data and ensure that users have access only to the resources and functionalities appropriate to their roles. In the next section, we will explore best practices for securing API communication in your React application.

Securing API Requests

Securing communication between your React application and back-end APIs is critical for maintaining the confidentiality and integrity of user data. This section outlines best practices for securing API requests, including the use of HTTPS, secure token management, and CSRF prevention techniques.

Using HTTPS

HTTPS (HyperText Transfer Protocol Secure) is essential for encrypting the data exchanged between the client and the server. It protects sensitive information, such as authentication credentials and API responses, from being intercepted by attackers. Modern browsers also flag HTTP websites as insecure, making HTTPS adoption a crucial security and trust factor for your application.

CHAPTER 15   SECURITY BEST PRACTICES

Securing Tokens

Authentication and authorization in web applications often rely on tokens such as **JSON Web Tokens** (JWT). Proper token management ensures these credentials remain secure. Some of the best practices for token security are listed below:

- **Short-Lived Tokens**: Use tokens with a short expiration time to limit the impact of token theft. Combine these with secure refresh token mechanisms for uninterrupted user sessions.

- **HttpOnly Cookies**: Store tokens in `HttpOnly` cookies to prevent client-side scripts from accessing them, thereby mitigating Cross-Site Scripting (XSS) attacks.

- **Secure Storage**: Avoid storing sensitive tokens in `localStorage` or `sessionStorage`, as these can be accessed by malicious scripts.

Preventing CSRF Attacks

Cross-Site Request Forgery (CSRF) is a vulnerability where attackers trick users into executing unwanted actions on a trusted site. Implementing CSRF prevention measures helps protect your application from such exploits. Best practices for CSRF preventions are listed below:

- **CSRF Tokens**: Generate a unique token for each user session and include it in API requests. Validate this token on the server side to ensure that the request originated from the authenticated user.

- **Server-Side Validation**: Always verify CSRF tokens on the server to confirm their authenticity before processing requests.

CHAPTER 15 SECURITY BEST PRACTICES

Example: CSRF Token Implementation

- Generate a CSRF token on the server and include it in the response headers or as a hidden field in forms.

- Send the token back with each API request using custom headers.

- Validate the token server side to ensure it matches the one generated for the user.

By implementing these security measures, including HTTPS, token best practices, and CSRF protection, you can safeguard API requests from common vulnerabilities. These practices are essential for building secure and trustworthy React applications that handle sensitive user data responsibly.

Data Protection

Protecting user data is paramount for maintaining trust and compliance with data security regulations. This section focuses on two critical practices: encrypting sensitive data and masking sensitive information, ensuring that data remains secure both in storage and during processing.

Encryption

Encryption is the process of converting sensitive data into an unreadable format that can only be deciphered with the appropriate decryption key. It is essential for safeguarding data both in transit (e.g., during API requests) and at rest (e.g., stored in databases). The best practices for encryption are shown below:

1. **In Transit**: Use HTTPS to encrypt communication between the client and server.

2. **At Rest**: Encrypt sensitive data, such as user passwords and credit card details, using strong encryption algorithms like AES-256 before storing them in databases.

3. **Key Management**: Securely manage and rotate encryption keys to prevent unauthorized access.

Masking Sensitive Information

Masking sensitive data, such as credit card numbers and Social Security Numbers (SSNs), minimizes exposure in user interfaces or logs. This ensures that only the necessary parts of the information are visible, reducing the risk of accidental data leakage. The example in Listing 15-5 demonstrates how to mask credit card numbers in a React input field.

Listing 15-5. Masking Input Fields

```
const MaskedInput = ({ value = "" }) => {
  const maskedValue = value.toString().replace(
  /\d(?=\d{4})/g, "*");
  return <input type="text" value={maskedValue} readOnly />;
}

//Example
<MaskedInput value="1234567890" />  // Displays: ******7890
<MaskedInput value="987654321" />   // Displays: *****4321
<MaskedInput value="" />            // Displays: (Empty input)
<MaskedInput value={null} />        // Displays: (Empty input)
```

In Listing 15-5, the `replace` method, combined with a regular expression, is utilized to mask all but the last four digits of the input value by replacing them with asterisks (*). Additionally, the `readOnly` attribute ensures that the user cannot alter the masked value, preserving its integrity. This approach is particularly effective for securely displaying sensitive information, such as credit card numbers, while maintaining partial visibility for validation purposes (e.g., "**** **** **** 1234").

By encrypting sensitive data and masking critical information in user interfaces, you significantly reduce the risk of data exposure. These practices help maintain user trust and comply with data protection standards such as GDPR and PCI DSS.

Dependency Management

Managing dependencies effectively is crucial for maintaining the security of a React application. Keeping dependencies updated ensures that known vulnerabilities are patched, reducing the risk of exploitation. Tools like `npm audit` or Snyk can help identify and mitigate security issues in the project's dependencies.

A practical example is the `npm audit fix` command in **Listing 15-6**, which scans installed dependencies for vulnerabilities and applies fixes where possible.

Listing 15-6. Running npm audit to Fix Security Vulnerabilities

```
# Check outdated dependencies before fixing security issues
npm outdated

# Scan dependencies for vulnerabilities
npm audit
```

```
# Automatically apply non-breaking security fixes
npm audit fix

# (Optional) Force fix breaking changes (Use with caution)
npm audit fix --force
```

While `npm audit fix` helps **patch vulnerabilities**, developers should **carefully review dependency updates**, especially when using `--force`, as it might introduce breaking changes. Beyond automated tools, it is essential to avoid installing untrusted packages from unreliable sources. Before adding a dependency, developers should check the package's reputation on platforms like GitHub and npm by reviewing factors such as stars, open issues, and the last update date.

Additionally, inspecting the source code can help identify potential security risks, ensuring that the package does not contain vulnerabilities or malicious scripts. Keeping dependencies minimal is another crucial practice, as reducing the number of third-party libraries decreases the overall attack surface. By regularly auditing dependencies, reviewing third-party packages, and adhering to best security practices, developers can significantly enhance the security posture of their applications.

Secure Deployment

Securing the deployment of your React application involves measures to protect your code and prevent attackers from gaining insights into its structure. Minifying and obfuscating the code in your production build reduces its readability, making it challenging for attackers to reverse-engineer and exploit your application. These steps ensure that your deployed application is both efficient and less vulnerable to malicious activities.

Additionally, it is critical to disable source maps in production. Source maps provide a mapping from the minified code back to the original source, which can be invaluable for debugging but poses a significant security risk if exposed publicly. By disabling source maps during the production build, you ensure that attackers cannot easily access your application's source structure.

Listing 15-7. Disabling Source Maps in Production

```
REACT_APP_GENERATE_SOURCEMAP=false npm run build
```

In Listing 15-7, setting the REACT_APP_GENERATE_SOURCEMAP environment variable to false prevents the generation of source maps during the build process. This practice enhances the overall security of your deployment and safeguards sensitive parts of your application.

Security Testing

Security testing is a crucial step in ensuring the robustness of your application against potential vulnerabilities and attacks. This process helps uncover security loopholes that could otherwise compromise user data or application functionality.

Static Analysis Tools

Static analysis tools like **SonarQube** and **ESLint (with security plugins)** can automatically scan your codebase for security vulnerabilities, unused variables, and unsafe coding practices. These tools provide **actionable recommendations** to mitigate identified risks early in development.

By integrating **static analysis into your CI/CD pipeline**, you ensure **consistent security enforcement** across your application. One way to achieve this is by using **ESLint with** `eslint-plugin-security`, which helps detect potential security flaws, such as unsafe object injection.

Listing 15-8. Configuring ESLint for Security Testing

```
npm install --save-dev eslint eslint-plugin-security
```

Then, configure ESLint in your .eslintrc.json file:

```
// .eslintrc.json
{
"extends": ["eslint:recommended", "plugin:security/recommended"],
  "plugins": ["security"],
  "rules": {
    "security/detect-object-injection": "warn"
  }
}
```

Run the analysis using

```
npx eslint ./src
```

For continuous security enforcement, consider integrating ESLint with **pre-commit hooks** using **husky** and **lint-staged** to ensure security checks before committing code. This can be set up with the command `npx husky-init && npm install`. Additionally, incorporating **CI/CD pipelines** such as **GitHub Actions** or **Jenkins** can help automate ESLint checks on every pull request, preventing insecure code from being merged. By adopting static analysis tools, automating security checks, and enforcing best practices, developers can significantly reduce security risks while maintaining high code quality.

Penetration Testing

Penetration testing involves simulating real-world attacks on your application to evaluate its security posture. These tests help uncover weaknesses that static analysis tools might miss, such as API endpoint misconfigurations or improper authentication flows. Regular penetration testing by security experts ensures your application can withstand various types of attacks, providing users with a secure and trustworthy experience.

Conducting Penetration Testing

1. **Use security testing tools** like **OWASP ZAP** or **Burp Suite** to scan your application for vulnerabilities.

2. **Simulate common attacks in a controlled testing environment**:

    - **SQL Injection (SQLi)**: Attempt to inject SQL commands into API endpoints or form inputs to check if the back end properly validates queries.

    - **Cross-Site Scripting (XSS)**: Inject malicious scripts into user input fields and observe whether they execute in the browser.

    - **Broken Authentication**: Test for issues like **token hijacking, weak session management, and improper Role-Based Access Controls (RBAC)**.

3. **Generate a penetration testing report** detailing

    - Identified **vulnerabilities** and their severity levels

    - **Recommendations** for fixing security gaps

After completing penetration testing, it is crucial to **patch vulnerabilities** and **retest** to ensure they are properly mitigated. By integrating penetration testing into your security strategy, you can **proactively defend against cyber threats** and strengthen the overall security of your application.

CHAPTER 15 SECURITY BEST PRACTICES

Summary

This chapter highlighted the critical need for securing React applications by providing actionable strategies to mitigate vulnerabilities and build secure web applications. It began with an overview of common threats, including Cross-Site Scripting (XSS), Cross-Site Request Forgery (CSRF), sensitive data exposure, and insecure API endpoints, setting the stage for understanding their potential impact.

Key techniques for securing React components were discussed, such as input sanitization with DOMPurify and leveraging React's automatic escaping output to prevent malicious scripts. Authentication and authorization best practices, like using OAuth or JWT and implementing Role-Based Access Control (RBAC), were explained with practical examples like protecting admin routes.

The chapter also focused on securing API requests by emphasizing HTTPS, secure token management using HttpOnly cookies, and preventing CSRF attacks through server-side validation. Data protection measures, including encryption and masking sensitive information, were outlined, along with examples to demonstrate these concepts in action.

Dependency management was covered, stressing the importance of regular updates, vulnerability scans with tools like npm audit, and avoiding untrusted packages. Secure deployment practices, such as minifying and obfuscating code and disabling source maps in production, were provided with clear steps to enhance application security.

Security testing was emphasized as a critical step in the development lifecycle, recommending tools like SonarQube and ESLint for static analysis and regular penetration testing to simulate and address potential vulnerabilities.

By implementing these security measures, developers can safeguard user data, build user trust, and ensure compliance with industry standards. In the next chapter, we will explore how to make your application inclusive for all users and adaptable for global audiences, ensuring it meets the needs of diverse populations.

CHAPTER 16

Accessibility and Internationalization

Modern web applications need to cater to diverse user bases. This includes ensuring usability for individuals with disabilities and adapting to linguistic and cultural preferences for a global audience. By addressing accessibility (A11Y) and internationalization (i18n) in your React applications, you enhance user experience, comply with legal standards, and broaden your application's reach.

This chapter explores core accessibility principles, such as semantic HTML, ARIA attributes, keyboard navigation, and screen reader compatibility, ensuring React applications are usable by individuals with visual, auditory, motor, or cognitive impairments. It also introduces automated testing tools like Axe DevTools, Lighthouse, and jest-axe, which help developers identify and fix accessibility issues.

Additionally, the chapter delves into internationalization, covering key concepts like language localization, currency formatting, and right-to-left (RTL) text support. Using react-i18next and FormatJS, we demonstrate how to dynamically switch languages, manage translations, and support multilingual user interfaces.

By the end of this chapter, you'll have the skills and tools to build inclusive, accessible, and globally adaptable React applications while adhering to modern web development best practices.

CHAPTER 16   ACCESSIBILITY AND INTERNATIONALIZATION

Introduction to Accessibility and Internationalization

Accessibility ensures that your application is usable by people with visual, auditory, motor, or cognitive impairments. It adheres to global standards, such as the Web Content Accessibility Guidelines (WCAG), which define best practices for creating accessible web applications. Moreover, accessibility enhances usability for everyone, including individuals with temporary disabilities, such as a broken arm, or situational impairments, like bright sunlight affecting screen visibility.

Internationalization enables applications to seamlessly adapt to various languages, currencies, and cultural norms without requiring extensive redevelopment. It supports localization (L10N), which involves translating and formatting content for specific regions or audiences. Additionally, internationalization allows applications to tap into global markets by creating a user-friendly experience for non-native speakers of the default language. Key challenges addressed in this chapter are as follows:

- Understanding accessibility standards like WCAG and ARIA (Accessible Rich Internet Applications)

- Implementing practical solutions for accessible navigation, forms, and interactive elements in React

- Using tools to test and validate your application's accessibility

- Managing multilingual content and regional formatting with tools like `react-i18next` and `formatjs`

- Integrating dynamic language switching without compromising performance

By the end of this chapter, you'll be equipped with practical skills and tools to build React applications that are inclusive and adaptable, making them accessible to a broader audience while adhering to modern standards.

CHAPTER 16   ACCESSIBILITY AND INTERNATIONALIZATION

Implementing Accessibility in React

Creating accessible React applications requires a thoughtful approach to forms, navigation, ARIA attributes, and keyboard interaction. By following best practices and leveraging modern tools, developers can ensure their applications are inclusive and meet accessibility standards.

One of the foundational steps in making forms accessible is to use `<label>` elements properly. Every input field should have a corresponding `<label>` that is linked via the `for` attribute to the input's `id`. This connection allows assistive technologies, like screen readers, to associate the label text with the input field. Additionally, focus management is crucial, especially for interactive elements like modals or forms. Developers can use `ref` in React or integrate libraries such as `react-focus-lock` to ensure the user's focus is directed to the correct element, enhancing usability for keyboard users and those with visual impairments.

Navigation is another critical area where accessibility must be prioritized. Semantic HTML elements like `<nav>` for navigation bars, `<main>` for main content, and `<button>` for actionable items add meaningful structure to the application. These tags inform assistive technologies about the purpose of different sections, making it easier for users to understand and navigate the content.

ARIA (Accessible Rich Internet Applications) attributes further enhance the accessibility of UI elements. For example, adding `aria-label` or `aria-labelledby` can provide additional context to elements, such as buttons or links, for screen readers. Similarly, `aria-describedby` can be used to link inputs to help text, offering guidance for users who may need more detailed information. For dynamic content, the `aria-live` attribute ensures that updates are announced to users without requiring manual intervention.

Keyboard navigation is an essential aspect of accessibility, particularly for users who cannot rely on a mouse. All interactive elements, such as buttons, links, and form fields, should be focusable using the `tab` key. Logical tab order ensures that users can navigate the interface intuitively,

CHAPTER 16 ACCESSIBILITY AND INTERNATIONALIZATION

while custom widgets like drop-downs or modals should include keyboard handlers to support interactions with keys such as Enter, Escape, and arrow keys. Listing 16-1 shows an example of an accessible form that implements these practices, and Figure 16-1 shows the rendered output.

Listing 16-1. Accessible Form Example

```
import React, { useRef, useEffect, useState } from "react";
import FocusLock from "react-focus-lock";
import "./AccessibleForm.css"; // Import styles

function AccessibleForm() {
  const [error, setError] = useState("");
  const firstInputRef = useRef(null);

  useEffect(() => {
    if (firstInputRef.current) {
      firstInputRef.current.focus();
    }
  }, []);

  const handleSubmit = (e) => {
    e.preventDefault();
    setError("Invalid username or password.");
  };

  const handleKeyDown = (e) => {
    if (e.key === "Escape") {
      setError(""); // Clear error message on Escape key
    }
  };

  return (
    <FocusLock>
      <div className="form-container">
```

CHAPTER 16 ACCESSIBILITY AND INTERNATIONALIZATION

```
<form onSubmit={handleSubmit} aria-
labelledby="formTitle">
  <h2 id="formTitle">Login Form</h2>

  <label htmlFor="username">Username</label>
  <input
    id="username"
    name="username"
    type="text"
    aria-required="true"
    aria-describedby="usernameHint"
    ref={firstInputRef}
    onKeyDown={handleKeyDown} // Listen for Escape key
  />
  <span id="usernameHint">Enter your username.</span>

  <label htmlFor="password">Password</label>
  <input
    id="password"
    name="password"
    type="password"
    aria-required="true"
    onKeyDown={handleKeyDown} // Listen for Escape key
  />

  {error && (
    <p id="errorMessage" role="alert" aria-
    live="assertive">
      {error}
    </p>
  )}
```

```
        <button type="submit" aria-describedby="submitHelp">
          Submit
        </button>
        <span id="submitHelp">Press Enter to submit the form.
        Press Escape to clear errors.</span>
      </form>
    </div>
  </FocusLock>
 );
}

export default AccessibleForm;
```

Figure 16-1. *Fully accessible React form with ARIA, focus management, and keyboard navigation*

In Listing 16-1, the form implements accessible design principles by using `<label>` elements linked to their corresponding input fields, ensuring compatibility with screen readers. The `aria-required` attribute indicates that the fields are mandatory, while `aria-describedby` provides additional guidance for users by linking input fields to contextual help text.

Furthermore, the focus management mechanism ensures that users navigating with keyboards or assistive technologies can seamlessly interact with the form. By incorporating `react-focus-lock`, the form maintains logical focus order, preventing users from unintentionally shifting focus outside of interactive elements.

With semantic HTML, ARIA attributes, and keyboard-friendly navigation, this implementation establishes a robust foundation for building accessible React forms that enhance usability for all users.

Testing for Accessibility

Ensuring that your application meets accessibility standards is a crucial step in the development process. While implementing best practices is essential, testing accessibility with reliable tools and automated tests ensures your application remains inclusive as it evolves. This section covers the most effective tools and techniques for testing accessibility in React applications. A variety of tools are available to audit and test the accessibility of your application. These tools can highlight areas of improvement and validate your efforts:

- **Axe DevTools**: A popular browser extension that provides a detailed report of accessibility violations directly within your browser's developer tools. It is easy to use and integrates seamlessly into your workflow.

- **Lighthouse:** Built into Chrome DevTools, Lighthouse offers an accessibility score and actionable recommendations to improve your app's usability. It also highlights areas like color contrast and semantic structure.
- **Jest-axe:** This JavaScript library enables automated accessibility testing during the development process. It integrates with Jest, a popular testing framework, and is particularly useful for unit testing React components.

Writing Automated Tests for Accessibility

Automated tests play a vital role in maintaining the accessibility of your React components. They ensure that updates or new features do not inadvertently introduce accessibility issues. The **jest-axe** library is a great tool for this purpose, as it works seamlessly with React components. The example in Listing 16-2 demonstrates how to write an accessibility test for the `AccessibleForm` component using Jest and jest-axe, and Figure 16-2 shows the result of running test cases.

Listing 16-2. Accessibility Test Using jest-axe

```
import React from "react";
import { render, screen, fireEvent } from "@testing-library/react";
import { axe } from "jest-axe";
import AccessibleForm from "./AccessibleForm";

describe("AccessibleForm Accessibility Tests", () => {
  // Test 1: Ensure the component has no accessibility violations
  it("should have no accessibility violations", async () => {
    const { container } = render(<AccessibleForm />);
```

CHAPTER 16   ACCESSIBILITY AND INTERNATIONALIZATION

```
  const results = await axe(container);
  expect(results).toHaveNoViolations();
});

// Test 2: Ensure all form elements are accessible by
screen readers
it("should have properly labeled input fields", () => {
  render(<AccessibleForm />);

  const usernameLabel = screen.getByLabelText("Username");
  const passwordLabel = screen.getByLabelText("Password");

  expect(usernameLabel).toBeInTheDocument();
  expect(passwordLabel).toBeInTheDocument();
});

// Test 3: Ensure focus starts on the first input field
it("should focus on the username input when the form
loads", () => {
  render(<AccessibleForm />);

  const usernameInput = screen.getByLabelText("Username");
  expect(usernameInput).toHaveFocus();
});
});
```

```
 PASS  src/components/chapter_16/Accessible.test.jsx
  AccessibleForm Accessibility Tests
    ✓ should have no accessibility violations (78 ms)
    ✓ should have properly labeled input fields (10 ms)
    ✓ should focus on the username input when the form loads (6 ms)

Test Suites: 1 passed, 1 total
Tests:       3 passed, 3 total
Snapshots:   0 total
Time:        0.54 s, estimated 3 s
Ran all test suites.
```

Figure 16-2. Automated test cases for accessibility

In Listing 16-2, the axe function is used to analyze the `AccessibleForm` component rendered by React Testing Library. The test checks for any accessibility violations and ensures that none are present. By incorporating such tests into your CI/CD pipeline, you can automatically catch and address accessibility issues before they reach production. Testing accessibility not only validates your implementation but also helps you identify gaps in your design. A combination of manual audits using tools like Axe DevTools and automated tests with jest-axe ensures that your application is robust and inclusive for all users.

Internationalization (i18n) in React

Internationalization, often abbreviated as **i18n**, plays a critical role in making applications accessible and adaptable to users worldwide. By enabling applications to support multiple languages, regional formats, and cultural preferences, developers can enhance the user experience and expand their reach to a global audience.

Internationalization allows users to interact with an application in their preferred language and format, breaking language barriers and creating a personalized experience. Beyond translation, it ensures that date, time, and currency formats are automatically adapted to the user's regional settings. For instance, while the United States may use a dollar symbol with commas separating thousands, European countries often use a comma as a decimal separator with the euro symbol.

React offers robust libraries to streamline the process of implementing internationalization. Two popular options include

- **react-i18next**: A powerful library that integrates seamlessly with React components, providing tools to handle translations, manage language switching, and support advanced features like interpolation

CHAPTER 16   ACCESSIBILITY AND INTERNATIONALIZATION

- **formatjs (React Intl)**: A comprehensive library that focuses on formatting numbers, dates, strings, and other locale-specific data, making it a great choice for projects with complex formatting requirements

Setting Up react-i18next

To demonstrate how internationalization can be implemented, I'll walk you through setting up **react-i18next** for a simple multilingual application.

Step 1: Install the library

Begin by installing the required libraries using npm:

```
npm install react-i18next i18next
```

Step 2: Create translation files

Define your translations in separate JSON files for each language. For instance, create en.json for English and es.json for Spanish in the locales folder:

```
// en.json
{
  "welcomeMessage": "Welcome to our website!"
}

// es.json
{
  "welcomeMessage": "¡Bienvenido a nuestro sitio web!"
}
```

Step 3: Initialize the i18n configuration

Configure i18n to load the translations and set the default language:

```
import i18n from "i18next";
import { initReactI18next } from "react-i18next";
import enTranslation from "./locales/en.json";
import esTranslation from "./locales/es.json";

i18n.use(initReactI18next).init({
  resources: {
    en: { translation: enTranslation },
    es: { translation: esTranslation },
  },
  lng: "en", // Default language
  fallbackLng: "en", // Fallback language if translation
  is missing
  interpolation: { escapeValue: false }, // React already
  escapes values
  detection: {
    order: ["localStorage", "cookie", "navigator"],
    caches: ["localStorage", "cookie"], // Stores selected
    language
  },
});

export default i18n;
```

In this configuration, the `resources` object specifies the translation files for each language. The `lng` property sets the default language, while `fallbackLng` ensures the app reverts to a default language if a translation is unavailable.

Step 4: Use the useTranslation hook in your components

The `useTranslation` hook from react-i18next makes it easy to access translation keys in your components:

```
import { useTranslation } from "react-i18next";

function Welcome() {
  const { t } = useTranslation();

  return <h1>{t("welcomeMessage", "Default Welcome
  Message")}</h1>;
}

export default Welcome;
```

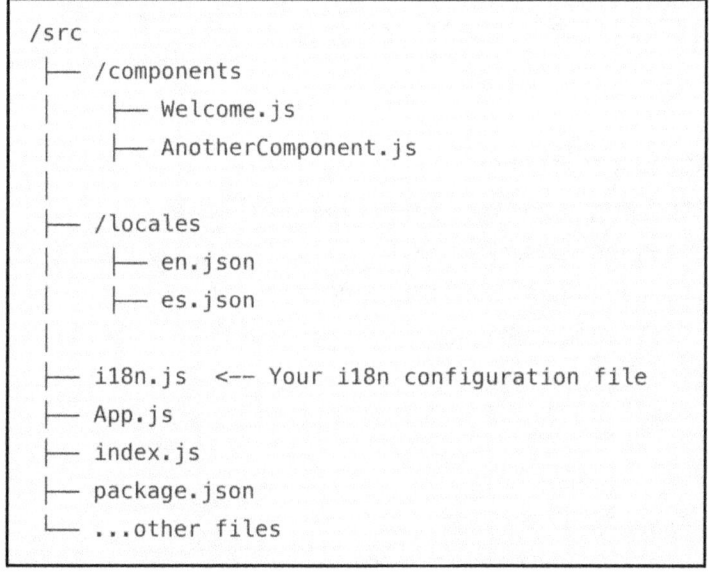

***Figure 16-3.** Recommended folder structure for locales and i18n.js*

In this example, the t function is used to fetch the translated text for the key welcomeMessage. Depending on the currently selected language, it will render either "Welcome to our website!" or "¡Bienvenido a nuestro sitio web!" Listing 16-3 shows a concise implementation of a multilingual React component using react-i18next, and the corresponding output is illustrated in Figure 16-4.

CHAPTER 16 ACCESSIBILITY AND INTERNATIONALIZATION

Listing 16-3. Multilingual React Application

```
import React from "react";
import { useTranslation } from "react-i18next";

const Welcome = () => {
  const { t, i18n } = useTranslation();

  const switchLanguage = (lang) => {
    i18n.changeLanguage(lang); // Dynamically change the
    language
  };

  return (
    <div>
      <button onClick={() =>
      switchLanguage("en")}>English</button>
      <button onClick={() =>
      switchLanguage("es")}>Español</button>
      <h1>{t("welcomeMessage")}</h1>
    </div>
  );
}

export default Welcome;
```

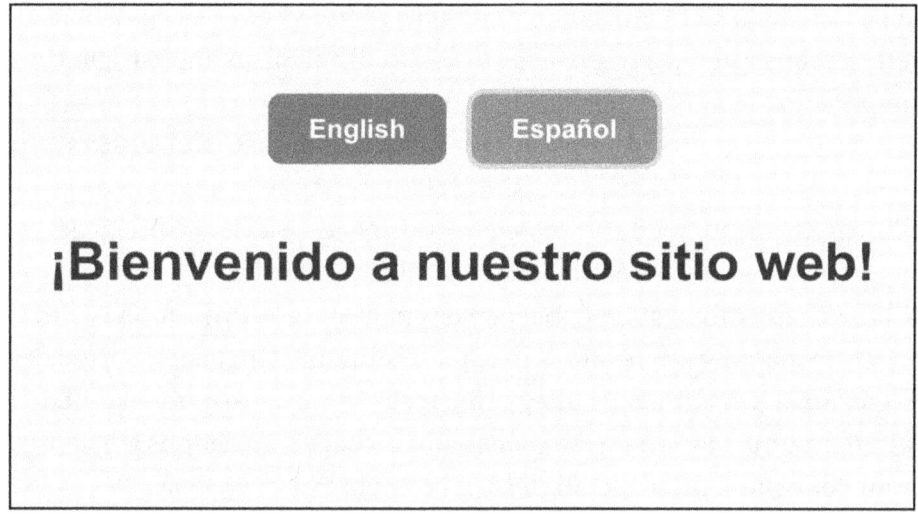

Figure 16-4. Multilingual React component

In Listing 16-3, this component allows users to switch between English and Spanish dynamically by clicking the respective buttons, demonstrating how react-i18next simplifies language handling in React applications. By following these steps, you can ensure that your React application provides a seamless and localized experience for users from diverse linguistic and cultural backgrounds. Whether you're building a small personal project or a large-scale enterprise app, internationalization is key to achieving a truly global reach.

Summary

In this chapter, we explored how to make React applications accessible and adaptable for users with diverse abilities and cultural backgrounds. Accessibility was highlighted as a critical aspect of modern web applications, ensuring usability for people with visual, auditory, motor, or cognitive impairments. Techniques such as using semantic HTML, proper labeling, ARIA attributes, and managing keyboard navigation were demonstrated to enhance the accessibility of forms and navigation components.

We also covered tools like Axe DevTools, Lighthouse, and jest-axe, which help identify and fix accessibility issues. A practical example showcased how to write automated tests using jest-axe to ensure React components remain accessible as the application evolves.

The chapter then shifted to internationalization (i18n), emphasizing its role in adapting applications to support multiple languages, currencies, and regional formatting. By integrating react-i18next, we demonstrated how to dynamically switch languages and manage translations efficiently. By implementing these techniques, developers can build React applications that are inclusive, user-friendly, and globally adaptable.

In the next chapter, we will transition to the process of preparing a React application for production. This includes optimizing the application for deployment, choosing the right hosting platforms, and setting up **Continuous Integration and Deployment** (CI/CD) pipelines.

CHAPTER 17

Deployment and Continuous Integration

In this chapter, we will explore the critical steps required to take React applications from development to production. Deployment is not merely about hosting an application; it involves preparing the application for optimal performance, ensuring it is secure, and deploying it to a platform that meets business needs. Continuous Integration and Deployment (CI/CD) further enhance this process by automating testing, building, and deployment workflows, ensuring stability and efficiency throughout the application's lifecycle.

Deploying a React application involves several considerations. First, developers must optimize their applications by **minifying assets**, **bundling code efficiently**, and utilizing techniques like **lazy loading** to enhance performance. Once optimized, the application needs to be configured for production with environment variables to securely handle sensitive data. These steps ensure that the application is ready for a smooth and efficient deployment.

Choosing the right deployment platform is another critical step. Platforms like **Netlify**, **Vercel**, and **AWS Amplify** provide seamless integration for hosting React applications. These platforms support

CHAPTER 17   DEPLOYMENT AND CONTINUOUS INTEGRATION

custom domain configurations, HTTPS, and offer unique features tailored to modern web development needs. The chapter will dive into the specifics of deploying React applications on these platforms, equipping developers with practical knowledge for different hosting scenarios.

Continuous Integration and Deployment (CI/CD) are indispensable for maintaining modern applications. By automating repetitive tasks such as testing, building, and deploying code, CI/CD pipelines enhance development speed and ensure stability. Setting up CI/CD pipelines with tools like GitHub Actions enables teams to deploy applications automatically after successful builds and tests, reducing manual effort and minimizing errors.

Post-deployment maintenance is equally vital. Monitoring tools like **Sentry** and **LogRocket** help track application performance and detect issues in production. Setting up alerts and dashboards ensures developers can respond quickly to errors or performance bottlenecks, maintaining a high-quality user experience.

By the end of this chapter, developers will have a comprehensive understanding of preparing, deploying, and maintaining React applications in production environments, as well as automating these processes for efficiency and reliability.

Preparing Your React App for Deployment

Deploying a React application involves more than simply hosting it; it requires optimizing the app for performance, configuring environment variables, and generating a production-ready build. Proper preparation ensures that the application runs smoothly, performs well, and meets production requirements.

CHAPTER 17 DEPLOYMENT AND CONTINUOUS INTEGRATION

Optimizing for Production

Optimization is a crucial step to ensure that the application loads quickly and efficiently for users. Several strategies can be implemented to achieve this:

1. **Code Minification**: Minifying JavaScript and CSS files reduces their file sizes, leading to faster load times. Tools like **Webpack** and **Vite** handle this automatically during the build process. Minification removes unnecessary whitespace, comments, and other non-essential elements from the code.

2. **Tree Shaking**: This process removes unused code from the final bundle. By eliminating dead code, tree shaking ensures that only the required components are included, reducing the bundle size. This technique is particularly effective when working with modular libraries like Lodash.

3. **Lazy Loading**: To enhance performance, components should be loaded dynamically only when they are needed. React provides built-in support for lazy loading through React.lazy() and Suspense. For example, Listing 17-1 demonstrates how to lazy load a component to minimize initial load times.

   Listing 17-1. Lazy Loading a React Component

   ```
   import React, { Suspense } from "react";

   const LazyComponent = React.lazy(() => import("./LazyComponent"));
   ```

```
const App = () => {
  return (
    <div>
      <Suspense fallback={<div>Loading...</div>}>
        <LazyComponent />
      </Suspense>
    </div>
  );
}

export default App;
```

4. **Image Optimization**: Optimized images significantly improve performance. Use compressed formats like WebP to reduce image sizes without compromising quality. Additionally, lazy loading images ensures that only images in the user's viewport are loaded initially, further speeding up the application.

Setting Up Environment Variables

Environment variables are essential for managing application configurations securely and efficiently across different environments (development, staging, production). These variables are typically stored in .env files to avoid hardcoding sensitive information like API keys. Examples of an .env file are listed below:

```
REACT_APP_API_URL=https://api.example.com
REACT_APP_API_KEY=your-secret-api-key
```

In React, environment variables must be prefixed with REACT_APP_ to be accessible within the application. Listing 17-2 illustrates how to use an environment variable in your application code. If you add or update environment variables, you must restart your React development server (npm start or yarn start).

Listing 17-2. Using Environment Variables in React

```
const apiUrl = process.env.REACT_APP_API_URL;
fetch(`${apiUrl}/endpoint`)
  .then((response) => response.json())
  .then((data) => console.log(data));
```

Creating a Build

The final step in preparing the application for deployment is to create a production-ready build. This build process optimizes the application by applying minification, bundling, and other performance enhancements. To generate a production build, use the following command:

```
npm run build
```

This command creates a `build/` directory containing static files that are ready to be deployed. These files include an optimized `index.html`, JavaScript bundles, and other assets necessary for running the application. Figure 17-1 describes the expected folder structure of the build directory.

CHAPTER 17   DEPLOYMENT AND CONTINUOUS INTEGRATION

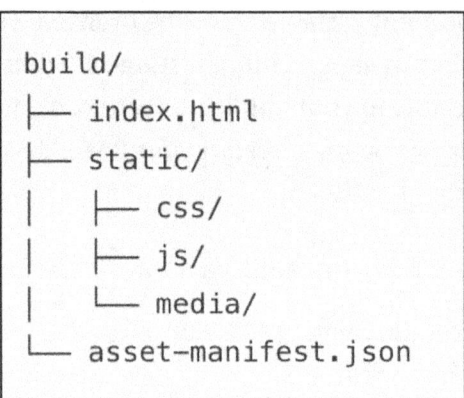

Figure 17-1. Build directory structure

This folder structure contains everything needed to deploy your React application to a hosting platform.

By following these steps, developers can ensure that their React applications are optimized, secure, and ready to be deployed in production environments. In the next section, we will explore various deployment platforms and their specific configurations to host React applications effectively. Let's move on to deployment platforms to complete the process.

Deployment Platforms

After preparing your React application for production, the next step is to deploy it to a hosting platform. Selecting the right deployment platform is critical to ensuring scalability, performance, and ease of management. This section explores popular deployment platforms, each tailored to different use cases, and provides step-by-step instructions for deploying your React app.

CHAPTER 17   DEPLOYMENT AND CONTINUOUS INTEGRATION

Popular Deployment Platforms

1. **Netlify**: Netlify is a powerful and easy-to-use platform for deploying modern web applications. Its seamless integration with Git repositories allows for automatic builds and deployments. Netlify supports serverless functions, custom domains, and HTTPS out of the box, making it a popular choice among developers.

2. **Vercel**: Vercel is specifically optimized for React applications and offers features like preview URLs for every commit, serverless functions, and fast global content delivery. It's an excellent choice for applications that require dynamic updates and real-time collaboration.

3. **AWS Amplify**: AWS Amplify is a scalable hosting platform with built-in CI/CD capabilities. It integrates deeply with other AWS services, making it ideal for applications that need back-end integration or require a cloud-native approach.

Deploying to Netlify

Netlify simplifies the deployment process by automatically building and deploying applications whenever code is pushed to a linked Git repository. Follow the steps below to deploy your React app:

1. **Push Your Code to a Git Repository**
   Ensure your React app is hosted on a Git platform such as GitHub, GitLab, or Bitbucket.

2. **Link the Repository to Netlify**
   Create a Netlify account and link your Git repository to it. Netlify will automatically detect the repository and import your project.

3. **Set the Build Command and Publish Directory**
   During the setup process, specify the build command as `npm run build` and the publish directory as `build/`.

4. **Deploy Automatically**
   Netlify will build and deploy your application automatically after every commit to the repository. This workflow ensures that your live application is always up to date. Listing 17-3 illustrates the Netlify Build Settings.

Listing 17-3. Netlify Build Settings

```
Build Command: npm run build
Publish Directory: build/
```

Deploying to Vercel

Vercel is another excellent platform for hosting React applications. It provides a simple CLI tool for deploying your applications in minutes.

1. **Install the Vercel CLI**
   Install the Vercel CLI globally on your machine using npm:

   ```
   npm install -g vercel
   ```

CHAPTER 17   DEPLOYMENT AND CONTINUOUS INTEGRATION

2. **Deploy the Application**
   Navigate to your project directory and run the vercel command:

   vercel

3. **Follow the Prompts**
   The first time you run Vercel, it will prompt you to log in if you are not already logged in. Next, it will ask you to select a project scope, allowing you to choose between a personal account or a team. Finally, Vercel will automatically detect your project type, such as React, and configure the deployment settings accordingly.

4. **Access Your Live Application**
   Once the deployment is complete, Vercel provides a live URL for your application, which updates dynamically with each new commit, for example, https://your-project.vercel.app. Listing 17-4 illustrates the Vercel Build Settings.

Listing 17-4. Deploying to Vercel

```
npm install -g vercel
vercel
```

Deploying your React application to these platforms ensures a reliable and professional hosting environment with minimal effort. Both Netlify and Vercel are developer-friendly and automate much of the deployment process, while AWS Amplify provides scalability and powerful back-end integrations for advanced use cases.

In the next section, we will explore how to integrate Continuous Integration and Deployment (CI/CD) pipelines to automate your builds and deployments further, ensuring efficiency and stability.

CHAPTER 17   DEPLOYMENT AND CONTINUOUS INTEGRATION

Continuous Integration and Deployment (CI/CD)

As React applications grow in complexity, manual deployment processes become inefficient and error-prone. Continuous Integration (CI) and Continuous Deployment (CD) are essential practices that automate the testing, building, and deployment of applications, ensuring consistency, reliability, and speed.

What Is CI/CD?

- **Continuous Integration (CI)**: CI automates the testing and merging of code changes into a shared repository. Developers can push their changes frequently without worrying about breaking the build, as CI ensures that all code is validated through automated tests.

- **Continuous Deployment (CD)**: CD takes automation a step further by deploying the application to production automatically after all CI checks pass. This practice eliminates manual intervention, ensuring faster and more reliable releases.

Setting Up CI/CD with GitHub Actions

GitHub Actions is a powerful automation platform that simplifies setting up **Continuous Integration and Continuous Deployment (CI/CD)** pipelines for React applications. By automating the build, test, and deployment process, you can ensure smooth, error-free updates to your Netlify-hosted application with every push to your repository.

Step 1: Creating a GitHub Actions Workflow File

To set up a CI/CD pipeline for deploying a React application to **Netlify**, you need to create a **workflow file** (deploy.yml) that defines the steps to build, test, and deploy your project automatically. Refer to Figure 17-2 for CI/CD workflow file location in your project. Place the file inside your project as .github/workflows/deploy.yml.

```
.github/
├── workflows/
│   ├── deploy.yml    <-- (Place the file here)
node_modules/
public/
src/
.gitignore
package.json
README.md
```

Figure 17-2. CI/CD workflow file location

Step 2: Writing the CI/CD Workflow Configuration

Listing 17-5 shows the complete GitHub Actions workflow file for deploying a React application to Netlify.

Listing 17-5. CI/CD Pipeline Workflow with GitHub Actions

```yaml
name: CI/CD Pipeline for Netlify

on:
  push:
    branches:
      - main

jobs:
  build:
    runs-on: ubuntu-latest
```

```yaml
steps:
  - name: Checkout Repository Code
    uses: actions/checkout@v4

  - name: Set Up Node.js
    uses: actions/setup-node@v4
    with:
      node-version: 18

  - name: Install Dependencies
    run: npm install

  - name: Run Tests
    run: npm test

  - name: Build the React Application
    run: npm run build

  - name: Deploy to Netlify
    uses: nwtgck/actions-netlify@v2
    with:
      publish-dir: ./build
      production-branch: main
      github-token: ${{ secrets.GITHUB_TOKEN }}
      deploy-message: "Deployed via GitHub Actions"
    env:
      NETLIFY_AUTH_TOKEN: ${{ secrets.NETLIFY_AUTH_TOKEN }}
      NETLIFY_SITE_ID: ${{ secrets.NETLIFY_SITE_ID }}
```

Step 3: Explanation of Steps

Each step in the workflow performs a critical role in automating the deployment process:

CHAPTER 17   DEPLOYMENT AND CONTINUOUS INTEGRATION

1. **Check Out Repository Code**: Retrieves the latest project files from the GitHub repository.

2. **Set Up Node.js**: Installs Node.js (version 18) to run the React application.

3. **Install Dependencies**: Runs npm install to install required project dependencies.

4. **Run Tests**: Executes automated tests using npm test to validate code changes before deployment.

5. **Build the React Application**: Runs npm run build to generate an optimized production-ready version of the application.

6. **Deploy to Netlify**: Uses the Netlify CLI action (nwtgck/actions-netlify@v2) to deploy the built application (./build folder) to **Netlify**. The **Netlify authentication tokens** (NETLIFY_AUTH_TOKEN and NETLIFY_SITE_ID) are securely stored as **GitHub Secrets**, ensuring a safe deployment process.

Step 4: Configuring Netlify Authentication Secrets

To allow GitHub Actions to deploy to Netlify, you must configure **authentication credentials** as **GitHub repository secrets**. Steps to add Netlify Authentication Tokens in GitHub are shown below:

- Go to your GitHub repository.
- Navigate to Settings ➤ Secrets and Variables ➤ Actions.
- Click "New Repository Secret."

CHAPTER 17   DEPLOYMENT AND CONTINUOUS INTEGRATION

- Add the following secrets:
  - NETLIFY_AUTH_TOKEN ➤ Found in Netlify ➤ "User Settings" ➤ "Personal Access Tokens."
  - NETLIFY_SITE_ID ➤ Found in Netlify ➤ "Site Settings" ➤ "Site Information."

Step 5: Pushing Changes to Trigger Deployment

Once the **workflow file (deploy.yml)** is committed to the repository, GitHub Actions will execute the deployment automatically **every time you push changes** to the main branch. To push changes and trigger deployment, run

```
git add .
git commit -m "Added GitHub Actions CI/CD for Netlify"
git push origin main
```

Step 6: Monitoring Deployment in GitHub Actions

After pushing your changes, you can monitor the workflow execution in **GitHub Actions** by navigating to your GitHub repository and clicking the **"Actions"** tab. From there, select the CI/CD pipeline workflow to track the status of each step in the deployment process. If the deployment is successful, Netlify will generate a live URL for your deployed React application.

Automating Tests and Builds

Automated testing and linting are integral to the CI process. Running these checks during CI ensures that issues are caught early, maintaining the quality and stability of the codebase. You can include Listing 17-6 script in your CI pipeline to run tests and lint the code.

Listing 17-6. Test and Lint Command

```
npm test && npm run lint
```

This command runs the project's test suite followed by linting checks. If any test fails or the code does not meet linting standards, the CI process halts, preventing a flawed build from being deployed.

By integrating CI/CD pipelines into your development workflow, you can automate the testing, building, and deployment processes, ensuring consistent and reliable releases. In the next section, we will explore how to monitor and track your application in production, enabling you to maintain a high-quality user experience.

Monitoring and Error Tracking in Production

Once your React application is live, monitoring and error tracking become essential for maintaining performance, identifying issues, and ensuring a seamless user experience. Monitoring tools provide insights into how the application performs in real-world conditions and help developers detect and resolve issues before they impact users.

Monitoring ensures that your application continues to perform optimally after deployment. It helps detect issues such as crashes, slow performance, or API failures early, allowing developers to address them proactively. By using monitoring and error-tracking tools, you can also analyze user behavior, identify bottlenecks, and improve the overall experience. Several tools are available for monitoring React applications in production, each catering to different needs:

1. **Sentry**: Sentry is a popular tool for tracking errors, performance issues, and user feedback. It integrates seamlessly with React and provides detailed error reports, stack traces, and context to debug issues effectively.

2. **LogRocket**: LogRocket records user sessions and logs front-end issues, making it easier to understand and reproduce bugs. By visualizing user interactions, it provides developers with actionable insights into UI problems.

3. **New Relic**: New Relic is a comprehensive monitoring solution that tracks both front-end and back-end performance. It offers metrics on application health, response times, and error rates, enabling end-to-end observability.

Setting Up Sentry for Error Tracking

Sentry is a powerful tool for error tracking and performance monitoring in React applications. It helps developers capture exceptions, track performance bottlenecks, and proactively resolve issues. This section demonstrates how to integrate Sentry into a React project.

Step 1: Installing Sentry in a React Project

To integrate Sentry, install the required dependencies using npm. These packages enable **error tracking** and **performance monitoring** within a React application.

```
npm install @sentry/react @sentry/tracing
```

Step 2: Initializing Sentry

Initialize Sentry in your application to start capturing errors and performance data. Place the initialization code in your app's entry file (e.g., `index.js` or `App.js`) as shown in Listing 17-7.

CHAPTER 17   DEPLOYMENT AND CONTINUOUS INTEGRATION

Listing 17-7. Initializing Sentry in a React Application

```
import * as Sentry from "@sentry/react";
import { BrowserTracing } from "@sentry/react";

Sentry.init({
  dsn: "https://your-dsn.sentry.io/", // Replace with your DSN
  from Sentry
  integrations: [new BrowserTracing()],
  tracesSampleRate: 1.0, // Adjust for performance monitoring
  replaysSessionSampleRate: 0.1, // Enables session replays
});
```

The DSN (Data Source Name) is a unique identifier assigned to your project in Sentry, allowing it to collect and organize error data. The tracesSampleRate defines the fraction of transactions captured for performance monitoring, helping track application performance metrics. Additionally, the replaysSessionSampleRate enables session replays, allowing developers to diagnose user issues by recording and analyzing interactions leading up to an error.

Step 3: Capturing Errors with Sentry

Use Sentry to capture exceptions and log errors programmatically. For example, wrap potentially error-prone code in a try-catch block and report errors to Sentry. To report errors programmatically, use Sentry.captureException() inside a try-catch block as shown in Listing 17-8.

Listing 17-8. Capturing Errors with Sentry

```
try {
  // Code that might throw an error
  throw new Error("An unexpected error occurred!");
} catch (error) {
  Sentry.captureException(error);
}
```

333

With this setup, any unhandled exceptions or errors logged with `Sentry.captureException` will be reported to your Sentry dashboard, providing detailed stack traces and debugging information.

By integrating monitoring tools like Sentry into your production workflow, you can maintain a high-quality user experience and proactively address issues. Tools like LogRocket and New Relic complement error tracking by offering user session replays and full-stack monitoring capabilities.

Summary

In this chapter, we covered the essential steps to prepare, deploy, and maintain React applications in production environments. We began by exploring optimization techniques like **code minification**, **tree shaking**, **lazy loading**, and **image optimization** to enhance application performance. Additionally, the use of environment variables for secure and flexible configuration management was discussed, followed by creating a production-ready build using the npm run build command.

The chapter then introduced popular deployment platforms like **Netlify**, **Vercel**, and **AWS Amplify**, each suited for specific hosting needs. Detailed steps for deploying applications to Netlify and Vercel were provided, highlighting features such as automatic builds, custom domains, and HTTPS support.

We also delved into **Continuous Integration** and **Deployment** (CI/CD) pipelines using GitHub Actions. By automating testing, building, and deployment processes, CI/CD ensures efficient workflows and reduces errors. A practical step-by-step example demonstrated setting up a pipeline to deploy a React app to Netlify, showcasing the benefits of automation.

CHAPTER 17 DEPLOYMENT AND CONTINUOUS INTEGRATION

Finally, the importance of monitoring and error tracking in production was emphasized. Tools like **Sentry** and **LogRocket** were introduced to track application performance, capture errors, and improve debugging. Setting up Sentry for error tracking was demonstrated with code examples to help developers maintain high-quality user experiences in production.

By the end of this chapter, developers gained a comprehensive understanding of deploying React applications, automating workflows with CI/CD, and monitoring applications in production.

In the next chapter, we will explore how to enhance React applications by **integrating third-party services and APIs**. This includes learning how to fetch data using libraries like Axios, manage asynchronous operations, and securely handle API keys.

CHAPTER 18

Integrating Third-Party Services and APIs

Integrating third-party services and APIs is essential for building modern, feature-rich React applications. This chapter explores how to enhance applications by fetching data from **REST APIs**, using **GraphQL** for efficient data queries, and integrating popular services like **Firebase and Stripe** for advanced capabilities.

We begin with techniques for fetching data using the **Fetch API** and libraries like **Axios**, focusing on handling asynchronous operations with Promises and async/await. You'll also learn how to manage loading and error states to improve the user experience. Next, we introduce GraphQL and demonstrate how to use **Apollo Client** to query and cache data in React applications efficiently.

The chapter then provides practical examples of integrating Firebase for authentication and real-time databases, as well as Stripe for secure payment processing. Each integration includes step-by-step guidance and best practices to ensure smooth implementation and configuration.

By the end of this chapter, developers will have a strong foundation for working with external APIs and third-party services, enabling them to build dynamic and scalable React applications with ease.

CHAPTER 18   INTEGRATING THIRD-PARTY SERVICES AND APIS

Introduction to Third-Party Services

Integrating third-party services is a powerful way to accelerate development and enhance the functionality of React applications. These services provide prebuilt solutions for common requirements, allowing developers to focus on building unique features rather than reinventing the wheel.

Why Use Third-Party Services?

1. **Saves Development Time**: Third-party services offer ready-to-use features like authentication, payments, and analytics. Developers can integrate these solutions with minimal effort, significantly reducing the time needed for custom implementations.

2. **Reliability**: Established services handle critical aspects like scaling, security, and maintenance, ensuring consistent performance and reliability for your application.

3. **Focus on Core Functionality**: By outsourcing common functionalities to third-party providers, developers can concentrate on building the core features that make their application unique.

Examples of Popular Services

1. **Firebase**: Provides tools for authentication, real-time databases, and hosting, making it ideal for rapid development of full-stack applications

2. **Stripe**: A popular solution for secure and flexible payment processing, supporting a wide range of payment methods

3. **Google Maps**: Offers powerful mapping and location services, ideal for applications requiring geolocation or navigation features

4. **SendGrid**: Simplifies sending transactional and marketing emails, with features like templates, analytics, and email tracking

By leveraging these services, developers can build robust applications with advanced capabilities while maintaining efficiency and reliability. In the next section, we will delve into the basics of working with APIs, starting with fetching data from REST APIs.

Working with REST APIs

APIs are the backbone of modern web applications, enabling communication between the front-end and external data sources or services. This section explores how to fetch data from REST APIs using `fetch` and `axios` in React, along with techniques for handling errors gracefully.

Fetching Data with fetch

The Fetch API is a built-in JavaScript method for making HTTP requests. Listing 18-1 shows an example of fetching data from a REST API and rendering it in a React component as illustrated in Figure 18-1.

CHAPTER 18 INTEGRATING THIRD-PARTY SERVICES AND APIS

Listing 18-1. Fetching Data with fetch

```
import React, { useEffect, useState } from "react";
const FetchExample = () => {
  const [data, setData] = useState(null); // Handle null case
  const [loading, setLoading] = useState(true);
  const [error, setError] = useState(null);

  useEffect(() => {
    fetch("https://jsonplaceholder.typicode.com/posts")
      .then((response) => {
        if (!response.ok) {
          throw new Error(`HTTP error! Status: ${response.
          status}`);
        }
        return response.json();
      })
      .then((data) => {
        setData(data);
        setLoading(false);
      })
      .catch((error) => {
        setError(error.message);
        setLoading(false);
      });
  }, []);
  if (loading) return <p>Loading...</p>;
  if (error) return <p>Error: {error}</p>;

  return (
    <ul>
      {data.map((item) => (
```

```
            <li key={item.id}>{item.title}</li>
        ))}
      </ul>
  );
}

export default FetchExample;
```

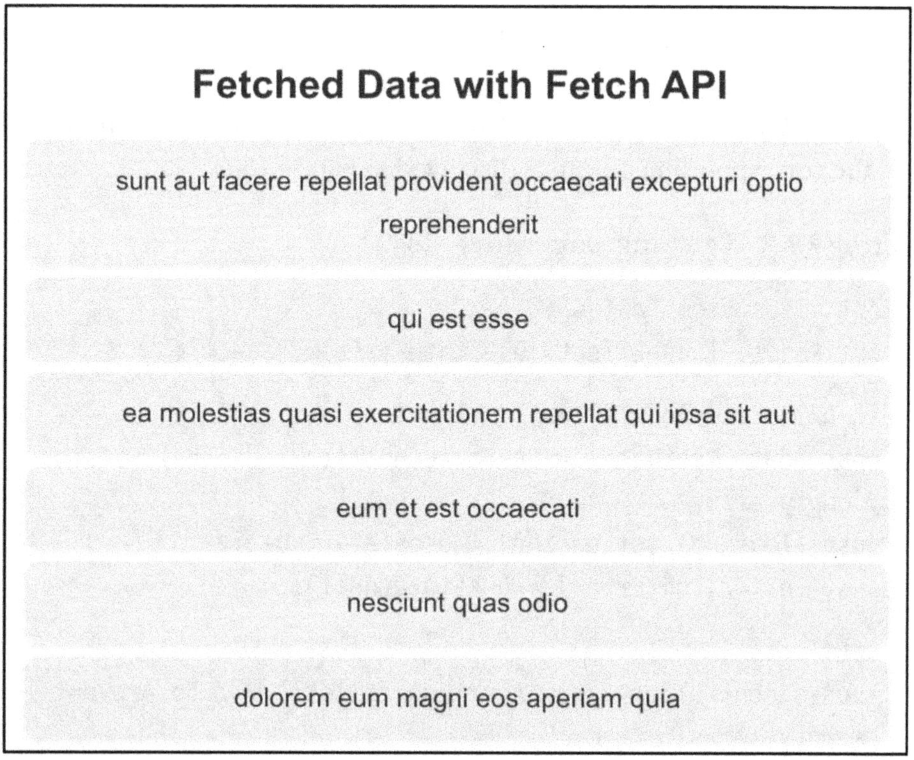

Fetched Data with Fetch API

sunt aut facere repellat provident occaecati excepturi optio reprehenderit

qui est esse

ea molestias quasi exercitationem repellat qui ipsa sit aut

eum et est occaecati

nesciunt quas odio

dolorem eum magni eos aperiam quia

Figure 18-1. Fetching data with Fetch API

The useEffect hook is used to fetch data as soon as the component mounts, ensuring the API request is triggered only once during the component's lifecycle. The API response is then converted to JSON format

CHAPTER 18   INTEGRATING THIRD-PARTY SERVICES AND APIS

and stored in the data state using the setData() function. Finally, the map() function iterates over the fetched data and dynamically renders it as a list, providing a simple and efficient way to display the retrieved information.

Using Axios for Fetching Data

Axios is a popular HTTP client that simplifies data fetching and provides advanced features like automatic JSON parsing and error handling. Install Axios if not already installed using npm install axios. The example in Listing 18-2 demonstrates using axios to fetch data with error handling, and the corresponding output is displayed in Figure 18-2.

Listing 18-2. Fetching Data with Axios

```
import axios from "axios";
import React, { useEffect, useState } from "react";

const AxiosExample = () => {
  const [data, setData] = useState(null); // Use null instead
  of empty array
  const [loading, setLoading] = useState(true);
  const [error, setError] = useState(null);

  useEffect(() => {
    const controller = new AbortController(); // To prevent
    memory leaks
    const fetchData = async () => {
      try {
        const response = await axios.get("https://
        jsonplaceholder.typicode.com/posts", {
          signal: controller.signal, // Attach signal for
          request cancellation
```

```
    });
    setData(response.data);
  } catch (error) {
    if (axios.isAxiosError(error)) {
      setError(`Error: ${error.response?.status || "Network
      Error"}`);
    } else {
      setError("Unexpected Error");
    }
    console.error("Error fetching data:", error);
  } finally {
    setLoading(false);
  }
};

fetchData();

return () => {
  controller.abort(); // Cleanup on unmount
};
}, []);

if (loading) return <p>Loading...</p>;
if (error) return <p>{error}</p>;

return (
  <ul>
    {data.map((item) => (
      <li key={item.id}>{item.title}</li>
    ))}
  </ul>
);
}

export default AxiosExample;
```

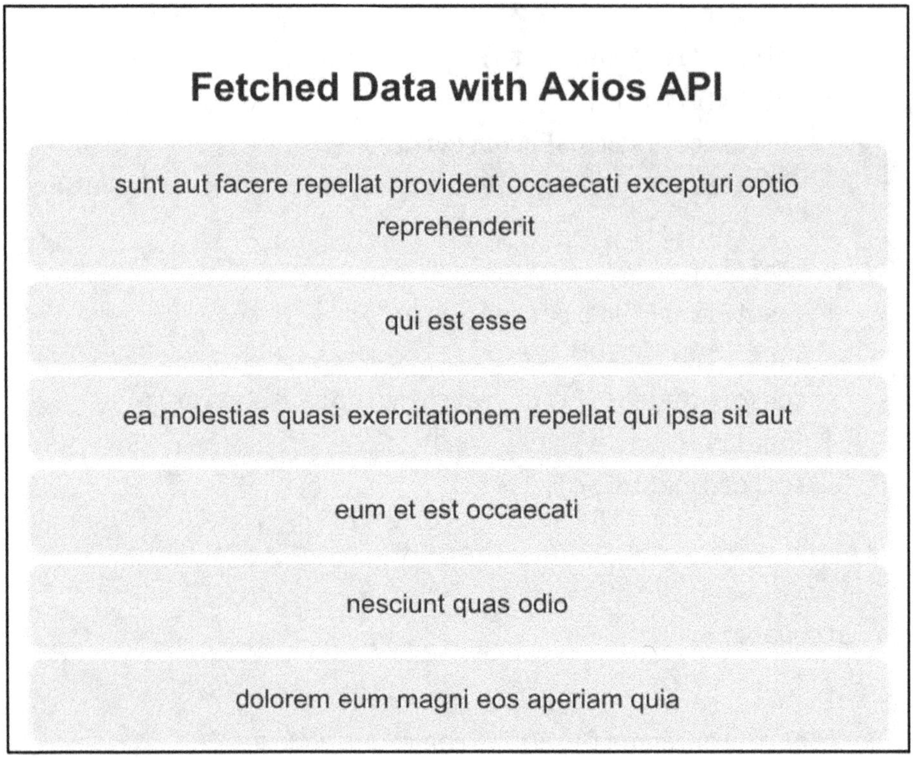

CHAPTER 18 INTEGRATING THIRD-PARTY SERVICES AND APIS

> **Fetched Data with Axios API**
>
> sunt aut facere repellat provident occaecati excepturi optio reprehenderit
>
> qui est esse
>
> ea molestias quasi exercitationem repellat qui ipsa sit aut
>
> eum et est occaecati
>
> nesciunt quas odio
>
> dolorem eum magni eos aperiam quia

Figure 18-2. *Fetching data with Axios API*

The `axios.get()` method is used to fetch data from the API, with the resulting response being stored in the `data` state. Any errors that occur during the API request are captured in the `catch` block and saved in the `error` state. If an error is encountered, it is displayed to the user through an appropriate error message, ensuring a better user experience and clear communication about issues with the API request.

Handling API Errors Gracefully

Error handling is crucial when working with APIs to provide a better user experience. See Listing 18-3 for retry logic example.

CHAPTER 18 INTEGRATING THIRD-PARTY SERVICES AND APIS

1. **Display Error Messages**: Show meaningful error messages to users instead of generic ones. For instance, "Unable to fetch data, please try again later."

2. **Fallback Data**: Use default or cached data as a fallback when the API is unavailable. This keeps the application functional even during outages.

3. **Retry Logic with Exponential Backoff**: For unreliable APIs, implement retry logic with increasing delays between attempts. This helps mitigate transient network errors.

Listing 18-3. Retry Logic Example

```
import axios from "axios";

async const fetchDataWithRetry = (url, retries = 3, delay = 1000) => {
  for (let i = 0; i < retries; i++) {
    try {
      const response = await axios.get(url);
      return response.data;
    } catch (error) {
      if (axios.isAxiosError(error)) {
        const status = error.response?.status;

        // Only retry for network-related or 5xx server errors
        if (status && status < 500) {
          console.error(`Client error ${status}: Not retrying`);
          throw error;
        }
      }
```

```
      if (i < retries - 1) {
        console.warn(`Retry ${i + 1}/${retries} in ${delay}
        ms...`);
        await new Promise((resolve) => setTimeout(resolve,
        delay));
        delay *= 2; // Exponential backoff
      } else {
        console.error("Max retries reached. Throwing error.");
        throw error;
      }
    }
  }
}

// Example usage
fetchDataWithRetry("https://jsonplaceholder.typicode.
com/posts")
  .then((data) => console.log("Fetched data:", data))
  .catch((error) => console.error("Final error:", error));
```

By mastering the techniques outlined above, developers can efficiently fetch data from REST APIs while handling errors gracefully. In the next section, we will delve into the world of GraphQL and explore how it provides a more flexible and efficient alternative to REST for data fetching in React applications.

GraphQL Integration

GraphQL offers a modern and flexible alternative to REST APIs by allowing clients to request precisely the data they need. With its query language and schema-based design, GraphQL enhances the efficiency of data fetching and minimizes over-fetching or under-fetching of data in React applications.

CHAPTER 18   INTEGRATING THIRD-PARTY SERVICES AND APIS

What Is GraphQL?

GraphQL is a query language for APIs that enables clients to specify the exact structure and fields of the data they need. Unlike REST, where predefined endpoints determine the data format, GraphQL provides a single endpoint and lets the client control the data retrieval. This flexibility makes GraphQL an excellent choice for dynamic and data-intensive applications. To integrate GraphQL into a React application, we use the Apollo Client, a popular library for managing GraphQL queries and caching. Below is the step-by-step instruction for setting it up.

Step 1: Install Apollo Client

To begin, install the necessary packages:

```
npm install @apollo/client graphql
```

Step 2: Configure Apollo Client

Next, configure Apollo Client with your GraphQL endpoint and caching mechanism. Wrap your application with the `ApolloProvider` to provide the client instance to all components in the app as shown in Listing 18-4.

Listing 18-4. Configuring Apollo Client

```
import { ApolloClient, InMemoryCache, ApolloProvider } from "@apollo/client";
import YourComponent from "./YourComponent"; // Import your component

// Configure Apollo Client
const client = new ApolloClient({
  uri: "https://example.com/graphql", // Replace with real GraphQL API
  cache: new InMemoryCache(),
```

```
  defaultOptions: {
    watchQuery: {
      fetchPolicy: "cache-and-network", // Fetch fresh data
      while using cache
      errorPolicy: "all", // Allows partial data when
      errors occur
    },
    query: {
      errorPolicy: "all",
    },
  },
});

// Main App Component
const App = () => {
  return (
    <ApolloProvider client={client}>
      <YourComponent />
    </ApolloProvider>
  );
}

export default App;
```

Step 3: Write GraphQL Queries

Write GraphQL queries using the gql template literal and execute them with the useQuery hook. The example in Listing 18-5 demonstrates fetching posts from a GraphQL API, and the corresponding output is shown in Figure 18-3.

Listing 18-5. Writing and Using GraphQL Queries

```
import { gql, useQuery } from "@apollo/client";
const GET_POSTS = gql`
  query GetPosts {
    posts {
      id
      title
      content
    }
  }
`;
const Posts = () => {
  const { loading, error, data } = useQuery(GET_POSTS, {
    fetchPolicy: "cache-and-network", // Uses cache first, but
    fetches fresh data
    errorPolicy: "all", // Allows partial results if
    errors occur
  });

  if (loading) return <p>Loading...</p>;
  if (error) return <p>Error: {error.message}</p>;
  if (!data || !data.posts || data.posts.length === 0)
    return <p>No posts available.</p>;

  return (
    <ul>
      {data.posts.map((post) => (
        <li key={post.id}>
          <strong>{post.title}</strong>
          <p>{post.content}</p>
        </li>
```

CHAPTER 18 INTEGRATING THIRD-PARTY SERVICES AND APIS

```
    ))}
   </ul>
  );
}

export default Posts;
```

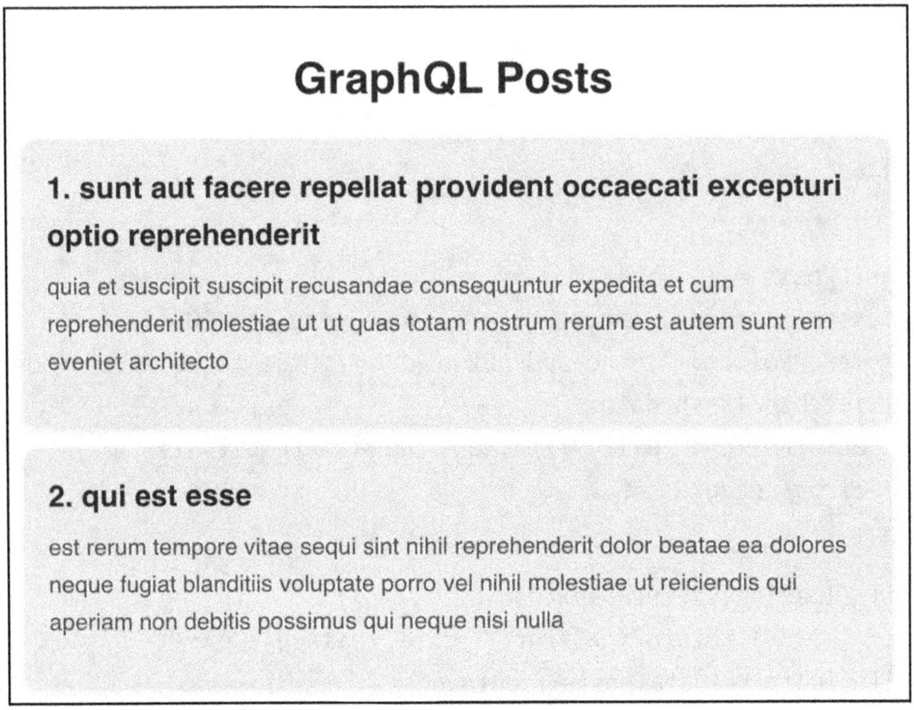

> **GraphQL Posts**
>
> **1. sunt aut facere repellat provident occaecati excepturi optio reprehenderit**
>
> quia et suscipit suscipit recusandae consequuntur expedita et cum reprehenderit molestiae ut ut quas totam nostrum rerum est autem sunt rem eveniet architecto
>
> **2. qui est esse**
>
> est rerum tempore vitae sequi sint nihil reprehenderit dolor beatae ea dolores neque fugiat blanditiis voluptate porro vel nihil molestiae ut reiciendis qui aperiam non debitis possimus qui neque nisi nulla

Figure 18-3. Fetching data with GraphQL

The GET_POSTS GraphQL query specifies the fields (id, title, and content) to be fetched for each post, ensuring that only the required data is retrieved. The useQuery hook is used to execute the query and provides three states—loading, error, and data—which help manage the UI based on the query's progress and results. Once the data is successfully fetched, it is dynamically rendered as a list, with each item generated from the data.posts array, creating an efficient and responsive display of the retrieved content.

By integrating Apollo Client, developers can efficiently manage GraphQL queries and caching in React applications. In the next section, we will explore integrating popular third-party services like Firebase and Stripe to add advanced functionality to your projects.

Payment Gateway Integration

Integrating a payment gateway into a React application is essential for enabling secure and seamless transactions. Stripe is a widely used payment gateway that provides an easy-to-integrate API and React library, making it an excellent choice for implementing payment functionality. The following steps demonstrate how to integrate Stripe into a React application to handle payment processing.

Step 1: Install Stripe Library

To start, install the required Stripe libraries using npm:

```
npm install @stripe/react-stripe-js @stripe/stripe-js
```

Step 2: Set Up Stripe Provider

Wrap your application with the Elements provider from Stripe and pass a stripePromise object created using the loadStripe method. This setup ensures that the Stripe context is available to all child components as shown in Listing 18-6.

Listing 18-6. Configuring Stripe Provider

```
import { loadStripe } from "@stripe/stripe-js";
import { Elements } from "@stripe/react-stripe-js";
import PaymentForm from "./PaymentForm";
```

```
const stripePromise = loadStripe(import.meta.env.VITE_STRIPE_
STRIPE_PUBLIC_KEY); // Secure key usage

const PaymentPage = () => {
  return (
    <Elements stripe={stripePromise}>
      <PaymentForm />
    </Elements>
  );
}

export default PaymentPage;
```

The `loadStripe` function initializes Stripe by using your publishable key, which is obtained from the Stripe dashboard. This key is essential for establishing a secure connection with Stripe's API. The `Elements` component acts as a provider, supplying the Stripe context to all child components within its scope. This setup ensures that all components can seamlessly access Stripe's features and functionality.

Step 3: Create a Payment Form

Design a payment form that includes a card input field and a submit button. Use Stripe's `CardElement` for securely collecting card details and the `useStripe` and `useElements` hooks for processing payments as illustrated in Listing 18-7. The corresponding output is displayed in Figure 18-4.

Listing 18-7. Creating a Payment Form

```
// PaymentForm.jsx
import { useState } from "react";
import { CardElement, useStripe, useElements } from "@stripe/
react-stripe-js";

const PaymentForm = () => {
```

```
const stripe = useStripe();
const elements = useElements();
const [error, setError] = useState(null);
const [loading, setLoading] = useState(false);

const handleSubmit = async (event) => {
  event.preventDefault();

  if (!stripe || !elements) {
    setError("Stripe is not properly initialized.");
    return;
  }

  setLoading(true);
  setError(null);

  const { error, paymentMethod } = await stripe.createPaymentMethod({
    type: "card",
    card: elements.getElement(CardElement),
  });

  if (error) {
    setError(error.message);
    setLoading(false);
  } else {
    console.log("Payment Success:", paymentMethod);
    setError(null);
    setLoading(false);
    alert("Payment Successful!"); // Simulate success message
  }
};

return (
  <form onSubmit={handleSubmit} className="payment-form">
```

```
      <CardElement className="card-input" />
      {error && <p className="error-message">{error}</p>}
      <button type="submit" disabled={!stripe || loading}
      className="pay-button">
        {loading ? "Processing..." : "Pay"}
      </button>
    </form>
  );
}

export default PaymentForm;
```

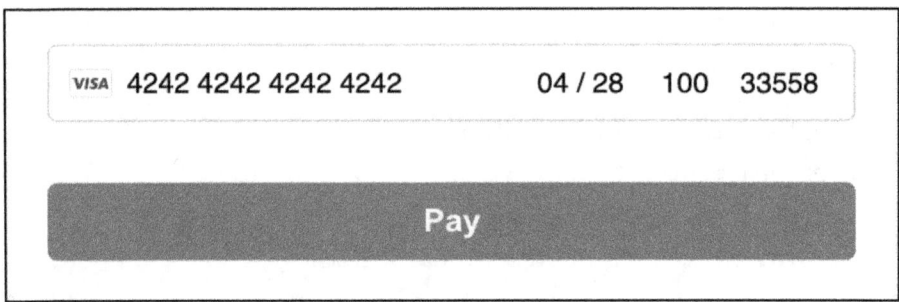

Figure 18-4. Payment gateway integration with Stripe

The CardElement component offers a prebuilt UI for securely capturing card details, ensuring compliance with security standards. The useStripe and useElements hooks facilitate seamless communication with Stripe's API while managing the form elements effectively. The createPaymentMethod function uses the card details entered by the user to generate a payment method, returning either a paymentMethod object upon success or an error if the process fails.

CHAPTER 18   INTEGRATING THIRD-PARTY SERVICES AND APIS

Integrating Firebase with React

Firebase is a **Backend-as-a-Service (BaaS)** platform provided by **Google** that helps developers build modern web and mobile applications **without managing servers**. It offers a suite of cloud-based tools, including **Firestore (database)**, **authentication**, **storage**, and **hosting**. For this project, we will be using **Firebase Firestore**, a **NoSQL cloud database** that allows real-time data storage and retrieval.

Firebase Firestore eliminates the need for a back end, allowing developers to store and retrieve data directly from the front end. It provides real-time updates, ensuring data synchronization across multiple devices instantly. Designed for scalability, Firestore efficiently handles applications ranging from small projects to enterprise-level databases. Additionally, it is secure and managed by Google, offering built-in authentication and customizable security rules. I will manually add multiple entries to Firestore and retrieve them in a React application in a step-by-step instruction.

Step 1: Install Firebase

First, install Firebase in your project:

npm install firebase

Step 2: Initialize Firebase

Create a firebase.js file in /src as shown in Listing 18-8.

Listing 18-8. Firebase Configuration File

```
//Firebase.js
import { initializeApp } from "firebase/app";
import { getFirestore, collection, getDocs } from "firebase/firestore";

// Replace this with your Firebase project config
const firebaseConfig = {
```

```
  apiKey: "YOUR_API_KEY",
  authDomain: "YOUR_PROJECT_ID.firebaseapp.com",
  projectId: "YOUR_PROJECT_ID",
  storageBucket: "YOUR_PROJECT_ID.appspot.com",
  messagingSenderId: "YOUR_SENDER_ID",
  appId: "YOUR_APP_ID"
};

// Initialize Firebase
const app = initializeApp(firebaseConfig);
const db = getFirestore(app);

// Export Firestore functions
export { db, collection, getDocs };
```

Step 3: Fetch Data from Firestore

Now, let's **fetch data** from a Firestore Product collection as shown in Listing 18-9.

Listing 18-9. Fetch Data from Firebase Database

```
// FetchData.jsx
import { useState, useEffect } from "react";
import { db, collection, getDocs } from "./firebase";

function FetchData() {
  const [data, setData] = useState([]);

  useEffect(() => {
    const fetchData = async () => {
      try {
```

CHAPTER 18 INTEGRATING THIRD-PARTY SERVICES AND APIS

```
      const querySnapshot = await getDocs(collection(db,
      "products")); // Replace with your collection name
      const items = querySnapshot.docs.map(doc => ({ id: doc.
      id, ...doc.data() }));
      setData(items);
    } catch (error) {
      console.error("Error fetching data:", error);
    }
  };

  fetchData();
}, []);

return (
  <div>
    <h2>Fetched Data from Firebase</h2>
    <ul>
      {data.map((item) => (
        <li key={item.id}>{item.name} - ${item.price}</li>
      ))}
    </ul>
  </div>
);
}

export default FetchData;
```

CHAPTER 18   INTEGRATING THIRD-PARTY SERVICES AND APIS

Figure 18-5.   Firebase integration with React application

In this example, we successfully integrated Firebase Firestore into a React application. We started by installing and initializing Firebase, ensuring that our project was correctly configured. Next, we created a Firestore collection (products) and added multiple entries manually through the Firebase Console. Finally, we retrieved the stored data and displayed it dynamically in our React application using Firestore queries. By leveraging Firestore, we eliminated the need for a back end while ensuring scalability, security, and real-time updates. This approach allows applications to store and fetch data seamlessly without managing servers.

Summary

In this chapter, we explored how to integrate third-party services and APIs into React applications to enhance functionality and streamline development. We began by discussing the advantages of third-party

CHAPTER 18   INTEGRATING THIRD-PARTY SERVICES AND APIS

services, such as saving development time, ensuring reliability, and allowing developers to focus on building unique application features.

We then covered working with **REST APIs**, showcasing how to fetch data using both the **Fetch** API and the **Axios** library. Error handling techniques, including retry logic and displaying fallback data, were introduced to improve reliability and user experience. A practical example demonstrated dynamically displaying data while effectively managing loading and error states.

The chapter also introduced **GraphQL** as a more efficient alternative to REST for data fetching. Using **Apollo Client**, we explored how to write queries, handle caching, and fetch precise data fields. A detailed example illustrated integrating Apollo Client into a React application and executing GraphQL queries.

Finally, we walked through integrating Stripe for payment processing. The steps included setting up the Stripe provider, creating a secure payment form, and processing payments with the `createPaymentMethod` function. The chapter concluded with a practical example that integrated a React example with a Firebase database, demonstrating how to build a comprehensive app that handles database interaction.

In the next chapter, we will explore **advanced component patterns** to enhance the scalability, maintainability, and flexibility of your React applications. Topics will include higher-order components, render props, compound components, and controlled vs. uncontrolled components. By mastering these patterns, you'll learn how to create reusable, modular, and efficient components for more robust application development.

CHAPTER 19

Advanced Component Patterns

This chapter delves into advanced component patterns that are vital for crafting scalable, maintainable, and flexible React applications. As applications grow in complexity, understanding and implementing these patterns becomes essential to manage code effectively. These advanced techniques empower developers to build reusable, modular, and efficient components that simplify development while improving application performance and user experience.

By mastering these patterns, developers can tackle intricate UI requirements with confidence, reducing redundancy and enhancing collaboration within teams. Each pattern discussed in this chapter addresses specific challenges faced in large-scale React applications, from sharing logic between components to creating dynamic, context-aware user interfaces. Whether you're building a simple feature or a comprehensive application, these patterns provide the tools and methodologies to achieve optimal results.

In the sections that follow, we will explore Higher-Order Components (HOCs), render props, compound components, controlled and uncontrolled components, and custom hooks. Through detailed explanations and practical examples, you'll learn how to leverage these patterns to design robust and maintainable applications.

CHAPTER 19   ADVANCED COMPONENT PATTERNS

Higher-Order Components (HOCs)

Higher-Order Components (HOCs) are advanced React patterns used to share functionality between components without duplicating code. They are functions that take a component as an argument and return a new component with additional behavior or properties. HOCs are particularly effective for abstracting logic and reusing it across multiple components, promoting cleaner and more maintainable code. For example, consider a scenario where you want to log the mounting of various components. Instead of adding `console.log` statements to each component individually, you can use an HOC to encapsulate this functionality, as demonstrated in Listing 19-1.

HOCs typically wrap components to modify their behavior or inject additional props. The example in Listing 19-1 demonstrates a simple HOC that logs when a component is mounted.

Listing 19-1. Logging Higher-Order Component

```
import React, { useEffect } from "react";
const withLogger = (WrappedComponent) => {
  return function EnhancedComponent(props) {
    useEffect(() => {
      console.log(`Component mounted: ${WrappedComponent.
      displayName || WrappedComponent.name || "Component"}`);
    }, []);
    return <WrappedComponent {...props} />;
  };
};
const ExampleComponent = () => <h2>Hello, World!</h2>;
const EnhancedExample = withLogger(ExampleComponent);
```

```
const App = () => {
  return <EnhancedExample />;
};

export default App;
```

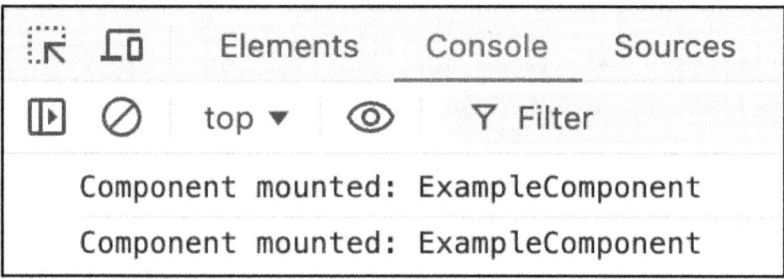

Figure 19-1. Higher-Order Component example

In this example, the `withLogger` HOC takes a `WrappedComponent` as its argument and returns a new component (`EnhancedComponent`). When the enhanced component is mounted, a message is logged to the console as shown in Figure 19-1. This allows you to easily add logging functionality to any component without modifying its implementation.

Use Cases and Limitations

Higher-Order Components (HOCs) are particularly useful for scenarios such as authentication and authorization, where they can ensure that only authorized users can access specific components. They are also widely used for data fetching, enabling developers to centralize logic and share it across multiple components, and for state management, where shared state or context can be injected into components. However, despite their versatility, HOCs come with certain limitations. They can introduce complexity in debugging, especially when multiple HOCs are nested, making it difficult to trace component hierarchies. Additionally, wrapping components with several HOCs can lead to verbose and cluttered code, often referred to as the "wrapper hell" problem, which can reduce code readability and maintainability.

Render Props

Render props is a design pattern that allows components to share logic by using a function passed as a prop. Instead of relying on wrapping components like HOCs, render props give developers the flexibility to define how a component should render based on its logic or state. This pattern promotes reusability and simplifies the sharing of state or logic between components.

A component implementing the render props pattern typically accepts a **function as a prop or child**. This function is responsible for rendering the desired output, based on the state or data managed by the component. Listing 19-2 demonstrates how to use the render props pattern effectively.

Listing 19-2. Mouse Tracker Using Render Props

```
import React, { useState, useEffect } from "react";

const MouseTracker = ({ children }) => {
  const [position, setPosition] = useState({ x: 0, y: 0 });

  useEffect(() => {
    const handleMouseMove = (e) => {
      setPosition({ x: e.clientX, y: e.clientY });
    };
    window.addEventListener("mousemove", handleMouseMove);
    return () => window.removeEventListener("mousemove",
    handleMouseMove);
  }, []);
```

```
    return children(position); // Using `children` instead of
`render`
};
const App = () => {
  return (
    <MouseTracker>
      {(position) => <p>Mouse Position: {position.x},
      {position.y}</p>}
    </MouseTracker>
  );
}
export default App;
```

Mouse Position: 343, 490

Figure 19-2. Render prop example

In this example, the MouseTracker component uses the useState hook to track the mouse position and updates it whenever the mouse moves, using the useEffect hook to manage the event listener. Instead of rendering its output directly, the MouseTracker component delegates the rendering responsibility to the function passed as children as shown in Figure 19-2. This makes the component flexible and reusable, as the parent component can define how the mouse position should be displayed.

Comparing Render Props with HOCs

Render props offer a more explicit and flexible alternative to HOCs. Instead of wrapping components, render props allow logic to be shared directly within the component's structure, making it easier to understand and control. However, they can sometimes lead to verbose or deeply nested code, especially when multiple render prop components are combined. For example, compare this pattern to the HOC approach in Listings 19-1 and 19-2. Render props eliminate the need for wrappers, providing more control over rendering, but at the cost of potentially more verbose JSX.

Compound Components

Compound components are a design pattern in React that allow multiple related components to work together to create flexible and reusable APIs. Instead of hardcoding relationships between parent and child components, compound components communicate implicitly through React's `children` props or Context API. This pattern is particularly effective for building complex, interactive UIs, such as tabs, drop-downs, or form wizards, while maintaining clean and declarative code. The following example demonstrates the parent-child relationship using the compound component pattern. The implementation is detailed in Listing 19-3.

Listing 19-3. Parent-Child Compound Component Illustration

```
import React, { useState } from "react";

// Parent Component
const Parent = ({ children }) => {
  const [value, setValue] = useState("Default Value");

  return (
    <div style={{ border: "1px solid black", padding:
```

```
      "10px" }}>
        <h2>Parent Component</h2>
        {React.Children.map(children, (child) =>
          React.cloneElement(child, { value, setValue })
          // Passing props automatically
        )}
      </div>
  );
}

// Child Component
const Child = ({ value, setValue }) => {
  return (
    <div style={{ marginTop: "10px" }}>
      <p>Child received: {value}</p>
      <button onClick={() => setValue("Updated from Child")}>Update Parent Value</button>
    </div>
  );
}

const App = () => {
  return (
    <Parent>
      <Child />
    </Parent>
  );
}

export default App;
```

CHAPTER 19 ADVANCED COMPONENT PATTERNS

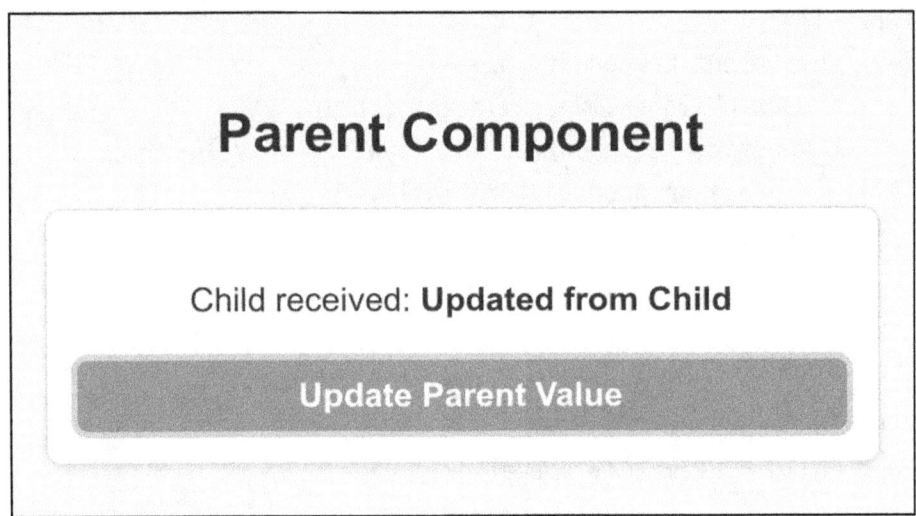

Figure 19-3. Compound component example

In this example, the Parent component maintains the state (value) and provides it to each Child component using React.cloneElement. Each Child receives the current value and a function to update it, ensuring all children remain in sync. When a Child component button is clicked, it updates the value in the Parent, causing all Child components to re-render with the updated state as illustrated in Figure 19-3. This approach enables seamless state sharing and coordination between the Parent and its child components, without requiring explicit prop drilling.

Compound components offer several advantages that make them a powerful pattern for building reusable and flexible UI elements. One key benefit is their clean and declarative API, which allows developers to define relationships between components using children or the Context API. This approach makes the code more intuitive and easier to understand and maintain. Additionally, compound components reduce coupling by enabling implicit interaction through a shared parent context. This minimizes the need for tightly bound dependencies between components, resulting in a more modular and maintainable codebase.

CHAPTER 19   ADVANCED COMPONENT PATTERNS

Controlled and Uncontrolled Components

Controlled and uncontrolled components are two approaches for handling user input in React. Controlled components rely on React to manage their state, ensuring that the component's value is always synchronized with the application's state. On the other hand, uncontrolled components rely on the DOM to manage their state, providing a more straightforward but less reactive solution.

Controlled components are ideal for scenarios where React needs to manage state and validation, such as complex forms or dynamic input fields. Since the component's state is fully controlled by React, developers can easily validate input, track changes, and implement custom logic. Conversely, uncontrolled components are more suitable for simple, unmanaged inputs or cases where you need to interact with non-React libraries. They are quicker to implement for lightweight use cases but offer less control over the component's behavior. Listing 19-4 shows an example of both approaches.

Listing 19-4. Controlled vs. Uncontrolled Input

```
import React, { useState, useRef } from "react";

// Controlled Component
const ControlledInput = () => {
  const [value, setValue] = useState("");

  return (
    <div>
      <h3>Controlled Input</h3>
      <input
        type="text"
        value={value}
        onChange={(e) => setValue(e.target.value)}
      />
```

CHAPTER 19 ADVANCED COMPONENT PATTERNS

```jsx
      <p>Current Value: {value}</p>
    </div>
  );
}
// Uncontrolled Component
const UncontrolledInput = () => {
  const inputRef = useRef();

  const handleSubmit = (e) => {
    e.preventDefault(); // Prevent default form submission
    alert(`Entered Value: ${inputRef.current.value}`);
  };

  return (
    <div>
      <h3>Uncontrolled Input</h3>
      <form onSubmit={handleSubmit}>
        <input type="text" ref={inputRef} />
        <button type="submit">Submit</button>
      </form>
    </div>
  );
}

Const App = () => {
  return (
    <div style={{ padding: "20px" }}>
      <ControlledInput />
      <UncontrolledInput />
    </div>
  );
}

export default App;
```

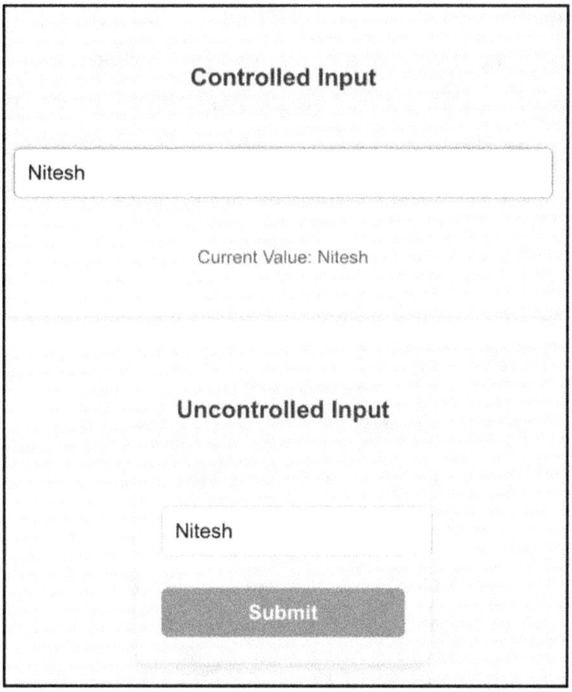

CHAPTER 19 ADVANCED COMPONENT PATTERNS

Figure 19-4. Controlled and uncontrolled component example

In the **ControlledInput** component, the `value` state is updated with every keystroke, keeping the input field synchronized with React's state. This makes it easy to implement validations or dynamic behaviors. In contrast, the **UncontrolledInput** component uses a `ref` to directly access the DOM element. The value is retrieved when needed, such as during form submission, making this approach less tied to React's lifecycle as shown in Figure 19-4.

Custom Hooks

Custom hooks are a powerful feature in React that enable developers to encapsulate and reuse logic across components. By extracting common functionality into custom hooks, developers can reduce redundancy and

CHAPTER 19 ADVANCED COMPONENT PATTERNS

improve code organization. Custom hooks are particularly useful for handling state management, API calls, and performance optimizations, making them an essential tool for building scalable React applications as illustrated in Listing 19-5.

Listing 19-5. Custom Hook for Fetching Data

```
import { useState, useEffect } from "react";
const useFetch = (url) => {
  const [data, setData] = useState(null);
  const [loading, setLoading] = useState(true);
  const [error, setError] = useState(null);

  useEffect(() => {
    let isMounted = true; // Prevents memory leaks if component unmounts

    async function fetchData() {
      try {
        setLoading(true); // Ensure loading state updates on new request
        const response = await fetch(url);
        if (!response.ok) throw new Error(`HTTP Error! Status: ${response.status}`);

        const result = await response.json();
        if (isMounted) setData(result);
      } catch (err) {
        if (isMounted) setError(err.message);
      } finally {
        if (isMounted) setLoading(false);
      }
    }
```

CHAPTER 19 ADVANCED COMPONENT PATTERNS

```
    fetchData();

    return () => {
      isMounted = false; // Cleanup to prevent state updates on
      unmounted component
    };
  }, [url]);

  return { data, loading, error };
}
const App = () => {
  const { data, loading, error } = useFetch("https://
jsonplaceholder.typicode.com/posts");

  if (loading) return <p>Loading...</p>;
  if (error) return <p>Error: {error}</p>;

  return (
    <ul>
 <h2> Custom Hook Fetch Data </h2>
      {data.map((post) => (
        <li key={post.id}>{post.title}</li>
      ))}
    </ul>
  );
}

export default App;
```

CHAPTER 19   ADVANCED COMPONENT PATTERNS

```
┌─────────────────────────────────────────────────────────┐
│                  Custom Hook Fetch Data                 │
│                                                         │
│  ┌───────────────────────────────────────────────────┐  │
│  │ sunt aut facere repellat provident occaecati excepturi optio reprehenderit │  │
│  └───────────────────────────────────────────────────┘  │
│                                                         │
│  ┌───────────────────────────────────────────────────┐  │
│  │                    qui est esse                   │  │
│  └───────────────────────────────────────────────────┘  │
│                                                         │
│  ┌───────────────────────────────────────────────────┐  │
│  │ ea molestias quasi exercitationem repellat qui ipsa sit aut │  │
│  └───────────────────────────────────────────────────┘  │
│                                                         │
│  ┌───────────────────────────────────────────────────┐  │
│  │               eum et est occaecati                │  │
│  └───────────────────────────────────────────────────┘  │
│                                                         │
│  ┌───────────────────────────────────────────────────┐  │
│  │                nesciunt quas odio                 │  │
│  └───────────────────────────────────────────────────┘  │
│                                                         │
└─────────────────────────────────────────────────────────┘
```

Figure 19-5. Custom hook fetch data example

In this example, the `useFetch` hook abstracts the logic for fetching data from an API. It initializes states for `data`, `loading`, and `error` using React's `useState` hook. The `useEffect` hook runs whenever the `url` dependency changes, triggering an asynchronous function to fetch the data. Errors are caught and stored in the `error` state, while the `loading` state tracks the progress of the fetch request. This hook can be reused across multiple components to standardize API interaction and simplify component logic.

Summary

In this chapter, we explored advanced component patterns that empower developers to build scalable, reusable, and maintainable React applications. We began with **Higher-Order Components (HOCs)**, which provide a way to enhance components by wrapping them with additional functionality. We then discussed the **render props** pattern, which enables

CHAPTER 19   ADVANCED COMPONENT PATTERNS

flexible logic sharing through a function prop. Following that, we covered **compound components**, a powerful pattern for building reusable APIs by allowing seamless communication between related components.

Next, we explored the differences between **controlled and uncontrolled components**, understanding when to use each approach for managing form inputs and user interactions. We also delved into **custom hooks**, which encapsulate reusable logic, such as state management and API calls, to simplify component functionality.

By mastering these advanced patterns, developers can create React applications that are modular, maintainable, and efficient, enabling them to tackle complex UI requirements with ease. In the next chapter, we will apply these patterns and concepts to **build a real-world retail store application**, demonstrating how to integrate React fundamentals with real-world requirements.

CHAPTER 20

Building a Real-World Retail Store App

Welcome to the final chapter of this book, where we bring everything together in an exciting, hands-on project! In this chapter, we'll build a **functional retail app** that demonstrates how the concepts you've learned throughout this book come together in a real-world scenario.

This app simulates a simple ecommerce platform and includes the following features:

- A **catalog of products** for users to browse
- A **product details page** with more information about each item
- A **shopping cart** for users to add, view, and manage selected items
- A **checkout process** where users can simulate payments using a mock payment gateway

To accomplish this, we'll use

- **React Router** to create a seamless navigation experience.

- **Redux** to handle application state, such as managing the cart
- **Stripe** to integrate a mock payment system in test mode

Rather than overwhelming you with the entire codebase, we'll walk through each feature step by step. You'll learn how to design reusable components, manage application-wide state, and handle navigation between different pages. Along the way, we'll also discuss best practices for organizing and structuring your code.

For those eager to dive deeper, the **full source code** of this app is available on our GitHub repository. You can use it to experiment, extend the functionality, and explore all the details that we might not cover explicitly in this chapter.

By the end of this chapter, you'll have a fully functional retail app and a deeper understanding of how to apply React concepts in a practical, real-world project. Let's dive in and build something amazing!

Setting Up the Project

To build our retail app, we need to set up the project environment, install required dependencies, and organize the folder structure. Follow these steps to prepare the groundwork for our app.

1. **Initialize the project**
   We will use `create-react-app` to quickly scaffold our React project. Run the commands in your terminal as illustrated in Listing 20-1.

Listing 20-1. Initializing the React App

```
npx create-react-app retail-app
cd retail-app
```

CHAPTER 20   BUILDING A REAL-WORLD RETAIL STORE APP

This command creates a new folder named retail-app with all the boilerplate code for a React application.

> **Note**   Ensure that Node.js and npm (or Yarn) are installed on your system. You can verify this by running node -v and npm -v.

2. **Install the required dependencies**
   To add routing, state management, and payment integration, install the dependencies in Listing 20-2.

Listing 20-2. Installing Required Dependencies

```
npm install react-router-dom redux react-redux @stripe/stripe-js @stripe/react-stripe-js
```

The react-router-dom library is used to enable seamless navigation between pages in our application, allowing users to move between product listings, details, the cart, and the checkout process. To manage the application-wide state, particularly for features like the shopping cart, we will use redux along with react-redux, which provides bindings for integrating Redux with React. Additionally, to simulate a payment system, we will use @stripe/stripe-js and @stripe/react-stripe-js, which facilitate integrating Stripe's payment gateway in test mode.

Folder Structure

To keep the project organized and scalable, we'll structure it as shown below. This structure separates reusable components, pages, state management (Redux slices), and data into different directories as in Figure 20-1.

379

CHAPTER 20   BUILDING A REAL-WORLD RETAIL STORE APP

```
src/
  components/
  pages/
  redux/
  data/
  utils/
  App.js
  index.js
  styles.css
```

Figure 20-1. Folder structure

- `components/`: Contains reusable UI components. These are independent building blocks, like `ProductCard`, `CheckoutForm`, and `NavBar`, which display individual product information.

- `pages/`: Contains page-level components, such as `HomePage`, `ProductDetailsPage`, `CartPage`, `CheckoutPage`, and `ConfirmationPage`. Each of these represents a route in the application.

- `redux/`: Contains Redux slices for managing global state, such as the shopping cart.

- `data/`: Holds static mock data for the products we will display in the app. This avoids the need for a back end or database.

- `utils/` (Optional): Helper functions, such as formatting utilities, can be added here if needed.

Why This Structure?

This folder structure is designed to promote reusability and scalability:

- **Modular Organization**: Each folder has a clear purpose, making it easy to locate and manage files as the app grows.

- **Separation of Concerns**: Components, state management, and static data are isolated for better maintainability.

- **Future Scalability**: If new features are added, such as user authentication, they can be easily accommodated without restructuring.

Adding Mock Data

To simulate product listings in our retail app, we will use mock data stored locally in a separate file. This approach allows us to focus on building and displaying the app's functionality without requiring a back end or database.

Creating the Mock Data File

1. **Create the** `data` **folder:**
   Inside the `src` directory, create a folder named `data` to store our mock data.

2. **Create the** `products.js` **file:**
   Inside the `data` folder, create a file named `products.js` and add the following code:

   ```
   const products = [
   ```

CHAPTER 20 BUILDING A REAL-WORLD RETAIL STORE APP

```
  { id: 1, name: "Laptop", price: 999,
  image: "/images/laptop.jpg" },
  { id: 2, name: "Phone", price: 499,
  image: "/images/phone.jpg" },
  { id: 3, name: "Headphones", price: 199,
  image: "/images/headphones.jpg" },
  { id: 4, name: "Smart Watch", price: 299,
  image: "/images/smart-watch.jpg" },
  { id: 5, name: "Tablet", price: 399, image:
  "/images/tablet.jpg" },
  { id: 6, name: "Gaming Console", price: 499,
  image: "/images/gaming-console.jpg" },
  { id: 7, name: "Wireless Mouse", price: 49,
  image: "/images/wireless-mouse.jpg" },
  { id: 8, name: "Bluetooth Speaker",
  price: 149, image: "/images/bluetooth-speaker.jpg" },
  { id: 9, name: "External Hard Drive", price: 89,
  image: "/images/external-hard-drive.jpg" },
  { id: 10, name: "Camera", price: 599, image:
  "/images/camera.jpg" },
];

export default products;
```

The mock data includes several key properties for each product. The `id` serves as a unique identifier, ensuring that each product can be individually referenced and managed within the app. The `name` represents the product's title, making it easily recognizable to users. The `price` specifies the cost of the product in USD, providing essential information for customers. Lastly, the `image` property points to the file path of the product's image, which will be stored in the `public/images` folder. This ensures that the app can display visual representations of the products alongside their details.

Organizing Product Images

To display product images in our app, store all the image files in the `public/images` directory. Ensure the following image files are saved in the directory:

- `laptop.jpg`
- `phone.jpg`
- `headphones.jpg`
- `smart-watch.jpg`
- `tablet.jpg`
- `gaming-console.jpg`
- `wireless-mouse.jpg`
- `bluetooth-speaker.jpg`
- `external-hard-drive.jpg`
- `camera.jpg`

The `public` folder is accessible from the root of the app, making the image paths in the products array (e.g., `/images/laptop.jpg`) functional without any additional configuration. This structure ensures that product images are easily accessible and can be displayed seamlessly across the application.

How Mock Data Fits into the App

The mock data will be used to

- Populate the product listing on the **HomePage**
- Provide details for the **ProductDetailsPage**
- Enable adding products to the shopping cart

This simple, static data source ensures we can focus on front-end functionality while maintaining flexibility for future enhancements like integrating real APIs. In the next section, we'll use this mock data to build the product listing page and display individual product cards.

Building Core Pages and Components

In this section, we will create the core pages and components of our retail app: the **Home Page**, the **Product Card component**, and the **Product Details Page**. These form the foundation of our application, allowing users to browse products, view their details, and prepare for the checkout process.

Product Page (Home)

The **Home Page** is the entry point of the app where users can browse all available products in a grid layout. The page dynamically renders each product using the reusable `ProductCard` component. We use the products array, imported from the mock data, to list all the products. By iterating through this array using the `map()` function, each product is passed as a prop to the `ProductCard` component. The grid layout is styled using Tailwind CSS for a visually appealing arrangement. Listing 20-3 shows the implementation of the **Home Page**.

Listing 20-3. Home Page: `src/pages/HomePage.js`

```
import React from "react";
import products from "./data/product";
import ProductCard from "./components/ProductCard";
import Navbar from "./components/NavBar";

const HomePage = () => {
```

CHAPTER 20   BUILDING A REAL-WORLD RETAIL STORE APP

```
  return (
    <div className="px-6 py-4 max-w-4xl mx-auto">
      <Navbar />
      <h1 className="text-2xl font-bold text-center mb-6"
      >Products</h1>
      {/* Responsive Grid: Max 2 items per row */}
      <div className="grid grid-cols-1 sm:grid-cols-2 gap-6">
        {products.map((product) => (
          <ProductCard key={product.id} product={product} />
        ))}
      </div>
    </div>
  );
};

export default HomePage;
```

Product Card

The ProductCard component is a reusable building block for displaying each product's information. It receives the product object as a prop, which contains the product's name, price, and image. The card uses this information to render a product's details in an attractive, standardized layout. Each card also includes a "View Detail" button which takes you to the product details page. This component ensures modularity, making it reusable across different pages, such as the Home Page and Product Details Page. Listing 20-4 shows the implementation of the ProductCard component.

Listing 20-4. Product Card: src/components/ProductCard.js

```
import React from "react";
import { Link } from "react-router-dom";
```

```jsx
const ProductCard = ({ product }) => {
  return (
    <div className="bg-white rounded-lg shadow-md p-4 w-64 flex
    flex-col items-center text-center transform transition
    duration-200 hover:scale-105 hover:shadow-lg">
      {/* Product Image */}
      <img
        src={product.image}
        alt={product.name}
        className="w-full h-44 object-cover rounded-md mb-3"
      />

      {/* Product Name */}
      <h3 className="text-lg font-semibold text-gray-800">
      {product.name}</h3>

      {/* Price */}
      <p className="text-gray-600 text-base mb-3">${product.
      price}</p>

      {/* View Details Button */}
      <Link to={`product/${product.id}`} className="w-full">
        <button className="w-full bg-blue-500 text-white
        px-4 py-2 rounded-md text-sm font-medium transition
        hover:bg-
        blue-600">
          View Details
        </button>
      </Link>
    </div>
  );
};

export default ProductCard;
```

CHAPTER 20 BUILDING A REAL-WORLD RETAIL STORE APP

Product Details Page

The **Product Details Page** provides detailed information about a selected product. This page uses React Router's useParams hook to retrieve the product ID from the URL. The products array is searched to find the corresponding product based on the id. If the product is found, its name, image, and price are displayed, along with an "Add to Cart" button. If no product matches the provided ID, an error message stating "Product not found" is displayed. This page demonstrates dynamic routing and conditional rendering, making it an essential part of the user experience. Listing 20-5 shows the implementation of the **Product Details Page**.

Listing 20-5. Product Details Page: src/pages/ProductDetailsPage.js

```
import React from "react";
import { useParams, useNavigate } from "react-router-dom";
import { useDispatch } from "react-redux";
import { addToRetailCart } from "../../store/retailCartSlice";
import { toast } from "react-toastify";
import products from "./data/product";
import Navbar from "./components/NavBar";

const ProductDetailsPage = () => {
  const { id } = useParams();
  const navigate = useNavigate();
  const dispatch = useDispatch();
  const product = products.find((p) => p.id === parseInt(id));

  if (!product) return <h2 className="text-center text-red-500 text-xl">Product not found</h2>;

  const handleAddToCart = () => {
    dispatch(addToRetailCart(product));
```

CHAPTER 20   BUILDING A REAL-WORLD RETAIL STORE APP

```
    toast.success(`${product.name} added to cart!`);
};

return (
  <div className="bg-gray-100">
    <Navbar />
    <div className="flex flex-col items-center px-4 py-6">
      <div className="flex flex-col md:flex-row items-center
      bg-white shadow-lg rounded-lg p-6 max-w-3xl w-full">
        {/* Product Image */}
        <img
          src={product.image}
          alt={product.name}
          className="w-64 h-64 object-cover rounded-lg
          border-2 border-gray-300 mb-4 md:mb-0 md:mr-6"
        />

        {/* Product Info */}
        <div className="flex flex-col items-center md:
        items-start text-center md:text-left">
          <h1 className="text-2xl font-bold text-
          gray-800">{product.name} Details</h1>
          <p className="text-xl text-gray-600 my-2">
            Price: <strong>${product.price}</strong>
          </p>

          {/* Buttons */}
          <div className="flex flex-col md:flex-row gap-4
          mt-4 w-full">
            <button
              onClick={handleAddToCart}
              className="bg-green-500 text-white px-5 py-3
              rounded-lg w-full md:w-auto text-lg font-medium
              transition hover:bg-green-600"
```

CHAPTER 20   BUILDING A REAL-WORLD RETAIL STORE APP

```
          >
            🛒 Shop
          </button>
          <button
            onClick={() => navigate(-1)}
            className="flex items-center text-blue-500
            hover:text-blue-700"
          >
            ← Back
          </button>
        </div>
      </div>
    </div>
  </div>
  );
};

export default ProductDetailsPage;
```

These core pages and components establish the user interface for browsing and interacting with products. In the next section, we will implement shopping cart functionality using **Redux** to enable state management across the app.

State Management with Redux

In this section, we will implement state management in our app using **Redux**. Redux allows us to manage global application state, such as the shopping cart, making it easier to share data between components. We will define a Redux store and Redux slice for managing cart functionality and connect it to our React application.

CHAPTER 20   BUILDING A REAL-WORLD RETAIL STORE APP

Setting Up Redux

To set up Redux, we need to define the state and actions for the shopping cart and integrate Redux with our React app.

1. Creating the Store

The `store.js` file in Listing 20-6 will configure the Redux store and combine all the reducers. This is particularly useful when you have multiple slices for managing different parts of the state.

Listing 20-6. Creating store.js: `src/redux/store.js`

```
import { configureStore } from '@reduxjs/toolkit';
import retailCartReducer from "./retailCartSlice";

const store = configureStore({
  reducer: {
    retailCart: retailCartReducer,
  },
});

export default store;
```

The `configureStore` function is used to create the Redux store with the required reducers. In this setup, the `retailCartReducer` is included under the `retailCart` key in the `reducer` object, allowing the store to manage the cart's state. By creating a dedicated `store.js` file, we establish a centralized entry point for managing all reducers. This setup simplifies state management, making it easier to add additional slices, such as `userSlice` or `productSlice`, in the future. This approach also enhances scalability, ensuring that the Redux store remains easy to configure and maintain as the application grows in complexity.

CHAPTER 20   BUILDING A REAL-WORLD RETAIL STORE APP

2. Creating the Retail Slice

The retailCartSlice will handle all cart-related actions, such as adding items to the cart, updating quantities, and removing items. This is implemented using the createSlice utility from Redux Toolkit, which simplifies the process of managing state and actions. In the src/redux folder, create a file named retailCartSlice.js and add the code shown in Listing 20-7.

Listing 20-7. Cart Slice: src/redux/retailCartSlice.js

```
import { createSlice } from '@reduxjs/toolkit';

// Load cart from localStorage to persist state
const loadCartFromStorage = () => {
  try {
    const cartData = localStorage.getItem("retailCart");
    return cartData ? JSON.parse(cartData) : [];
  } catch (error) {
    console.error("Error loading cart from localStorage:", error);
    return [];
  }
};

const initialState = {
  retailCart: loadCartFromStorage(), // Separate cart for retail app
};

const retailCartSlice = createSlice({
  name: 'retailCart',
  initialState,
  reducers: {
```

```
    addToRetailCart: (state, action) => {
      const existingItem = state.retailCart.find((item) =>
      item.id === action.payload.id);
      if (existingItem) {
        existingItem.quantity += 1;
      } else {
        state.retailCart.push({ ...action.payload,
        quantity: 1 });
      }
      localStorage.setItem("retailCart", JSON.stringify(state.
      retailCart));  // Save to separate localStorage key
    },
    removeFromRetailCart: (state, action) => {
      state.retailCart = state.retailCart.filter((item) =>
      item.id !== action.payload.id);
      localStorage.setItem("retailCart", JSON.stringify
      (state.retailCart));
    },
    clearRetailCart: (state) => {
      state.retailCart = [];
      localStorage.removeItem("retailCart");  // Clear only
                                                retail cart
    },
  },
});

export const { addToRetailCart, removeFromRetailCart,
clearRetailCart } = retailCartSlice.actions;
export default retailCartSlice.reducer;
```

The retail cart slice begins with an initial state where the `items` array is empty, representing an empty shopping cart. The reducers within the slice handle the cart's primary actions. The `addToRetailCart` reducer adds a new item to the cart or increments the quantity of an existing item if it is already in the cart. The `removeFromRetailCart` reducer, on the other hand, removes an item from the cart by filtering out the item with the specified ID. Both reducers ensure that the cart's state is managed dynamically based on user actions. Finally, the `addToRetailCart` and `removeFromRetailCart` actions are exported from the slice, making them accessible for use in the app's components to interact with the cart's state effectively.

3. Connecting Redux to the App

To use the cart slice, we need to set up the Redux store and provide it to the React app. The store will manage the global state and make it accessible to all components. Update the `src/index.js` file as shown in Listing 20-8.

Listing 20-8. Connecting Redux Store: `src/index.js`

```
import React from "react";
import ReactDOM from "react-dom";
import { Provider } from "react-redux";
import store from "./redux/store";
import App from "./App";

ReactDOM.render(
  <Provider store={store}>
    <App />
  </Provider>,
  document.getElementById("root")
);
```

The Redux store is created using the `configureStore` function, which initializes the store with the `retailCartReducer`. This reducer manages the cart's state, handling actions such as adding or removing items. To make the Redux store accessible throughout the application, the `Provider` component from `react-redux` is used. By wrapping the `App` component with the `Provider`, the store is passed down to all child components, enabling them to access and interact with the global state seamlessly. This setup ensures efficient state management across the app.

Now that Redux is set up, we can integrate the cart functionality into our app. In the next section, we will build the **Cart Page**, which will display the items in the cart, along with options to update quantities or remove items. Finally, we will integrate the **Checkout Page** with Stripe to enable a simulated payment process. This will complete the core functionality of our retail app.

Checkout with Stripe

In this section, we will implement a **checkout process** for our app, enabling users to add items to their cart and proceed to checkout. Using Stripe's test mode, we will simulate payment functionality. Finally, we will create the **Cart Page**, **Checkout Page**, and **Checkout Form** to handle payment processing.

1. Installing Stripe Dependencies

Before integrating Stripe, ensure the required libraries are installed. These libraries enable secure payment handling and integration with Stripe's API as shown in Listing 20-9.

Listing 20-9. Installing Stripe Libraries

```
npm install @stripe/stripe-js @stripe/react-stripe-js
```

This command installs the core Stripe library (`@stripe/stripe-js`) and its React integration (`@stripe/react-stripe-js`), which we will use to build the payment form.

2. Cart Page

The **Cart Page** enables users to review their selected items, adjust quantities, and remove products before proceeding to checkout. Serving as a crucial step between adding items to the cart and finalizing a purchase, it enhances the overall shopping experience. In this section, we will implement the **Cart Page** and integrate it with **Redux** to manage the cart state efficiently. Additionally, it will display the total price and include a **Checkout** button, as illustrated in Listing 20-10.

Listing 20-10. Cart Page: `src/pages/CartPage.js`

```
import React from "react";
import { useSelector, useDispatch } from "react-redux";
import { removeFromRetailCart, clearRetailCart } from "../../
store/retailCartSlice";
import { useNavigate } from "react-router-dom";

const CartPage = () => {
  const cart = useSelector((state) => state.retailCart.
  retailCart);
  const dispatch = useDispatch();
  const navigate = useNavigate();

  const handleRemove = (id) => {
    dispatch(removeFromRetailCart({ id }));
```

```
};

const handleContinueShopping = () => {
  navigate("/example/34/"); // Redirect back to product page
};

const totalPrice = cart.reduce((total, item) => total + item.
price * item.quantity, 0);

return (
  <div className="flex flex-col items-center bg-gray-100
  py-8 px-4">
    <h1 className="text-3xl font-bold text-gray-800 mb-6">
    Your Cart</h1>

    {cart.length === 0 ? (
      <div className="bg-white shadow-md p-6 rounded-lg
      text-center">
        <p className="text-gray-600 text-lg">Your cart is
        empty. Start shopping now!</p>
        <button
          className="mt-4 px-6 py-3 bg-blue-500 text-
          white font-medium rounded-lg hover:bg-blue-600
          transition"
          onClick={handleContinueShopping}
        >
          🛍 Continue Shopping
        </button>
      </div>
    ) : (
      <div className="w-full max-w-3xl bg-white shadow-lg
      rounded-lg p-6">
        {/* Cart Items List */}
```

```jsx
<div className="space-y-6">
  {cart.map((item) => (
    <div key={item.id} className="flex items-center
    justify-between bg-gray-100 p-4 rounded-lg
    shadow-sm">
        <img src={item.image} alt={item.name}
        className="w-20 h-20 object-cover rounded-md
        border" />

        {/* Added fixed width here */}
        <div className="w-64 ml-4">
          <h3 className="text-lg font-semibold
          text-gray-700">{item.name}</h3>
          <p className="text-gray-600">Qty: {item.
          quantity}</p>
          <p className="text-gray-800 font-bold">$
          {(item.price * item.quantity).toFixed(2)}
          </p>
        </div>

        {/* Remove button no longer stretches */}
        <button
          className="px-3 py-2 w-24 bg-red-500
          text-white rounded-md hover:bg-red-600
          transition text-sm font-medium"
          onClick={() => handleRemove(item.id)}
        >
          ✖ Remove
        </button>
    </div>
  ))}
</div>
```

```jsx
{/* Total Price */}
<h2 className="text-2xl font-bold text-gray-900 mt-6
text-center">Total: ${totalPrice.toFixed(2)}</h2>

{/* Buttons */}
<div className="flex flex-col sm:flex-row gap-4 mt-6
justify-center">
  <button
    className="px-6 py-3 bg-gray-500 text-white
    font-medium rounded-lg hover:bg-gray-600
    transition w-full sm:w-auto"
    onClick={() => dispatch(clearRetailCart())}
  >
    🗑 Clear Cart
  </button>
  <button
    className="px-6 py-3 bg-blue-500 text-white
    font-medium rounded-lg hover:bg-blue-600
    transition w-full sm:w-auto"
    onClick={handleContinueShopping}
  >
    🛍 Continue Shopping
  </button>
  <button
    className="px-6 py-3 bg-green-500 text-white
    font-medium rounded-lg hover:bg-green-600
    transition w-full sm:w-auto"
    onClick={() => navigate("/example/34/checkout")}
  >
    💳 Checkout
  </button>
</div>
```

```
        </div>
      )}
    </div>
  );
};

export default CartPage;
```

The **Cart Page** integrates seamlessly with Redux to manage and display cart items. The `useSelector` hook retrieves the list of cart items from the Redux store, ensuring the page dynamically reflects the current state of the cart. The `useDispatch` hook is used to dispatch the `removeFromRetailCart` action, enabling users to remove items from the cart with ease. The total price is calculated dynamically by iterating over the cart items and summing up the product of each item's price and quantity using the `reduce()` method, providing users with an accurate total cost.

The page is designed to handle both empty and populated cart states effectively. If the cart is empty, a user-friendly message is displayed, along with a link to return to the Product Home Page to continue shopping. If there are items in the cart, they are presented in a detailed list, showing the product name, quantity, price, and an option to remove items. Additionally, a "Checkout" button is provided, linking users to the Checkout Page (`/checkout`), where they can finalize their purchase. This structured design ensures a smooth and intuitive shopping.

3. Creating the Checkout Page

The **Checkout Page** in Listing 20-11 is where users can review their cart items and input payment details. It uses Stripe's `Elements` component to provide the payment context to its child components, such as the **Checkout Form**.

Listing 20-11. Checkout Page: src/page/CheckoutPage.js

```
import React from "react";
import { useSelector } from "react-redux";
import { Elements } from "@stripe/react-stripe-js";
import { loadStripe } from "@stripe/stripe-js";
import CheckoutForm from "./components/CheckoutForm";

const stripePromise = loadStripe("your-stripe-public-key-here");

const CheckoutPage = () => {
  const cart = useSelector((state) => state.retailCart.retailCart);
  const totalPrice = cart.reduce((total, item) => total + item.price * item.quantity, 0);

  return (
    <div className="min-h-screen flex flex-col items-center bg-gray-100 py-10 px-4">
      <h1 className="text-3xl font-bold text-blue-600 mb-4">Checkout</h1>
      <h2 className="text-xl font-semibold text-gray-700 mb-6">Total: ${totalPrice.toFixed(2)}</h2>

      {/* Stripe Elements Wrapper */}
      <div className="w-full max-w-md bg-white shadow-md rounded-lg p-6">
        <Elements stripe={stripePromise}>
          <CheckoutForm />
        </Elements>
      </div>
```

```
    </div>
  );
};

export default CheckoutPage;
```

The **Checkout Page** serves as the entry point for the payment process. It initializes Stripe using the `loadStripe` function and wraps the payment form in the `Elements` component, which provides a secure Stripe context. By encapsulating the **checkout form** within the Stripe environment, we ensure that sensitive payment details are handled securely and in compliance with industry standards.

4. Creating the Checkout Form

The **CheckoutForm** component in Listing 20-12 handles the payment form and submission logic. Users can input their card details using Stripe's `CardElement`.

Listing 20-12. Checkout Form: `src/components/CheckoutForm.js`

```
import React, { useState } from "react";
import { useStripe, useElements, CardElement } from "@stripe/react-stripe-js";
import { useDispatch } from "react-redux";
import { clearRetailCart } from "../../../store/retailCartSlice";
import { useNavigate } from "react-router-dom";

const CheckoutForm = () => {
  const stripe = useStripe();
  const elements = useElements();
  const dispatch = useDispatch();
  const navigate = useNavigate();
```

CHAPTER 20   BUILDING A REAL-WORLD RETAIL STORE APP

```
  const [isProcessing, setIsProcessing] = useState(false);
  const [message, setMessage] = useState("");

  const handleSubmit = async (event) => {
    event.preventDefault();

    if (!stripe || !elements) {
      return;
    }

    setIsProcessing(true);

    // Mock Payment Intent (replace with backend API call in
    real-world)
    setTimeout(() => {
      setIsProcessing(false);
      dispatch(clearRetailCart());
      navigate("/example/34/confirmation");
    }, 2000);
  };

  return (
    <form onSubmit={handleSubmit} className="bg-white shadow-lg
    rounded-lg p-6 max-w-md w-full">
      <h2 className="text-xl font-semibold text-gray-800
      mb-4">Enter Payment Details</h2>

      {/* Card Element Wrapper */}
      <div className="border border-gray-300 rounded-md
      p-3 mb-4">
        <CardElement className="w-full" />
      </div>

      {/* Payment Button */}
      <button
```

```
              type="submit"
              disabled={!stripe || isProcessing}
              className={`w-full py-3 rounded-md text-white font-
              semibold transition ${
                 isProcessing ? "bg-gray-400 cursor-not-allowed" :
                 "bg-blue-500 hover:bg-blue-600"
              }`}
           >
              {isProcessing ? "Processing..." : "💳 Pay Now"}
           </button>

           {/* Error Message */}
           {message && <p className="text-red-600 text-center
           mt-3">{message}</p>}
        </form>
     );
};

export default CheckoutForm;
```

The CheckoutForm component handles the user interaction for entering payment details and submitting the payment. It uses Stripe's CardElement component, which provides a secure and customizable input field for credit card information. The useStripe and useElements hooks simplify interaction with Stripe's API. To provide a better user experience, the isProcessing state is used to disable the form during submission, preventing multiple payments. Figure 20-2 shows the Cart Page.

CHAPTER 20   BUILDING A REAL-WORLD RETAIL STORE APP

Figure 20-2. Cart Page illustration

Routing

Routing is an essential part of our app, enabling users to navigate between different pages seamlessly. In this section, we will set up routes for our application using **React Router**. The routes will allow users to access the **Home Page**, the **Product Details Page**, and, later, additional pages like the **Cart Page** and **Checkout Page**.

Adding Routes

To enable routing, we use react-router-dom to define the paths for different components. We'll configure routes in the src/App.js file, as shown in Listing 20-13.

CHAPTER 20 BUILDING A REAL-WORLD RETAIL STORE APP

Listing 20-13. Setting Up Routes in `src/App.js`

```
import { BrowserRouter as Router, Routes, Route } from "react-router-dom";
import HomePage from "./pages/HomePage";
import ProductDetailsPage from "./pages/ProductDetailsPage";
import CartPage from "./pages/CartPage";
import CheckoutPage from "./pages/CheckoutPage";

const App = () => (
  <Router>
    <Routes>
      <Route path="/" element={<HomePage />} />
      <Route path="/product/:id" element={<ProductDetailsPage />} />
      <Route path="/cart" element={<CartPage />} />
      <Route path="/checkout" element={<CheckoutPage />} />
    </Routes>
  </Router>
);

export default App;
```

1. **React Router Setup**

    - The Router component wraps the application and enables routing. It ensures that the routes defined within the app are properly handled by React Router.

2. **Routes**

    - The Routes component contains all the defined Route components, each specifying a path and the corresponding component to render.

3. **Home Page Route**
   - The / path is linked to the HomePage component, allowing users to view the list of products as soon as they open the app.

4. **Product Details Route**
   - The /product/:id path is linked to the ProductDetailsPage component. The :id is a dynamic segment, allowing React Router to pass the product ID from the URL to the component via useParams.

5. **Dynamic Navigation**
   - With this setup, users can navigate to a specific product's details by visiting a URL such as /product/1, where 1 corresponds to the product ID.

Deployment

In this section, we will deploy our React app to a hosting provider, making it accessible to users. We'll focus on deploying the app to popular platforms like **Netlify**, which offer seamless integration for modern web apps.

1. Building the App

Before deploying, we need to create an optimized production build of the application. This is done using the following command.

Build the App

```
npm run build
```

The `npm run build` command generates a `build` folder in the project directory, which contains all the static files necessary for deployment. These files include minified JavaScript, optimized CSS, and other assets that are ready for production use. It is important to ensure there are no errors during the build process. If any issues occur, carefully review the console output, identify the problems, and resolve them before proceeding with the deployment.

2. Deploying to Netlify

Step 1: Sign Up/Log In to Netlify

- Visit Netlify and create an account if you don't already have one.
- Once logged in, go to the Netlify dashboard.

Step 2: Create a New Site

- Click the "Add New Site" or "New Site from Git" button.
- You can either connect a GitHub repository or manually upload the build folder.

Step 3: Manual Deployment

- If you prefer manual deployment
    1. Drag and drop the build folder into the Netlify dashboard.
    2. Netlify will process the files and generate a unique URL for your app.

Step 4: Configure the Domain (Optional)

- You can configure a custom domain for your app by linking it to Netlify from the domain settings.

3. Testing the Deployed App

After deploying, open the provided URL (e.g., https://your-app-name.netlify.app) in your browser and test the app. Ensure the following features work correctly:

- Navigation between pages
- Adding items to the cart and updating quantities
- Proceeding to the checkout and completing a payment simulation

Summary

Congratulations on reaching the end of this book! Together, we've built a fully functional retail app, incorporating essential concepts of React, Redux for state management, routing with React Router, and a seamless checkout experience using Stripe. Throughout this journey, we've walked through the key steps required to create a robust, modern web application while emphasizing modularity, scalability, and best practices in React development.

For the complete source code, you can access the GitHub repository. This project is just the beginning—you now have a solid foundation to build upon. Consider extending the app by adding advanced features such as filtering and sorting products, implementing search functionality, or persisting the cart data using localStorage or a back-end service. These enhancements will not only improve the app but also deepen your understanding of full-stack development.

Thank you for following along, and we hope this book has empowered you to create even more dynamic and interactive applications in the future. Happy coding!

Index

A

Accessibility, 144
    challenges, 302
    definition, 302
    form, 304–306
    implementation, 303–307
    principles, 301
    testing, 164, 307 (*see also* Testing accessibility)
Accessible Rich Internet Applications (ARIA), 302, 303
Add-to-cart functionality, 123–125
Apollo Client, 337, 347
App component, 4–6, 10, 58, 394
ARIA, *see* Accessible Rich Internet Applications (ARIA)
Array indices, 110
Assistive technologies, 303, 307
Asynchronous validation, 224
Authentication, 287, 288
Automated testing
    accessibility, 308–310
    CI/CD process, 330, 331
AWS Amplify, 317, 323
Axe DevTools, 301, 307, 316
Axios, 337, 342–344
axios.get() method, 344

B

Backend-as-a-Service (BaaS), 355
Block Element Modifier (BEM), 164, 165
Blog application, 241, 245
Bootstrap, 143, 159, 161, 162
Bracket Pair Colorizer, 36
Broadcast data, 184
Broken authentication, 299
BrowserRouter component, 230, 231
Build directory structure, 321, 322
Burp Suite, 299
Button component, 4, 128

C

Callback functions, 57, 250
Calling functions, 75, 76
CardElement component, 354
cart.map function, 201
Cart page, 395–399, 404
Checkout form, 220–224, 401–403
Checkout page, 399–401
CI/CD, *see* Continuous integration and deployment (CI/CD)
Class components, 4, 46, 47, 53, 55, 92, 93, 128, 132

© Nitesh Upadhyaya 2025
N. Upadhyaya, *Advanced Front-End Development*,
https://doi.org/10.1007/979-8-8688-1318-4

INDEX

Class name collisions, 146
Cleanup function, 177–180
Client-side validation, 212–214
Code bloat, 161
Code minification, 319
Code splitting, 252, 253
Complex data structures, 113–115
Component-based approach
   advantages, 128
   best practices, 135
   challenges, 140, 141
   create, 44
   definition, 43
   designing shopping cart page
     CartSummary component, 138
     composing page, 138
     header component, 136
     modular components, 136
     output, 140
     product component, 137
     ProductList component, 137
   folder structure, 44
   props, 48–51
   reusability and composition, 133, 134
   steps, 129–131
   types, 44–47, 131, 132
   understanding, 127, 128
Component-based architecture, 3–7
componentDidCatch method, 169
componentDidMount, 16, 170, 174
componentDidUpdate, 16, 171
componentWillUnmount, 171
Composition, 133, 134
Compound components, 366–368
Conditional rendering, 12, 75, 80, 85, 89, 90, 104, 387
   user experience, 96
   using if statements, 96, 97
   using logical && operator, 98
   using ternary operator, 97
configureStore function, 189, 190, 390, 394
Conflict-free approach, 151
Consistency, 160, 164
constructor, 170
Context API, 193, 254
Continuous integration and deployment (CI/CD), 317
   automated testing and linting, 330, 331
   definition, 326
   GitHub Actions, 326–330
   pipelines, 298, 318
   workflow configuration, 327
   workflow file location, 327
Contrast ratios, 144, 164
Controlled components, 203–205, 207, 369–371
Counter slice, 191
createPaymentMethod function, 354, 359
Create-react-app tool
   configuration, 25
   create first React app, 25, 26
   file structure, 27, 28

INDEX

initial terminal output, 26
running development
    server, 28–30
stopping server, 30
success message, 26
terminal output, 29
understanding project
    structure, 27, 28
Credit card numbers, 294, 295
Cross-Site Request Forgery (CSRF),
    281, 282, 292, 293
Cross-Site Scripting (XSS), 281,
    282, 285, 299
CSRF, *see* Cross-Site Request
    Forgery (CSRF)
CSRF token implementation, 293
CSS-in-JS libraries
    definition, 152
    dynamic styling, 153, 154
    styled-components and
        emotion, 152
    template literals, 153
    theming support, 154, 155
CSS media queries, 144, 161
CSS modules
    advantages, 151
    definition, 149
    disadvantages, 151
    implementation, 150, 151
CSS styling, 104
Custom Hooks, 15, 16, 371–374
Cyber threats, 299
Cypress, 267, 269, 273, 274, 279
cy.visit function, 274

D

Data protection
    encryption, 293, 294
    masking sensitive information,
        294, 295
Data Source Name (DSN), 333
Declarative navigation, 233
Declarative programming
    paradigm, 71
Declarative syntax
    defined, 11
    reasons, 12
Default props, 51, 57, 58
Dependency management,
    295–296, 300
Deployment
    building app, 407
    considerations, 317
    creating build process, 321, 322
    environment variables, 320, 321
    Netlify, 323, 324, 407, 408
    optimization, 319, 320
    platforms, 317, 323
    security, 296, 297
    testing, 408
    Vercel, 324, 325
    workflow process, 328
Destructure props, 57
Diffing, 8, 10, 248
Document Object Model (DOM), 8
DOMPurify, 284, 285
DOMPurify.sanitize function, 285
Dynamic lists, 111–113

413

INDEX

Dynamic parameter with
useParams, 232
Dynamic routing, 232, 234,
244, 245, 387
Dynamic styling, 148, 153, 154

E

Encryption, 293, 294
End-to-end (E2E) testing,
266, 272–274
Environment variables, 320, 321
Error handling, 239, 241, 344, 346
Error tracking
needs, 331, 332
Sentry, 332–334
ES7 React, 36
Escaping output, 285–287
ESLint, 36, 297, 298
Event handling
class components, 92, 93
combined event, 209, 211
definition, 90
form submission and logout
actions, 104–106
functional components, 90, 91
onChange event, 207, 208
onSubmit event, 208, 209
passing parameters
arrow functions, 94
conditional rendering, 96–98
context-specific actions, 93
multiple parameters, 95
user greeting, 94
Event object, 211

F

Fallback mechanism, 239
Fetch API, 337, 339, 341, 342
fetch.mockResolvedValueOnce()
function, 278
fetchProducts function, 260
filter() method, 111
Firebase, 337, 338, 355–358
Firestore, 355, 358
FixedSizeList component,
122, 257
Focus management, 303, 307
Folder structure, 379, 380
Formatjs, 311
Formik, 216–218
Form validation
client-side validation, 212–214
real-time validation, 214, 215
Fragments, 69, 78, 79
Functional components, 4, 44, 46,
52, 53, 90, 91, 128, 132

G

Generic designs, 161
Git
configuration, 38
download and installation, 37
repository, 38, 39
workflow
commit changes, 39, 40
push to remote
repository, 40
stage changes, 39, 40

GitHub Actions, 298, 326–330
GitLens, 36
Global styles, 154, 165
Google Maps, 339
GraphQL, 36, 337
    definition, 347
    fetching data, 350
    setting up, 347, 348
    states, 350
    writing and using queries, 348
Grid system, 162, 163

H

handleChange function, 215
handleMouseEnter function, 262
handleSubmit function, 224
Higher-order components (HOCs), 16, 249
    example, 363
    functionality, 362
    logging, 362
    use cases and limitations, 363
HMR, *see* Hot module replacement (HMR)
HOCs, *see* Higher-order components (HOCs)
Hooks, 44
    challenges and solutions, 179
    functional components, 172
    lifecycle scenarios, 175, 176
    timer component, 176–179
    useEffect, 172, 174
    useState, 174, 175

Hot module replacement (HMR), 34
HTTPS, *see* HyperText Transfer Protocol Secure (HTTPS)
HyperText Transfer Protocol Secure (HTTPS), 291

I

Image optimization, 320
Images
    lazy loading, 257
    responsive, 258
Immutable updates, 111
Imperative approach, 11
Infinite loops, 179, 180
Inline styling, 164
    advantages, 148, 149
    definition, 147
    disadvantages, 149
    JSX, 79
    properties, 148
Insecure API endpoints, 283
Integration testing, 266, 271, 272
Interactive login form, 100–105
Internationalization (i18n)
    applications, 310
    concepts, 301
    definition, 302
    folder structure, locales and i18n.js, 313
    implementation, 310
    react-i18next, 311–315
Intuitiveness, 143

J

JavaScript expressions, 70
    calling functions, 75, 76
    conditional rendering, 75
    embedding variable, 74
JavaScript XML (JSX), 132
    advantage, 68
    applying CSS classes, 79
    definition, 67
    expressions, 74-76
    fragments for grouping elements, 78, 79
    inline styling, 79
    invalid and valid expression, 68
    logical && operator, 80
    props, 76, 77
    rendering elements, 71-74, 81
    rules, 68-71
    self-closing expression, 70
    snippet, 68
    spread attributes, 80
    user dashboard, 81-86
Jenkins, 298
Jest, 267, 268
Jest-axe, 301, 308
jest-fetch-mock library, 277
JSON Web Tokens (JWT), 287, 292
JSX expressions, 71

K

Keyboard navigation, 303
Keys
    defined, 107, 109
    management, 119
    mistakes, 110
    unique and stable identifiers, 110

L

Lack of reusability, 149
Lazy loading, 122, 237-239, 252, 253, 257, 319
Lifecycle, React
    class components, 169-172
    management, 180
    methods, 167
    phases, 167, 168
        mounting, 168-170
        unmounting, 169, 171, 172
        updating, 168, 171
Lighthouse, 301, 308
Linting, 330, 331
Lists
    add and remove items, 112
    add-to-cart functionality, 123-125
    data collection, 107
    dynamic items, 111-113
    lazy loading, 120
    management, 119
    nested lists and complex data structures, 113-115
    recursion, 116-118
    rendering, 108
    rendering objects, 108, 109
    virtualization, 121, 122

INDEX

loadStripe function, 352, 401
Localization, 302
LogRocket, 318, 332
Long-term support (LTS), 22

M

map() function, 111, 384
Masking sensitive data, 294, 295
Media, 257, 258
Media queries, 161, 164
Memoization, 247
Mock data, 381, 382
    usage, 383, 384
Mocking, 276–279
Mocking API calls, 277–279
Monitoring tools, *see* Error tracking
Mounting phase, 168–170
MouseTracker component, 365
Multilingual React component,
    313, 315

N

Navigation, 233, 234, 303
Nested lists, 113–115
Nested routes, 234–236
Nested state structures, 254
Netlify, 317, 323, 324, 327, 329,
    407, 408
Network performance
    prefetching data, 261, 262
    React Query, 259, 260
New Relic, 332

Node.js
    download and installing, 22
    output, 23
    updating, 24
    verify installation, 23
    version, 22
Node Package Manager
    (npm), 22, 24
Node Version Manager (nvm), 24
NotFound component, 240
npm audit fix command, 295

O

OAuth, 287
onBlur event, 209, 210
onChange event, 207, 208
onFocus event, 209, 210
onSubmit event, 208, 209
Optimization, deployment,
    319, 320
Over-componentization, 140
OWASP ZAP, 299

P, Q

Parent-child relationships, 113, 366
Payment form, 352–354
Payment gateway, 351–354
Penetration testing, 298, 299
Performance bottlenecks
    identification tools, 249
    symptoms, 248
    user experience, 248

INDEX

Performance optimization
   bottlenecks (*see* Performance bottlenecks)
   challenges, 247
   code splitting and lazy loading, 252, 253
   images and media, 257, 258
   large lists, 255–257
   network performance, 259–262
   preventing unnecessary re-renders, 249–252
   state management, 254, 255
   virtual DOM, 247
Personally identifiable information (PII), 283
PII, *see* Personally identifiable information (PII)
Post-deployment maintenance, 318
Prefetching data, 261, 262
Preprocessors (SCSS/SASS)
   features
      functions and operations, 158
      mixins, 157
      nesting, 156
      variables, 156
   installing, 158
   streamline styling workflows, 155
Prettier, 36
ProductCard component, 385
ProductDetails component, 239
Product details page, 387–389
Product images, 383, 384
ProductItem component, 130
ProductList component, 130
Product page (home), 384
Programmatic navigation, 233
Prop drilling, 184, 186
Props, 48–51, 76, 77
   best practices, 57, 58
   vs. state, 56
ProtectedRoute component, 237
Protected routes, 236, 237
Pseudo-classes, 153

R

RBAC, *see* Role-based access control (RBAC)
React app
   accessibility, 303–307
   component-based architecture, 3–7
   components, 2
   deploy (*see* Deployment)
   frameworks, 17
   history, 3
   initializing project, 378
   inline styling, 147–149
   internationalization, 310–315
   lifecycle (*see* Lifecycle, React)
   state management, 183, 184
   structure, 18
   styling, 143–145
   virtual DOM, 7–11
React Context API, 183–186
React development

INDEX

recommended extensions, 36
VS Code, 35
ReactDOM.render method, 72
React Hook Form, 218, 219
React Hooks, 3, 167
    concepts, 13–15
    counter example, 14
    custom, 15, 16
    reasons, 13
    side effects, 13
React-i18next, 310–315
React Intl, 311
React.lazy function, 252
React.memo, 249, 250
React-Native Snippets, 36
React Profiler, 247
React Query, 259, 260
React-redux, 187, 196, 379, 394
React Router, 19
    blog application, 245
    built-in mechanisms, 239
    concepts, 231–234
    configuration, 230
    declarative approach, 229
    definition, 229
    installation command, 229
    libraries, 227
    setting up, 229–231
React testing library, 267, 268
Real-time validation, 214, 215
Reconciliation, 8, 11, 110, 247
Recursion, 113, 116–118
reduce() method, 399

Redux, 36, 111, 187
    selectors, 254, 255
    setting up
        connecting app, 393, 394
        creating retail slice, 391–393
        creating store, 390
    state management, 389
Redux Toolkit, 183, 184
    configuring store, 189
    connecting React components, 191, 192
    vs. context API, 193
    creating slice, 188, 189
    features, 187–191
    install dependencies, 187
    providing store, 190
    shopping cart
        building component, 197–201
        configuring store, 196
        creating cart slice, 194, 196
        providing store, 196, 197
    streamlines, 187
Regression prevention, 265
Reliability, 265, 338
Rendering elements
    arguments, 71
    definition, 71
    efficient, 73
    multiple element, 72, 73
    single element, 72
Render props, 364–366
    vs. HOCs, 366
replaysSessionSampleRate, 333

INDEX

Responsive design techniques, 144, 161–164
Responsive frameworks, 162
Responsive images, 258
Responsiveness, 144
REST APIs, 337
    Axios, 342–344
    error handling, 344, 346
    fetching data with fetch, 339, 341, 342
Retail app, 389
    adding mock data, 381, 382
    building core pages and components
        home page, 384
        product card, 385
        product details page, 387–389
    checkout with stripe (*see* Stripe)
    deployment, 406–408
    features, 377
    folder structure, 379, 380
        reusability and scalability, 381
    organizing product images, 383, 384
    project setting up
        initializing react app, 378
        installing required dependencies, 379
    routing, 404–406
    source code, 378 *See also* Redux
Retail slice, 391–393
Retail store application, 19
Retry logic, 344, 346
Reusability, 133, 134, 141
Reusable components, 136
Reusable functions, 99, 100
Reusing styles, 164
Robust navigation system, 229
Role-based access control (RBAC), 288–291
Route matching, 232
Routing, 227, 229, 404–406
    error handling, 239, 241
    lazy loading, 237–239
    and navigation features, 227
    nested routes, 234–236
    page implementations, 243–245
    protected routes, 236, 237
    SPAs, 228, 229
    structure, 241
        See also React Router

S

Sanitization, 284, 285
SASS, *see* Syntactically Awesome Style Sheets (SASS)
screen.getByText function, 271, 272
Security
    API requests
        data protection, 293–295
        HTTPS, 291
        preventing CSRF attacks, 292, 293
        tokens, 292
    authentication, 287, 288

INDEX

concerns, 281
dependency management, 295, 296
deployment, 296, 297
disabling source maps, 297
RBAC, 288–291
React components
   escaping output, 285–287
   user input sanitization, 284, 285
risks, 282, 283
testing, 297–299
vulnerabilities, 281
Selectors, 254, 255
Semantic HTML elements, 303
SendGrid, 339
Sensitive data exposure, 283
Sentry, 318, 331–334
Sentry.captureException(), 333
setCount function, 175
setData() function, 342
setTheme function, 186
Shopping cart page, 136–139
ShoppingCartPage component, 130
Shopping cart, Redux Toolkit
   building component, 197–201
   configuring store, 196
   creating cart slice, 194, 196
   providing store, 196, 197
shouldComponentUpdate, 171
Single-page applications (SPAs), 227–229, 233
Single responsibility principle, 135
Snapshot testing, 274–276

Social security numbers (SSNs), 294
SonarQube, 297
Source maps, 296
SPAs, *see* Single-page applications (SPAs)
SQL Injection (SQLi), 299
SSNs, *see* Social security numbers (SSNs)
State
   best practices, 57, 58
   class components, 53, 55
   functional components, 52, 53
   vs. props, 56
Stateless components, 133, 134
State management, 85, 104, 141, 205
   best practices, 193, 194
   event handling, 89
   libraries, 111
   nested state, 254
   in React, 183, 184
   Redux, 389
   selectors, 254, 255
   useState hook, 174
Static analysis tools, 297, 298
Stripe, 337, 339
   cart page, 395–399
   creating checkout form, 401–403
   creating checkout page, 399–401
   installing dependencies, 394
   libraries, 351
   payment gateway, 351, 354
   provider, 351

Stubbing, 276–279
Styling, 86
    best practices, 164, 165
    CSS-in-JS libraries, 152–155
    CSS modules, 149–151
    frameworks, 159–161
    inline, 147–149
    intuitive design, 143
    libraries, 144
    preprocessors (SCSS/SASS), 155–159
    in React applications, 143–145
    responsive design, 161–164
    traditional CSS, 145–147
    web development, 143
Suspense component, 238, 241
Synchronization, 204
Syntactically Awesome Style Sheets (SASS), 155

T

Tailwind CSS, 143, 159–163
TaskItem.jsx, 86
TaskList.jsx, 86
Testing
    advantages, 265
    E2E tests, 272–274
    environment, 267–269
    integration, 271, 272
    mocking and stubbing, 276–279
    pyramid, 266
    requirements, 267
    snapshot, 274–276
    tools, 265
    unit, 269–271
Testing accessibility
    automated tests, 308–310
    tools, 307
ThemeContext, 186
ThemeProvider, 154, 186
Theming support, 154, 155
Third-party libraries, 276, 296
    Formik, 216–218
    React Hook Form, 218, 219
Third-party services
    examples, 338, 339
    reasons, 338
Timer component, 176–179
toggleActivity function, 61
Toggle button, 92, 99
toggleUserActivity function, 58, 62
toJSON() method, 276
toLocaleTimeString() method, 178
tracesSampleRate, 333
Traditional CSS
    advantages, 146
    definition, 145
    disadvantages, 146, 147
    external stylesheets, 145
Tree shaking, 319
Trigger deployment, 330

U

Uncontrolled components, 205, 206, 369–371
Unit testing, 266, 269–271

Unmounting phase, 169, 171, 172
Unnecessary re-renders
    functional component, 249
    React.memo, 249, 250
    useCallback and useMemo,
        250, 252
Updating phase, 168, 171
useCallback, 250, 252
useEffect hook, 172, 174, 178
useLayoutEffect hook, 175
useMemo, 250, 252
User dashboard, 81–86
useRef hook, 175
User experience (UX), 143
UserHeader.jsx, 86
User interface (UI), 8, 203
User list application, 58–63
UserProfile component, 6
useState hook, 174, 175, 178
Utility functions, 269
Universally unique identifier
    (UUID), 110

V

Validation
    asynchronous, 224
    errors, 223
    form (*see* Form validation)
    logic, 212
    rules, 216
    techniques, 203
validationSchema, 217
Vercel, 317, 323–325

Virtual DOM, 2, 3
    benefits, 9, 10
    definition, 8
    UI and, 8
    visualizing process, 10
Virtualization, 122, 256, 257
    lists, 121, 122
Visual appeal, 144
Visual impairments, 303
Visual Studio Code (VS Code), 35
Vite, 319
    completion message and
        commands, 32
    vs. create-react-app, 34
    displayed in browser, 34
    installing and creating
        project, 31, 32
    running development
        server, 32, 33

W, X, Y

waitFor function, 279
Web browsers, 8
Web Content Accessibility
    Guidelines (WCAG),
    144, 302
Webpack, 150, 151, 319
Wildcard route, 239, 240, 245
"Wrapper hell" problem, 364

Z

Zustand, 111

GPSR Compliance

The European Union's (EU) General Product Safety Regulation (GPSR) is a set of rules that requires consumer products to be safe and our obligations to ensure this.

If you have any concerns about our products, you can contact us on

ProductSafety@springernature.com

In case Publisher is established outside the EU, the EU authorized representative is:

Springer Nature Customer Service Center GmbH
Europaplatz 3
69115 Heidelberg, Germany

www.ingramcontent.com/pod-product-compliance
Lightning Source LLC
LaVergne TN
LVHW010333260326
834688LV00036B/687